Adele Briscoe Looscan

Daughter of the Republic

Laura Lyons McLemore

THE TEXAS BIOGRAPHY SERIES / NUMBER 4

A Joint Project of the Center for Texas Studies at TCU
and TCU Press / Fort Worth, Texas

Library of Congress Cataloging-in-Publication Data

Names: McLemore, Laura Lyons, 1950- author.
Title: Adele Briscoe Looscan : Daughter of the Republic / Laura Lyons McLemore.
Other titles: TCU Texas biography series ; no. 4.
Description: Fort Worth, Texas : TCU Press, [2016] | ©2016 | Series: The Texas biography series ; number 4 | Includes bibliographical references.
Identifiers: LCCN 2015036227 | ISBN 9780875654423 (alk. paper)
Subjects: LCSH: Looscan, Adele B., 1848-1935. | Women in public life--Texas--Biography. | Historians--Texas--Biography. |Texas--Biography. | Daughters of the Republic of Texas--History--20th century. | Texas State Historical Association--History--20th century. |Texas--History--1846-1950.
Classification: LCC F391.L86 M35 2016 | DDC 976.4/05092--dc23
LC record available at http://lccn.loc.gov/2015036227

TCU Press
TCU Box 298300
Fort Worth, Texas 76129
817.257.7822
www.prs.tcu.edu
To order books: 1.800.826.8911

Contents

Adele Briscoe Looscan as a young woman.
RGA13-1813, Houston Public Library, HMRC

Editor's Foreword

THROUGH ITS RICH and colorful history, Texas has been home to countless fascinating figures. Some of the state's great works of historical literature, such as Eugene C. Barker's biography of Stephen F. Austin and Marquis James's study of Sam Houston, have chronicled the lives of Texas's larger-than-life leaders. Yet there remain many important personalities who have not yet found their biographer, and many more whose stories are in need of fresh examination in a scholarly biography. The Texas Biography Series, jointly published by the TCU Press and the Center for Texas Studies at TCU, offers a venue for telling their stories. Another major goal of the series is to broaden the body of biographical literature in Texas historiography beyond its traditionally heavy emphasis on the "great men" (which has often meant "great white men on horseback"). While the series certainly includes biographies of nineteenth-century political and military leaders, it also strives to encourage biographers to examine the full range of historical actors who have shaped the destiny of the Lone Star State, including women, members of racial and ethnic minorities, and figures from the worlds of business, the arts, science, religion, and even sports. In doing so, the series will contribute to keeping the field of Texas history vital and relevant in the twenty-first century.

As the fourth volume in the series, Laura Lyons McLemore's biography of Adele Briscoe Looscan fulfills several of these goals. Looscan was a woman, operating successfully in what in most respects was a man's world. Although related to military men, she made her mark as a researcher, writer, and activist in the fields of history and historical preservation. As a civic leader in Houston, she played an important role in the cultural life of one of the state's principal cities. McLemore's thoroughly researched, gracefully written study provides new ways of understanding Texas's cultural history and presents an incisive study of women's lives in the nineteenth and early twentieth centuries.

This book and its predecessors in the Texas Biography Series owe their existence to several important institutions. The TCU Press and its staff continue to furnish the editorial and production expertise to create books equal to those of the leading national publishing houses. The Center for Texas Studies at TCU is a critical partner in launching, funding, and publicizing the series. And finally, Houston Endowment, the Summerlee Foundation, and the Carl and Florence King Foundation have provided generous grants to underwrite the costs of the series. As editor, I am grateful to all of these partners who continue to make the series a success.

Gregg Cantrell
Erma and Ralph Lowe Chair in Texas History
Texas Christian University

Introduction

When Adele Looscan opened her copy of the *San Antonio Express* that had arrived earlier in the day, March 3, 1915, her own name jumped out at her. "Mrs. Looscan Made President," the headline read in bold capital letters. "Houston Woman Elected President of the Texas Historical Society."[1]

Two days later, having recovered from her initial shock, Mrs. Looscan sat at her writing desk and penned a letter to Eugene C. Barker, director of the Texas State Historical Association (TSHA), expressing her surprise and curiosity as to "how this strange thing came about."[2] The answer, though not the one he gave her, was that Barker needed help recruiting women members for the association, and Adele Looscan had been a founding member of the Daughters of the Republic of Texas (DRT) and a charter member of the Texas Woman's Press Association, and she had remained active in patriotic societies such as the Daughters of the American Revolution (DAR) and United Daughters of the Confederacy (UDC). She was a well-connected woman with a demonstrated devotion to Texas history. To Adele, Barker wrote a simpler and more flattering explanation: "Judge [Zachary T.] Fulmore did not want to be re-elected—and in looking over the membership list, he and I could find no one who had taken more effective interest in the Association than you. I think you deserve it by all odds."[3]

Thus, in 1915, at a time when women still had no formal access to the political process and were still striving within the realm of women's clubs to develop their autonomy, express their identity, and make a lasting contribution, Adele Lubbock Briscoe Looscan became the first woman president of the Texas State Historical Association, which, despite Barker's recognition of the need to include women, essentially was and long remained a predominantly male society. Mrs. Looscan would go on to become the longest-serving president in the association's history. Unquestionably, this lengthy tenure set Adele Looscan apart from her peers, both female and male. Yet, in many ways, her life, activities, and accomplishments were typical for women of her era. A closer examination, however, reveals several factors that make her difficult to categorize and challenges some long-held assumptions about a "woman's sphere" in the nineteenth and early twentieth centuries.

Early nineteenth-century prescriptive literature and, in fact, nineteenth-century essays, articles, and sermons generally were replete with references to a "woman's sphere." The writing of Catharine Beecher and others in the early nineteenth century nurtured the idea of separate spheres for men and women, and this notion became a way of imposing order in the disorderly world of the Industrial Revolution. Writing in the mid-1960s, Barbara Welter and other historians reinforced the metaphor of separate spheres by identifying a nineteenth-century stereotype that Welter labeled the "cult of true womanhood."[4] She identified the attributes of "true womanhood" by which a woman judged herself and was judged by her spouse, her friends, and society, as piety, purity, submissiveness, and domesticity.[5] These earlier scholars accepted the ideology of separate spheres largely as fixed entities and asked only how a particular female or feminine institution represented acquiescence to or rebellion against domesticity.[6] By the 1990s, women's history scholars had begun to acknowledge that such generalizations belied the "complexity of the experience of women in all their diversity." As historian Elizabeth Fox-Genovese wrote in 1993, "The concept of separate spheres, as most of us now acknowledge, was a myth. We have further learned that innumerable women rejected the myth as an adequate description of their own lives and, especially, their ambitions." It was "no longer even safe to assume that the ideology of separate spheres, which had long been taken to articulate the experience and values of white, middle-class women, faithfully captured the reality of any women's lives. Since our primary responsibility," Fox-Genovese went on to say, "remains to recapture the voices of discrete women and groups of women with as much immediacy as possible, we should do better to avoid generalizations entirely." She went so far as to argue that "any adequate theory of women's history must simultaneously attend to similarity and differences, always asking similar to and different from whom, and in which ways."[7] Mary P. Ryan has contended that the ideology of separate spheres that divided the world into public/private and male/female was not an accurate description of actual behavior but an attempt to impose an orderly system, or the perception of a system, on a disorganized world.[8] Other scholars have argued that the terms "public" and "private" are not adequately defined and are, therefore, inadequate to accurately describe activities that were neither exclusively domestic nor exclusively governmental, neither exclusively female nor exclusively male.[9] Adele Looscan is an example of the women whose lives and activities have led twenty-first-century historians to the realization that large numbers of women did not reflect the tenets of the "separate spheres" paradigm.

Adele Briscoe Looscan certainly considered herself a "lady" by the standards of her day—"a moral and domestic creature who embodied the desirable traits of loving maternity, intuition, and sensitivity."[10] In that respect, she was no different from her peers. However, unlike some of her wealthier counterparts, her social standing and that of her family derived primarily from their pioneer heritage, as did the social influence of others of her generation who claimed a direct connection to the Republic of Texas. Repeatedly, the exclusivity of membership in the Daughters of the Republic of Texas was emphasized by the organization itself and by the newspapers that reported its activities. As the *Galveston Daily News* reported on November 7, 1891, "Those qualified for membership are wives and lineal descendants of lineal male descendants of all persons eligible for membership of the Texas Veteran[s] Association." Nearly a decade later, the *Brenham Daily Banner* queried in its reporting of Texas Independence Day exercises, "Who would not be proud to be eligible [for] membership in this patriotic organization?"[11] As the granddaughter of John Richardson Harris, from whom Harris County gets its name, and the daughter of Capt. Andrew Briscoe, a veteran of the Battle of San Jacinto, Adele Briscoe was the youngest of a female dynasty in Houston that began with her grandmother, Jane Birdsall Harris.[12] Economically, her immediate family could best be described as middle class, in which "ladies" in the second half of the nineteenth century were judged not only by their amusing charms but by their supposedly natural qualities of domesticity and morality, and were distinguished by fulfilling the duties of their sphere, as Adele herself expressed in an address to her school classmates in 1864.[13] Adele's mother and grandmother, even though widowed most of their adult lives, were devoted to their homes and the rearing of their children. In the mid-nineteenth century, the role of dutiful daughter was clearly defined and urged upon girls from their earliest years. A daughter was expected to help her mother in tasks recognized as "female," and mothers were advised to subtly direct their daughters toward those skills that would be most useful to them in maturity. Whether as a result of her prolonged widowhood, the reality of living on a rapidly expanding frontier, or both, Mary Jane Briscoe had her own notion of what skills would be most useful to her daughters and perhaps emphasized less passive ideals than might be considered the American norm at the time. Adrienne Caughfield, in her study of women and westward expansion, has noted that very little that women did was actually passive when dealing with expansionism, regardless of the roles they had been assigned by society. She notes that women actively promoted the Texas Revolution and contributed supplies and even labor during various other crises—examples that challenge the idea of women as being solely passive.[14]

While Adele's ideals may have matched the female role prescribed for true womanhood—piety, purity, submissiveness, and domesticity—her real-life experiences were more complex. Born at a time when opposition to this stereotype was culminating in the Seneca Falls Convention, she grew up in a household dominated by women who were anything but passive; their circumstances would not allow it. Having no children of her own, Adele became the nurturer of an extended family and fulfilled the role of devoted daughter longer than most of her friends. She was thirty-three when she married, forty-nine when she was widowed, and eighty-seven when she died. For more than half her life she managed her own financial affairs, either with male assistance or without it, as her mother and grandmother had done before her. In fact, so great was her mother's influence that Adele had a difficult time becoming someone with her own identity rather than just Mary Jane Briscoe's daughter. She followed her mother's lead into church work, benevolent societies, literary societies, patriotic societies, and historic preservation initiatives, as often described in histories of the women's club movement. Like many other women of her generation in Texas, she pursued her love of education and writing by involving herself in study clubs, advocating for libraries, and writing articles for newspapers. Her devotion to history, Texas history in particular, and, more important, historical method, took priority over other interests, and that pursuit eventually distinguished her from fellow members of the Texas Woman's Press Association or federated women's clubs and even from the Daughters of the Republic of Texas that she had helped to found. In many ways, she was a typical clubwoman of the late nineteenth and early twentieth centuries, with a keen interest in preservation, patriotic heritage, education, and self-assertion. However, her life took a slightly different turn from pursuit of those goals exclusively within the company of other women—a turn that led her, by March 1915, to become president of an organization dominated by men. As Julie Des Jardins has noted in her study of women historians from 1880 through 1945, women who, like Adele, turned to historical enterprise "did not differ from the tens of thousands across the country who made up the rank and file of local preservationist groups by the nineteenth century. Indeed all manifestations of the historical enterprise—collected and written, preserved and taught, enacted and studied—had fallen into the universe of the white, middle-class domestic woman by the turn of the twentieth century." The key, Des Jardins has suggested, may have been timing.[15] Adele Looscan was a woman of her times who, for a variety of reasons, did not fit neatly into generalizations about women. During her lifetime she witnessed and experienced rapid economic, social, cultural, and political changes of major proportions. She was among those women who had one foot firmly planted in tradition and the other in modernity. In some ways she fit every mold; in other ways she created her own.

The most critical factor shaping Adele Looscan's destiny was her family background and the milieu in which she was reared. She was, both literally and figuratively, a daughter of the Republic of Texas. Adele Lubbock Briscoe was born in early 1848. She was named in honor of Adele Baron of New Orleans, wife of Francis R. Lubbock, who was a close family friend and later governor of Texas. Her mother was the daughter of a Texas pioneer, John R. Harris, one of Austin's Old Three Hundred, whose family had deep roots in New York and Pennsylvania. Her father, Andrew Briscoe, was a southerner, a fortune hunter, would-be entrepreneur, and veteran of the Texas Revolution who died while Adele was still an infant. She and her three siblings thus grew up in a single-parent home with more or less support at various times from members of her extended family. From birth, she lived in a household dominated by independent women and the ghosts of her father and grandfather. They cast long shadows.

Another major formative influence in Adele Looscan's life was her education. Both her parents were anxious that their children be classically educated. Aside from the obvious advantages of literacy, education was a marker of gentility and class distinction. At least in part to obtain better educational opportunities for his children, Andrew Briscoe moved his family from Texas to New Orleans when Adele was about a year old. Concern for their continued education was a determining factor in Mary Jane Briscoe's return to Texas after her husband's death. During a time when higher education was affordable only for the wealthiest ranks of society, Mary Jane Briscoe made certain that her children, both boys and girls, received the best education available to them while they were growing up. In her study of women's education in America between 1780 and 1840, Margaret A. Nash has noted that for most white, middle-class young women, education was a critical component of forging or maintaining a class identity. Education became a key part of the white, middle-class struggle to define itself. Gender differentiation within the class, Nash observes, was less important than differentiating between the middle class and the socioeconomic classes above and below it. She did not argue that curricular differences for males and females did not exist within the white middle class but that "such differences were minor compared to the distance the white middle class wanted to create between itself and people of color and people of other classes."[16]

In the Northeast, where Mary Jane (Harris) Briscoe had been reared, women such as Emma Willard, Catharine Beecher, and Mary Lyon encouraged female education in subjects such as ancient languages, science, mathematics, theology, philosophy, geometry, and anatomy. As historians have noted, the schools promoted by these reformers, in addition to producing teachers, missionaries, and feminists, provided girls "with models of self-sufficient unmarried women and with firm friendships, self-confidence, and ambition."[17] In writing about nineteenth-century women, Barbara Welter has observed that, as that century unfolded, sharp differences in the external upbringing of women and men, especially in such areas as education, diminished. High schools and colleges, including female seminaries and colleges, offered the same level of education to young men and young women.[18] Studies of higher education for women suggest that assumptions regarding women's work as wives and mothers did not result in curricular ideals very different from those held for men. Margaret Nash found that few academies and seminaries of the early national or antebellum eras taught courses directly related to "women's work," such as childrearing techniques or domestic management. She maintains that most educators believed a general liberal arts curriculum, similar to that for men, was good preparation for any life role. Students, teachers, and school founders alike largely concurred with Catharine Beecher in believing that a broad-based education was as valuable to women as to men. Formal learning outside the home had begun to increase in the Northeast by the late eighteenth century. The broad and diffuse discourse of civic republicanism following the American Revolution provided support for academies as opposed to home tutoring.[19]

As Megan Seaholm points out in her study of Progressive-Era clubwomen in Texas, new educational opportunities for women and the success of women's educational enterprises, such as the new colleges for women, were a significant challenge to widely held beliefs regarding female intellectual inferiority.[20] As Harris County grew and became increasingly urban, academies and seminaries opened, often with highly educated professors who were graduates of East Coast or European universities. Although most of these educational institutions existed only briefly, some became well established. Mary B. Brown opened her Young Ladies' Seminary and Day School in Houston on property she owned on the corner of Franklin and Caroline Streets in the 1840s. She taught many prominent Houstonians, including Adele; Elizabeth Fitzsimmons Ring, a founder of the Museum of Fine Arts, Houston; and Mrs. Phillip Fall, a founder of the Ladies' Parish Association at Christ Episcopal Church. Miss Brown's school provided instruction in spelling, penmanship, grammar, geography, arithmetic, natural philosophy, chemistry, astronomy, botany, rhetoric, and French; Greek, Roman, and Hebrew biography and history; and ancient geography, history, and mythology. By the time Adele graduated in 1866, she had obtained a substantial academic foundation in addition to the requisite training in manners and etiquette expected of all refined young ladies.[21]

Texans' desire for better education was part of a national phenomenon. Frederick Eby recognized this trend as he prepared his book on the history of the development of education in Texas. "Early in the fifties the people of Texas for the first time became genuinely aroused on the subject of education. There arose a strong and widely spread desire that something adequate be done to provide educational facilities in order to realize the dream of the fathers of the Republic," he wrote.[22] A number of universities were established in Texas prior to the Civil War, usually with provisions for a female department. "The immediate effects of the Civil War on the schools were destructive and caused Texas to flounder in chaos for twenty years, before the new era dawned," Eby wrote.[23] In 1866, upon graduating from Miss Brown's seminary and day school, Adele's options were severely limited. The University of Texas would not formally open until 1883, and study abroad was financially beyond reach. It is also entirely likely that Mary Jane Briscoe wanted to keep her younger daughter close by. In this regard, Adele and her sister were no different from the vast majority of their peers. Few young women in the 1860s could afford to be educated in female seminaries or universities. Thus, classical training did not lead to a college education for Adele, but it prepared her for her lifelong pursuit of independence, her passion for the study of history, and for the next major influence on her life: her association with women's clubs.

To a great extent, Adele was led to association and leadership in the women's club movement in Texas through the compelling influence of her mother. As early as the 1820s and 1830s, women's church activities had begun to expand beyond attendance and preparations for church functions to raising funds to purchase literature, to help domestic missions and the poor, and to provide scholarships for theology students. Women in New York and New England had set up moral reform societies even before Mary Jane Harris moved to Texas. The Civil War years provided an opportunity for women to strengthen skills they had acquired in religious and educational reform efforts by forming volunteer associations to assist soldiers. The war period also provided them an opportunity to work with other women outside their homes.[24] In the decades following the Civil War, women in unprecedented numbers created or joined organizations.[25] Mary Jane Briscoe was among that number. When the Ladies' Sewing Circle and the Ladies' Parish Association at Christ Episcopal Church in Houston were organized in 1871, she became a member and an exemplar for her daughters. A decade later, in her mother's parlor, Adele and one of her school friends, along with women from the ladies' associations of Christ Episcopal Church and First Presbyterian Church, organized a reading and study club along the lines of those that had begun forming more than a decade earlier in the Northeast, such as Sorosis and the New England Woman's Club, organized in 1868 for the purpose of providing an intellectual and social self-improvement program outside the realm of the household.[26] One thing led to another, and Adele, along with her mother, became involved in a host of activities associated with the Sheltering Arms Association, Woman's Exchange, the City Federation of Women's Clubs, the Texas Veterans Association, Houston Pen Women, Texas Woman's Press Association, Texas Historical and Landmarks Association, and the Daughters of the Republic of Texas, which was the first of the patriotic and preservation societies organized in Texas.

That Adele would have been acquainted with developments in society and culture in the Northeast following the Civil War seems certain. With formal schooling behind her, she accompanied her mother on an extended trip around the country in May 1870 to visit relatives and conduct business connected with the Harris estate, her grandmother having died the previous year. Their first destination was California, where Adele's uncle, Lew Harris, had settled in 1849. After spending the summer on the California coast, the two women boarded a steamer en route to western New York. They arrived in Seneca Falls, her mother's childhood home, in October. From there they visited family and friends in Penn Yan and Albany for several weeks before beginning the journey south toward Houston. It was their first trip to the East during the decade of the 1870s but not the last, as Adele traveled with her sister's family to the Centennial celebration in Philadelphia in 1876 and, together with her mother, returned to New York again in 1879.

Mary Jane Briscoe, along with her older son, Parmenas, and younger daughter, Adele, moved her primary residence to Houston proper from the original settlement of Harrisburg in 1874 and quickly became a leader in early women's organizations there. However, even before she and Adele hosted the organizational meeting of Houston's first women's study club in 1885, there had been a literary association in Harrisburg attended by both men and women. It not only provided inspiration for Adele's involvement in the Houston Lyceum and what came to be called the Ladies' Reading Club, but it was also the scene, in 1871, of a moving address by Houston's young county attorney, Michael Looscan, whom Adele Briscoe would marry within a decade.[27] Once married to a successful and popular husband, Adele engaged energetically in the burgeoning women's club movement in Houston. The Ladies' Reading Club offered her the opportunity to pursue the intellectual attainment and sophistication for which her upbringing had prepared her. As a married woman, she was very much like other women of her class who were enthusiastically joining the club movement. As Megan Seaholm has observed, Texas clubwomen were both traditional and progressive in their outlook and in their work. Seaholm also notes that while the club movement in Texas introduced women into the public sphere in new and different ways, it never wavered from promotion of a woman's role as wife, mother, and homemaker.[28] Adele Looscan fulfilled the role of wife and homemaker faithfully during her marriage to Michael Looscan and seemed to share what Carl Degler has described as a companionate relationship.[29] The fact that the couple did not have children freed Adele to pursue club work, various studies, writing, and, most of all, historical research into Texas history and concomitantly her own family's history. It was this focus and priority on history that defined Adele Looscan's participation in women's organizations and distinguished her from many if not most of her cohorts.

When Adele, Carrie Ennis Lombardi, and several acquaintances from the ladies' associations of Christ Episcopal and First Presbyterian Churches of Houston met in Mary Jane Briscoe's parlor on a wintry February day in 1885 for the purpose of creating a society in which women could enjoy both intellectual and social stimulation and self-improvement, they adopted the name Ladies' History Class. That the organization was exclusively for women "having a literary taste" gave credence to the notion of the woman's sphere, and the subsequent history of the class, which was soon renamed the Ladies' Reading Club, followed the course of similar organizations across Texas and the nation. Adele Looscan was appointed president pro tempore. When women were admitted to the Houston Lyceum in 1887, she led the reading club ladies in pressing for the establishment of a public library, in keeping with her own interests and in line with the national trend of women promoting education and libraries. As early as 1896, 90 percent of the federated clubs in Vermont were actively promoting the building of libraries. At the New York State Federation (of Women) convention in Buffalo in 1901, the literary sessions dealt not with literature but with organizing libraries. The Rhode Island Federation began its library activity in 1903.[30] When the Texas Federation of Women's Clubs appeared on the scene in 1897, Adele Looscan was appointed third vice president. The organization's first library committee was headed by Mrs. J. C. Terrell, whom Texas clubwomen referred to as the "Mother of Texas Libraries." Terrell's committee wrote in 1899, "The first and most important work of the clubs is to agitate the question of local libraries, thus fostering and educating public sentiment in this direction until the radiating influence shall compass the State, compelling more favorable legislation."[31]

Historic preservation had become another focus of activity for women's clubs by the mid-nineteenth century. The first history of architecture in the United States was written by Louisa Tuthill, who dedicated her book, *History of Architecture from the Earliest Times: Its Present Condition in Europe and the United States; With a Biography of Eminent Architects and a Glossary of Architectural Terms,* "to the Ladies of the United States of America, the acknowledged arbiters of taste." Tuthill's book, published in 1848, the year of Adele Looscan's birth, urged women to promote American architecture.[32] In 1853 Ann Pamela Cunningham and the Mount Vernon Ladies' Association led the way. As Annette K. Baxter notes in her preface to Karen Blair's examination of the clubwoman as feminist, these drives went deeper than the political need to participate; they arose from an emotional need to express one's identity and make a lasting contribution.[33] Efforts by women in Texas for historical preservation began as early as 1884, when Mary Jane Briscoe became an honorary member of the Texas Veterans Association and joined their efforts to purchase the San Jacinto battleground and erect monuments to the participants in that battle. From much the same motivation, Adina De Zavala in San Antonio organized a group of San Antonio women in 1889 to "discuss" Texas and its heroes, thus forming one of the first women's societies in the state organized expressly for patriotic purposes. De Zavala spearheaded the preservation of four former Franciscan missions and the Spanish governor's palace in San Antonio and encouraged the recognition of March 2 as Texas

Independence Day.[34] The preservation of the San Jacinto battleground was a deeply personal cause for Adele, her mother, and many other widows and daughters of veterans in Houston, Galveston, and their vicinity. It spurred Adele's intellectual interest in history to become a lifelong cause. And it prompted her, along with her mother and the daughters of other veterans, particularly Betty Ballinger and Hally Bryan, to organize the forerunner of the DRT, the Daughters of the Lone Star Republic, in late 1891—again in Mary Jane Briscoe's parlor—to perpetuate the memory and spirit of participants in the fight for Texas independence and to encourage historical research into the earliest records of Texas, especially those relating to the period of the revolution and republic. Mary Jane Briscoe was elected first vice president and Adele was elected historian. The purpose of the organization aligned with the traditional role of southern women and women across the country who claimed as their own the work of conserving and cultivating "culture."[35] Julie Des Jardins, in her detailed analysis of women and the historical enterprise, noted that in the nineteenth century American women embraced their role as the custodians of national history. They studied the past from the books they kept in home libraries and preserved family relics of bygone years, all to prepare themselves for their maternal duty to raise civic-minded children and future citizens.[36] One might assume that individual women could have multiple motivations. Any sense of maternal duty Adele may have had she exercised vicariously; her concern was for all future citizens of Texas and for preserving the memory of her own heroes. The work of the Daughters of the Republic of Texas became a priority for Adele, as its purpose aligned not only with her intellectual interests but also with her sense of identity.

Like women all over the United States, women in Texas enjoyed extraordinary success through their writing. Texas newspapers in the 1880s became outlets for their short stories, sketches, poems, and opinions. By 1893, Aurelia Hadley Mohl, whose journalistic career had begun in the mid-1850s and who had been a charter member of the Ladies' Reading Club of Houston, had called on women writers from all over Texas to form the Texas Woman's Press Association. Adele had been writing articles for the organs of the Woman's Exchange, the *Texas Messenger* and *Gulf Messenger.* Her association with the Texas Woman's Press Association, and later the Houston Pen Women, did not set her apart from her friends and associates, many of whom were also members of the Ladies' Reading Club, the Lyceum, and the Daughters of the Republic of Texas.

The year 1897 marked the beginning of many critical changes in Adele Looscan's life. Early in the spring she received an invitation from George P. Garrison at the University of Texas to join a group of people in forming an association for the collection and preservation of documents for the use of researchers and future historians of Texas. Although she accepted the invitation, she did not attend the organizational meeting as her husband, Michael, had fallen ill at about the same time. In May, Adele had been elected third vice president of the newly formed Texas Federation of Women's Clubs but found it necessary to resign when Michael became increasingly ill and her mother fell and sustained incapacitating injuries. Michael died in August, leaving her to settle his estate and provide for his siblings in the Northeast, whom he had been supporting. She was no longer a woman "of leisure" or a wife. She found herself, out of necessity, engaged in the business of managing her own affairs without regard to gender roles.

As Karen Blair has observed, not all women moved easily from culture to reform.[37] Although Adele continued to be involved in clubs and associations, she did not expand her activities to involvement in causes such as temperance, suffrage, women's rights, or even municipal housekeeping as did many others within the club movement. Adele's club activities remained within the realm she had already established for herself—education, libraries, history, and historic preservation. On one hand, this lack of change perhaps signaled how traditional she really was. On the other hand, while Adele had accepted unquestioningly the ideology of the "lady," she was by habit autonomous and comfortable in her associations with men as well as women. As she became more active in the Texas State Historical Association, she deferred to the authority of professionally trained historians, who were men, and sought the tutelage that Prof. George P. Garrison offered, but she was not hesitant to express her own opinions or maintain her own priorities. The loss of her husband and her mother within a period of six years certainly marked a turning point in her life. For better or worse, she was in charge of her own life and free to be whoever she wanted to be.

Another decisive turning point occurred several years later when, with her close friend and colleague in promoting Texas history, Adina De Zavala of San Antonio, she became embattled in an effort to preserve the historic Alamo. De Zavala's particular cause since moving to San Antonio in the 1880s had been the preservation of the Spanish missions. The two women's collaboration in attempting to preserve Mission San Antonio de Valero, commonly known as the Alamo, brought Adele's traditional values into direct conflict with the new socioeconomic order that accompanied modernization and "progress" in Texas, as personified by Clara Driscoll and her vision for making the Alamo a symbol to legitimate the social transformation and economic development in Texas that followed independence.[38] The conflicting visions of De Zavala and Driscoll with regard to the preservation of the Alamo touched off a destructive and painful battle within the Daughters of the Republic of Texas that resulted in Adele Looscan being sued and the De Zavala Chapter being expelled from the state organization. Recriminations within the organization were bitter and particularly hurtful because they came from erstwhile friends and destroyed the sense of sisterhood that had developed over many years. Adele continued to be active in the Texas Federation of Women's Clubs, the press women's associations, and the patriotic societies—the Daughters of the American

Revolution and United Daughters of the Confederacy. She associated with the Daughters of the Heroes of Texas, which Adina De Zavala reconstituted in San Antonio after the break with the Daughters of the Republic of Texas, and with the Texas Folklore Society, Texas Historical and Landmarks Association, and the Texas State Historical Association, all of which included both men and women in their membership. After 1910, these groups became the focus of her attention and energy. The Daughters of the Republic of Texas she left behind.

Of course, Adele was not the only woman to affiliate with the Texas State Historical Association. In fact, some of her associates in the Texas Woman's Press Association served on the first executive council, and women from the Daughters of the Republic of Texas and the press association numbered among the membership, including Clara Driscoll by 1909. The difference between Adele and most of the clubwomen who became members of the TSHA was her active contribution to the organization's quarterly journal. By the time she was elected to the executive council in 1912, she had contributed a dozen articles to the *Quarterly.* By contrast, Anna J. Pennybacker, author of a popular history of Texas for schools, had contributed none, though she was elected a TSHA Fellow for her promotion of Texas history. Women contributed articles to the *Quarterly* beginning with the first issue. Many of these pieces consisted of memoirs, reminiscences, or biographical sketches. Adele contributed her share of such works, and although her articles tended to be sympathetic to her subjects, they evidenced thorough research and assiduous collection of original sources.

When Adele Looscan found herself elevated to the office of president of the Texas State Historical Association in 1915, she was stepping into a role that none of the other women members of the association, either clubwomen or professional historians, had occupied. When she left the office ten years later, in 1925, it would be almost fifty years before another woman would become president of the

TSHA. Adele brought to the office qualities that were critical at that moment in the existence of the association—her devotion to Texas history, her connections with the women of the state who got things done, her political connections, her business connections, and her own combination of tradition and progressivism. She provided a steady and attentive hand that enabled executive director Eugene C. Barker to focus his energies on dealing with a string of existential crises, including World War I and the conflict between Gov. Jim Ferguson and the University of Texas. She personally sought out primary sources of Texas history to add to the association's collection; she supported the organization financially at critical junctures, and she worked tirelessly to help secure its future.

Adele Briscoe Looscan was indeed a woman of her time, a combination of nineteenth-century tradition and twentieth-century progressivism. She flourished in the society of both women and men. She earned the respect of both. She was shaped by circumstance and by her heritage as a daughter of the Republic of Texas and was motivated throughout her life by her dedication to it. Hers is a story worth telling. Aside from what it reveals about women and culture in nineteenth- and early twentieth-century Texas, Adele's story reveals something fundamental about the nature, origins, and shaping of Texas's modern identity. It is a story that cannot be fully understood without understanding its beginnings.

Chapter One

ANTECEDENTS

ON A NOVEMBER DAY in 1836, seventeen-year-old Mary Jane Harris stood on the deck of the schooner *Julius Caesar* as it approached the mouth of the Brazos River.[1] Pewter swells curled into frothy white ribbons where the bow pushed through them. Layers of flat, silvery clouds made the otherwise mild day seem cool and damp. If the chilly breeze off the Gulf of Mexico teased wisps of dark hair from their pins and whipped them across her face, Mary Jane ignored them. As she gazed toward the horizon, her expression must have contained a mixture of anxiety, anticipation, and curiosity. So many members of the Harris family, some she had never met, had been drawn to Texas. In addition to her parents and brothers, her grandmother, Mary Richardson Harris, had migrated to Texas with her sons, William Plunkett Harris and David Harris, in about 1830 following John Harris's death. Her mother's brother, E. B. Birdsall, had been stationed with the army at nearby Fort Jesup, Louisiana, in January 1836. In short, most of her immediate family had preceded her to Texas.

Her grandparents, Lewis and Patience Birdsall, her uncle Maurice, and her cousin, George Babcock, who had accompanied her on the trip, remained in the salon as the ship approached the Texas shore, but Mary Jane had waited all her life for her first glimpse of Texas; she could not brook such confinement today. She thought of home, the friends who had gathered to see her on her way, and the happy days she had spent with them. One of those friends, Jane Ingersoll, had wished her well on her trip to Texas: "Dearly beloved Harris, you will undoubtedly enjoy yourself having always had a lovely perception of the beauties of nature."[2] Jane was a former classmate from Albion, New York, located on the Erie Canal about an hour from Seneca Falls. Their correspondence bespoke a shared appreciation for and educated awareness of the world. Mary Jane might never see her friends again. There was little choice but to shake off the twinge of nostalgia, wrap her shawl closer against the chill wind, and, breathing deeply of the salt air, plant her feet and squint into the horizon toward the new land and a future that was far from certain.

It had been an interminably long trip from her grandparents' home in Seneca Falls, New York, fully a month since their departure in early October 1836. She had endured the teeth-rattling stagecoach ride to Buffalo. Fearful gales on Lake Erie meant the trip would have to be made overland. By a tedious route of slow transit and many changes, they had reached New Orleans on the first of November. After a week visiting in that city, they had boarded the *Julius Caesar* for Texas, but Mary Jane would have to wait longer still to see Harrisburg, the settlement her father, John Richardson Harris, had established in 1824 as one of empresario Stephen F. Austin's earliest settlers. The Harris home, briefly host to the provisional government of the new Republic of Texas, had been burned by the Mexicans several months earlier, so her party would land at Quintana, a busy port at the mouth of the Brazos River.[3]

As the sand dunes of Quintana beach drew closer, Mary Jane tried to take in the "beauties of nature"—the beaches that would make Quintana a popular resort in the decades to come. They featured reddish dunes adorned with wispy sea oats bending gracefully in the wind. Sea birds soared and called as if announcing the ship's arrival, but excitement and the desire to set her feet on Texas soil distracted her from the view. At length the ship arrived at the dock, and a ramp was lowered for debarking both passengers and goods destined for the merchant firm of Thomas F. McKinney and Samuel M. Williams. Mary Jane, accompanied by her grandparents and uncle and trailed by hands bearing their trunks and valises, made her way down the rough wooden ramp and onto Texas soil.[4]

The travel-weary entourage rode up the dirt street from the wharf to the town proper, which consisted of a few roughly hewn houses. The most comfortable looking of these was a two-story boardinghouse, which, happily, proved to be their destination. The group stayed there for a few days, meeting and being introduced to many men who had made their names famous in action during the late revolution. Not all company was fit for young ladies, and Mary Jane found herself excused from the presence of some less savory visitors. Undaunted by admonitions and burning with curiosity, she found a vantage point at a wide crack in the wall and with rapt fascination watched the notorious slave smuggler and swindler Monroe Edwards, in rich and gaudy attire with diamonds flashing on his fingers, as he sat eating his meal of sweet potatoes.[5]

After a brief stay, Mary Jane and her family entourage boarded the steamer *Yellowstone* for Brazoria. There they remained two weeks at the boardinghouse of Jane Long, the widow of filibuster James Long. Jane Long was a legendary figure in those parts, and her taste for recounting her romantic adventures was rivaled only by her guests' appetite for hearing them. Mary Jane sat transfixed as Mrs. Long, who was said to have given birth to the first Anglo American child born in Texas, regaled the party with her stories. Jane Long was a study in contrasts, at once a regal figure and an impish one. The grooves that bracketed her mouth belied her relatively young age. Her deep-set eyes sparkled with humor and worldly wisdom. Tall and shapely, she moved with deceptively feminine grace and yet exuded a masculine energy and self-assurance. As she animatedly recounted one adventure after another, she seemed to be inwardly laughing at a secret joke.[6] Adding to the newcomers' excitement, the first congress of the Republic of Texas was in session at nearby Columbia, and President Sam Houston and other distinguished men were frequent visitors.[7]

At last, the erstwhile New Yorkers set out on the last leg of their journey to reunite with their daughter-mother-sister, Jane Harris, and Mary Jane's brothers, Lewis (Lew) Harris and DeWitt Clinton (Clint) Harris, in Harrisburg. After her brother Clint rode out to meet them with a saddle horse for her, the final stage of the trip proceeded on horseback accompanied by an ox-drawn wagon carrying their personal effects. It was a journey of about fifty miles, nearly every step of which was covered with water, as heavy rains had saturated the prairies. Mrs. Harris, spying them while still at a distance, waited impatiently in her doorway for the group to arrive.

Mary Jane Harris had arrived to claim her birthright. Texas was her father's legacy, all she would ever have of him. Born in 1819, she was but a toddler when John Harris left his family in 1823 to join his former neighbors, the Austins, in Texas. By 1829, he was dead of yellow fever. Mary Jane hardly remembered him at all. She had only the larger-than-life memory, given to her by her mother, of his pioneer spirit, his bravery, and his accomplishments, embodied in this community of twenty or so cabins and a sawmill.[8]

Mary Jane Harris's first impression of Harrisburg was of a beautiful location, banks sloping gently down to the bayou, and the woods all around filled with magnolia trees, which, in full bloom, would perfume the air with their lemony, sweet fragrance.[9] But on this day in mid-November it was too damp and cold to linger outdoors dreaming of spring. The house her mother currently occupied was the only house in the vicinity spared by the Mexicans when they burned the town a few months earlier. It escaped the torch only because it stood on the edge of the prairie and went unnoticed by the marauders. Her own home had been destroyed. Her brothers were engaged in having it rebuilt by Mexican prisoners, who had been assigned to Mrs. Harris for that purpose. When finished, the house

Mary Jane expected to call home would not be entirely unfamiliar to her. It would be the same size and shape as her grandfather's home in Seneca County, New York, though not as tall. It was a sturdy house divided into four rooms, with a twelve-foot-wide center hall. The front piazza afforded a scenic view of the bayou and the magnolia trees that lined the opposite bank. Clint and Lewis had built the house on large oak blocks several feet from the ground, making "4 pens and a passage," until they got the proper height for the first story. The roof consisted of peeled pine poles hewed on one side, with split laths on which were laid split boards three feet long. The structure was barely in a condition to be occupied when their family members arrived. They had built a kitchen of logs about eighteen by twenty feet with a loft, where they had lived for some time before the big house was ready to occupy. The kitchen had a large fireplace in one end and a chimney of sticks plastered with clay.[10] On that day in mid-November, the smoldering coals would have radiated inviting warmth to road-weary travelers and filled the air with just a hint of pungent wood smoke.

On this site in the early 1820s, John Richardson Harris had located a league of land, including the Harrisburg townsite, which was considered to be the very head of navigation on Buffalo Bayou, about twenty miles from Galveston. Here, vessels that could cross Redfish and Clopper's Bars would stop; they could go no further.[11] The area encompassed both prairie and forest. The bottoms along the waterways were thick with hardwoods and conifers. The remaining lands were prairie. Canebrakes covered many acres, with cane reaching twenty feet in height. Flamingos and other waterfowl waded gracefully through the marshes surrounding the confluence of Buffalo Bayou and the San Jacinto River. Deer were plentiful. Several hundred people had settled there, mostly in the timbered areas along the waterways.[12] News of this "most beautiful" site soon spread. By the early 1830s, it had attracted the attention of land developers and mercantile interests infected with "Texas fever." Three towns had been laid out in the vicinity, Harrisburg being the most permanent. In 1834 or 1835, Nathaniel Lynch, who lived opposite the junction of Buffalo Bayou and the San Jacinto River, divided and platted his land and named it Lynchburg. Meanwhile, James Morgan, representing a new land company called the New Washington Association, purchased sixteen hundred acres of land on Clopper's Point across Galveston Bay with the intent of founding a city and developing it commercially and agriculturally. He renamed the point for himself and laid out the town of New Washington. The area also attracted the attention of merchant interests and land speculators in Nacogdoches and Anahuac, including James and Henry Prentiss, Henry Raguet, and Augustus C. and John K. Allen.[13]

In Port Gibson, Mississippi, Andrew Briscoe, one of twelve children of Parmenas Briscoe, Mississippi pioneer, planter, and state politician, had contracted "Texas fever," too. At twenty-three, Andrew was anxious to make his way in the world. Restless and seeing little opportunity in sharing with eleven siblings, the dark-haired, intense Andrew was easily captivated by all the land excitement on the Mexican frontier. He made a few scouting trips between 1830 and 1833, during which he registered as a citizen of the Mexican province of Coahuila and Texas, garnered a good many contacts, initiated some business deals, and began making preparations to relocate. Thus, in late January 1834, he informed the Allen brothers at Fort Jesup (eighty miles due east of Nacogdoches) of unavoidable delays in his business that induced him to postpone his immigration to Texas until October, but he sent money to Henry Teal to pay Henry Raguet's account in Nacogdoches.[14] Among other matters delaying his relocation was some research he intended to do. Having grown up on a plantation with nearly a hundred slaves, he saw the slave trade as a real potential moneymaker in Texas, what with Stephen F. Austin and others hoping to attract colonists from the planter class across the South. He wanted to explore the possibilities. He had not yet been to New Orleans, so he could provide no information with regard to the importation of slaves, but he meant to inform himself completely as soon as he arrived there. He waited anxiously to hear from the Allens as to whether they had arranged the two dollars per labor (177.1 acres) land-purchase price with Don Vicente Aldrete as they had promised, and to find out how his friend Carbajal was managing in his business.[15] Don Aldrete, probably the largest landowner in the Refugio area at the time, was land commissioner of the province of Coahuila and Texas. Andrew's arrangements with the commissioner would depend on the information he received from the Allens. If, when he got to New Orleans, he found that the slave trade could be carried on with profit, he assured the Allens he would write to them his views on the subject. He urged his business partners to keep him apprised of developments.[16]

It was little more than a year later when Andrew Briscoe arrived in Texas ready to launch himself, full bore as usual, into business at Anahuac. Only, as usual, everything did not go exactly as he planned, and he was instantly outraged. Hence, in April 1835, with palpable angst he penned a letter to John K. Allen: "Four weeks in this place and some damned rough usage having my goods landed against my will by military force. The people would calmly stand by and see me lose all—god damn them," he fumed. He went to Velasco to get justice and failed—"the roughest fare and most dangerous excursions unpaid." His business was delayed; the deputy collector, backed by forty soldiers, seized some of his provisions as contraband and demanded the payment of duties on the remaining goods, withholding them until the duties were paid. "When I talk of resistance the people blame me and talk of a jury trial and the devil knows what all," he huffed. But, in the end, he calculated that he would get through it with little more than the loss of time.[17]

In fact, young Andrew in his hubris had underestimated Mexican customs officials. When he intentionally taunted them by loading his boat in such a manner as to excite curiosity, stowing bricks rather than smuggled goods in the hull, the new commander, Antonio

Tenorio, arrested him and DeWitt Clinton Harris, to whom he had tried to trade his "contraband" without paying national tariffs.[18] The two were released when William B. Travis and Patrick Jack arrived to drive Tenorio out of office, but Briscoe would not let it go and continued to fume, eventually finding an outlet for his outrage by joining the military action against Mexico.[19]

But on this particular April day in 1835 Briscoe merely wrote to John K. Allen. He was in need of the balance owed him, some $720, and he appealed to Allen to send it to him, along with his horse, which he also stood in need of, and promised to pay all the expenses of transport. He could not say with certainty when he would arrive at Nacogdoches, but he expressed the hope he would be there sometime during the summer. "Tell the ladies that I am not married, but am a candidate and hope to be elected in the course of the next five years," he joked half seriously. He expected to reach Nacogdoches in July or August and would, "of course," hunt for a wife. The sooner his business with the Allens was brought to a close, the better.[20]

Thwarted in his original business plans, Andrew Briscoe entered into resistance against Mexico with energy and enthusiasm. In October 1835, he was elected captain of the Liberty Volunteers in time to lead them into the Battle of Concepción at the end of that month and on to San Antonio in December. Within a year of his arrival in Texas, he had been elected, along with Lorenzo de Zavala, "the most interesting man in Texas" according to William Fairfax Gray, as a delegate from Harrisburg to the convention that was to assemble in Washington, which only days beforehand was invaded by the Mexican army. After signing the Texan Declaration of Independence there, he departed before the convention ended, apparently anxious to get back to soldiering. He raised a company of regulars for the army, and he commanded Company A during the Battle of San Jacinto, in April 1836. In the aftermath of battle, Harrisburg, like other places in Texas, offered the market Briscoe had been angling for. Items of all kinds, from foodstuffs to clothing to crockery, were in high demand. From New Orleans, he had goods sent to his store in Lynchburg and instructed his clerks to raise the prices as high as the market would bear. Not long after the war ended, he was appointed chief justice of Harris County, and not long after that, he fulfilled his prediction to the Allen brothers by finding himself a wife. As fortune would have it, his business partner's young, beautiful, and unmarried sister arrived in Harrisburg in November 1836, just in time for the holidays.[21]

Indeed, Dewitt Clinton Harris's sister, Mary Jane, had acquired a reputation as the belle of Buffalo Bayou in the vicinity of Harrisburg. She was lively and full of fun that New Year's Eve in Harrisburg. She had taken dancing lessons in New York but never tried to dance because her lessons had never gone beyond learning the steps, but there was no hugging the wall on that festive evening. There were too few females to go around as it was. She did her first dancing on a puncheon floor in a room with three beds in it. The fiddler's strings often reduced to one, but she didn't care. She was young and carried away with excitement. With great agility they all jumped the large cracks in the floor as the new year came in. Those were happy times that winter, when the family all lived in one room and cooked out of doors, and if she needed to change her dress, she would go to the smokehouse and get in a corner away from the dripping bacon to complete her toilette.[22]

No question about it, Mary Jane Harris brought an uncommon degree of glamour and charm to Harrisburg. It was probably inevitable that she would capture the attention of Andrew Briscoe that New Year's Eve. The house throbbed with the vitality of the crowd gathered in the great room. Furniture was pushed back against the walls; the floor was swept smooth. Flames danced and crackled in the fireplace, casting animated shadows on the walls and providing a background for the hum of voices punctuated occasionally by sharp bursts of laughter. Briscoe, who had been made county judge of Harrisburg (later Harris) County just a few days earlier, felt slightly uncomfortable in his own skin and disguised the fact by cloaking his insecurity in boisterousness. He gravitated naturally toward the vivacious, black-haired Mary Jane. She was far and away the prettiest girl at the party, and he was in the market for a wife anyway. Moreover, through his business and military exploits with her brother, he already possessed a vested interest in Harrisburg and was virtually part of the family.[23]

The New Year's Eve festivities marked not only the end of a momentous year for Texas but the beginning of another for the inhabitants living along Buffalo Bayou. Within a few weeks of the Battle of San Jacinto, the Allen brothers had purchased land just fifteen or so miles from the battlefield, at the junction of Buffalo and White Oak Bayous, and they hoped to sell it to the new Republic of Texas as a site for the capital. They named their new city after the hero of San Jacinto, Sam Houston, and they promoted it shrewdly. They intended it to be a full-blown city from the start. They hired Gail Borden Jr. and his brother, Thomas, to survey and lay out the town with wide streets and reserves identified as Court House Square, Congress Square, Church, and School, and they advertised the plan in the newspapers of Europe and the United States. Their efforts were rewarded when Houston was chosen as the capital of the Republic of Texas on November 30, 1836. As the new year dawned, it was a city of tents but already exploding with growth.

By April 1837, Houston was a town of five hundred people, most of them male.[24] On April 21, they celebrated the first anniversary of the Battle of San Jacinto with a grand ball. Invitations printed on white satin went out to neighboring plantations. Guests came from miles around, accompanied by manservants and ladies' maids and garbed in elegant ball costumes from New Orleans. President Houston dressed for the occasion in black velvet trimmed in gold cording, with a ruffled shirt and scarlet cassimere waistcoat. His boots were equally fine, with short red tops laced and folded down to just above his ankles and finished at the heels with silver spurs. He included in his party, in addition to the British consular officer, Joseph Tucker Crawford, Mary Jane Harris, to whom he had taken quite a fancy, and her cousin John Birdsall, as well as Francis and Adele Lubbock and the Moseley Bakers. They all met at Capt. Moseley Baker's house, a one-room clapboard with a fine carpet covering a bare dirt floor. At sundown they proceeded together to the ball.[25]

Dancing had already begun when they arrived, this time to the music of violin, bass viol, and fife instead of the one-string fiddle. The large room filled with guests from Brazoria, Columbia, San Felipe, Harrisburg, and the adjoining country. When the presidential party entered, the orchestra struck up "Hail to the Chief." The crowd parted and, with General Houston and Mrs. Baker in the lead, the Harrisburg contingent advanced to the upper end of the room. Mary Jane felt like a princess in a fairy tale. She carefully laid aside her wrap, changed shoes for dancing slippers, and joined the cotillion led by General Houston with Mrs. Baker, gowned in white satin and black lace. Mrs. Sidney Sherman wore a breathtaking white velvet ball gown she had brought from Kentucky. There were gowns of white mulls and colored satins, low cut with spreading skirts, every bit as elegant as those worn in the capitals of Europe. Women wore feathers or exotic Mexican flowers in their hair.[26] To a seventeen-year-old girl, it was a dazzling display. The atmosphere was charged with expectation. Something big and important was about to happen; she could feel it, and she wanted to be part of it. These memories of being the belle of a ball attended by the most prominent people in Texas would remain with Mary Jane for a lifetime and be recounted to her children.

Not to be outdone, the gentlemen had put on their finest plumage as well. Colonel Sherman wore the blue broadcloth uniform, lined in gold satin and trimmed in gold braid, that he had worn in the battle. The other gentlemen wore formal evening dress in the style of Beau Brummel. Their cravats of white muslin or silk were tied just below the points of their very high collars. Their cutaway evening coats revealed ruffled shirts, handsome waistcoats, and tight pantaloons ending above their ankles. In contrast to this elegant display the ballroom itself was an unfinished, two-story room with bare beams. Sperm oil candles in wooden chandeliers lighted the ballroom, but there was no roof on the building.[27]

At midnight they all adjourned to the hotel of Ben Fort Smith, a two-room log building without floor or carpet. There, a lavish supper was laid out: turkeys, venison, cakes and a profusion of other sweets, rich coffee, and sparkling wines. There were witty toasts and hearty laughter. When the fare had been consumed, they returned to the ball, launched into a lively Virginia reel, and danced until dawn. Never at a loss for admiring partners, Mary Jane found it truly a magical and memorable night, filled with excitement and promise.[28]

Like the new city of Houston, romance blossomed in winter, and the following August, on Mary Jane Harris's eighteenth birthday, she and Andrew Briscoe were married. Since the county seat had been fixed at Houston and Andrew was county judge, the couple, along with Mary Jane's brothers, Lew and Clint, removed there, where Clint served as county clerk and Lew went into his office as deputy.[29] Andrew, for all his bravado in challenging Mexican customs officials at Anahuac two years prior, suffered an attack of self-doubt as he prepared to take office. After all, he had no legal training. How could he presume to handle law business correctly? "It is extremely awkward to undertake a kind of business of which one is entirely ignorant of the rules and form of proceedings. I believe I am a good soldier; but I shall make a very indifferent probate judge or notary public," he wrote to Secretary of State Thomas Rusk.[30]

Despite his qualms, Andrew assumed his duties as county judge, and the Briscoes took up residence in Houston. Young Briscoe purchased a two-story house being built on Main Street one block from the capitol, the first two-story house in Houston. He discharged his duties as a civil officer intelligently and efficiently but always with an edge. Regardless of the prestige that might be attached to the position of chief justice, civil service was never Andrew Briscoe's ambition. He wanted more, much more, and in 1838, a year into his appointment, an intriguing new opportunity began to take shape. His erstwhile business associates Augustus and John Allen and several others of his acquaintance had become involved in a railroad and banking venture. At about the same time, the Republic of Texas chartered three other companies interested in the construction and operation of railroads.[31] In short order, the railroad ventures were tied to the promotion of municipal real estate.[32] The fourth railroad chartered by the Republic of Texas, the Harrisburg Railroad and Trading Company, was the by-product of a real estate promotion scheme, and it was too close to home for Andrew to resist. In June 1838, the final claims against the estate of John Richardson Harris were settled. The beneficiaries of the settlement formed a trust, the Harrisburg Town Company, the stock of which was divided among the heirs of John Richardson Harris, one of whom, of course, was Mary Jane Briscoe. When the stockholders met for the first time, they appointed Andrew Briscoe as agent. He resigned his position as chief justice early, on May 2, 1839. Along with Mary Jane's brother Lew, and her grandfather, Lewis Birdsall, he became convinced that building a railroad from Harrisburg to the Brazos would greatly increase the value of the company's stock.[33] All expenses incurred by the railroad construction project would be paid from the sale of Harrisburg town lots.

Andrew and Mary Jane Briscoe returned to Harrisburg, built a two-story brick home, and welcomed their first son, Parmenas. Andrew assumed the role of gentleman farmer. The prairies of the area were well suited to cattle raising. Mary Jane, fond of horseback riding from childhood, accompanied Andrew on excursions to the prairies during which he tended to his cattle business. She acquired a fine black horse as full of spirit as she and entertained herself by thundering across the prairies in joyous abandon while Andrew was away tending to his real estate interests in Austin.[34] His neighbor,

Francis Lubbock, remembered, "Briscoe's home was three miles from ours. He was county judge of Harris County, and a man to be admired—firm, brave, and just. His wife was from the State of New York, General Sherman's from Kentucky, and mine from Louisiana. These were all good friends, for the women as well as the men who came here were true Texans."[35] As the tumultuous decade of the 1830s drew to a close, the Briscoes, their extended families, and their neighbors in Harrisburg and vicinity seemed to have settled into a peaceful and idyllic existence that was, in actuality, a thin veneer. Mexico had not given up on Texas, and to the consternation of many Texans, the United States did not immediately embrace it either.

Texas in the 1840s was a place full of high hopes and equally high anxieties, successes and hardships, opportunities and uncertainties, dangers and difficulties. Although enterprises flourished and population increased, both were threatened by hostile Indians as well as Mexico, for whom the outcome of the late Texas Revolution was far from settled. Defense had to be provided from an empty treasury while political leaders feuded among themselves and some even sought to extend the disputed western boundary even farther.[36] "Land and inclosed Plantations plenty but no provisions—times have never been so hard in Texas, like they are now. I have never known the want of two bits untill now.—!!!!!" fretted Adolphus Sterne in March 1842.[37]

In Harrisburg, a town of some fourteen hundred souls by 1840 and one of the earliest successful settlements in Austin's Colony, Andrew Briscoe raised cattle and cast about for investment opportunities. His idea of establishing a slave-trading enterprise never went anywhere. In fact, he never acquired more than four slaves himself. His most recent venture, the private railroad enterprise, had not gone particularly well, due in large part to the unsettled political and economic climate in Texas. Although Andrew began promoting his Harrisburg and Brazos Railroad in 1839, by 1840 only about two miles of road had been laid owing to his inability to secure funding. The failure to realize sufficient funding reflected the uncertain climate of the Republic of Texas. Initial land sales went badly. Subsequent sales held in Houston and in Harrisburg also failed to raise sufficient capital. By May, the company realized that land sales would not produce the revenue necessary for the construction of even a short-line route from the Brazos River to Harrisburg. There was little doubt that the slow sale of property and "the impossibility of enlisting foreign capital because of the unsettled condition of the country" spelled the demise of the railroad. A Mexican invasion seeming probable at any time, the project was abandoned.[38]

That same year Briscoe drafted a complete plan for building a railroad from Harrisburg to San Diego, California, and in 1841 he secured a charter from the Republic of Texas for the Harrisburg Railroad and Trading Company, of which he was president. He continued to cast about for some way of financing the route. In the meantime, he occupied himself in a number of ways. He obtained a license from the county court to operate a ferry across Bray's Bayou at Harrisburg. The following month, in July 1841, he announced his candidacy to represent Harris County in Congress but changed his mind in August, claiming that the only way he could win would be to buy the election, which he refused to do. In 1843, he and Mary Jane's uncle, William Plunkett Harris, entered into a contract designed to raise capital by selling land around Harrisburg to French immigrants. This scheme never came to fruition either, and in 1847 the Harrisburg Town Company transferred all unsold lots and lands to Sidney Sherman for $150,000. Sherman succeeded in persuading northern investors to provide capital for his enterprise, which was the building of a railroad from Harrisburg westward.[39] By 1848, disappointed and feeling betrayed by Sherman, Briscoe began looking for a new venture. By this time, Andrew and Mary Jane Briscoe were the parents of five children: Parmenas, Andrew Birdsall, Byron, Jessie Wade, and the youngest, Adele.

Adele Lubbock Briscoe, the namesake of Adele Baron, wife of Francis R. (Frank) Lubbock, was born February 5, 1848, three days after the Treaty of Guadalupe Hidalgo ended the Mexican-American War, recognized the annexation of Texas to the United States, and settled the boundary between Texas and Mexico from the Gulf of Mexico up the main channel of the Rio Grande to the southern boundary of the Mexican province of New Mexico. It seemed that prospects in Harris County were looking up. The flow of newcomers to the area never slowed during the war. Business was brisk. Construction, commerce, and banking all thrived. Frank Lubbock's mercantile business was doing so well that he bought four hundred acres on Sims Bayou from Andrew Briscoe, who was acting as agent for the Harris heirs, and took up cattle ranching. "The little town of Harrisburg," Lubbock recalled, "gave us a pleasant set of neighbors. We had plenty of good country fare." Lubbock noted that Gen. Sidney Sherman, who lived at Harrisburg, "with all the energy of a very energetic man, was striving to build up that town." Why, then, with the promise of Texas at last about to be realized, would Andrew Briscoe decide to seek his fortune elsewhere just at that time? A legal dispute arose with Sherman involving business transactions going back a decade and a fire that damaged or destroyed the Briscoe home. Later, in a letter to James Briscoe, Mary Jane spoke of the case against Sherman, stating her belief that "if the shrubbery had not been removed, the house would not have burned." Furthermore, the year 1849 was long remembered as a "black year" for Texas farmers. A late killing frost followed by severe drought took a harsh toll. These reverses of fortune as well as a restless spirit might explain why Briscoe, who was raising cattle, became disillusioned and resolved to move his family to New Orleans.[40] The real answer to that question, though, may have lain beyond Texas. The California gold rush, which had begun in 1848, brought forty-niners through Houston, where they bought supplies for the gold fields. And the gold bug was contagious.[41]

The bug that bit Andrew Briscoe, however, drew him eastward, initially, instead of westward. In what seemed an abrupt decision, especially considering his poor health, he decided to move his family from Harrisburg to New Orleans with the idea of going into banking and finance. He wrote to his brother, James, in Richmond, Texas, enclosing his will and laying out his longer range plans to go west. This plan involved selling a large portion of his movable property, acknowledging that, should he die in California, his family "would probably be left with very little active means on which to live." Andrew's letter revealed a good deal about himself and his state of mind. His will gave James absolute control of his affairs in the event of his death. "You may probably think it would have been more natural that I had delegated these large powers to my wife in whose good sense and honor you know I very justly place great confidence," he wrote, "but I have preferred giving them to you, from the fact that all women on business matters require and follow advice, and she would most naturally consult her brothers, who would consider her and her children their proper prey." Having admitted that what he proposed to do would leave Mary Jane in an awkward financial position, he assured his brother that "previous to my departure if such a thing is practical, I will have my life insurance in a sum at least equal to the value of the property sold, which will place my family in as good a position as it was at the time of making the enclosed will, except that they will be without a home. If I live any length of time in California, I shall permit her funds from time to time of which I will regularly advise you, that in case of my death you may know what there ought to be, of my estate." As chauvinistic as these statements sounded, they were not the only plans Andrew had made without consulting his wife. "You will observe," he wrote, "that in my will, is a restriction against Mary's marrying—this is deliberately done, as I cannot contemplate the idea of a stepfather for my children, or that the proceeds of my labor and my father's labor, should support another man's children or grandchildren, and though Mary would now treat a second marriage as an impossible absurdity, and though she is really wiser than other women, I suppose that a disagreement with you, poverty, or ambition would tempt her, as most other women, to contemplate in course of time, an event which would at first seem absurd." He went on to explain some assets he held in trust for others, making reference to a judgment against Sidney Sherman pending in the Supreme Court, and then observed, "Money will probably be much more plenty in a few years than it ever has been, in which case the provision will be very small for my wife, but if I die any way soon, it is as much as she has any right to expect my estate to pay, and if I should live a few years, I shall have plenty of time to alter the provision to suit the case."[42]

In the meantime, he intended to raise cash through his New Orleans enterprise despite an inauspicious start. Mary Jane, with the fortitude that had seen her through several ventures already with Andrew and the birth of five children, took leave of her mother and brothers and stoically moved her family and household to New Orleans in the dead of winter, keeping her misgivings to herself. But secretly she was filled with doubt and fear. She had just suffered the loss of her youngest boy, Byron, to illness. The whole family was more or less unwell. Andrew had been quite ill. He had certainly chosen a dull season of the year to commence a new business, especially with insufficient capital. The expense of relocating had been enormous. Andrew was depressed, and vexed, and harried. The children were cross; the baby, Adele, was suffering with an unpleasant rash that made her doubly fussy. They knew almost no one in New Orleans. Rent was high and income was uncertain while Andrew struggled to establish his business. She could not voice her trepidation to Andrew, whose stress level made him edgier and more sensitive than ever.[43]

Mary Jane was not alone in her concern. Her father-in-law, Gen. Parmenas Briscoe, had grave doubts of his own. Unlike Mary Jane, he did not hesitate to express his concerns and to plead with his son: "I wish that you had come on here and let your family stay here until fall. I am very fearful that you and family will be sick. Your poor brother Sam is dead—he and fifteen of his negroes died the same week, all of cholera. We have plenty of house room, and plenty of milk and butter, so do not hesitate but bring your family."[44]

General Briscoe's words proved no more persuasive than Mary Jane's silence. Andrew determined stubbornly to persevere. With renewed optimism he wrote to his father in April from Saint Louis, the first stop on a whirlwind business tour that included Louisville, Cincinnati, New York, and Boston: "My health is excellent. I think I am recovering some of my lost flesh. Certainly I am recovering confidence in myself. Success in making favorable impressions on men that I have seen very little of and in forming acquaintances rapidly has in a great measure restored my lost confidence in myself, and I now feel that I shall succeed." Although disappointments in his Texas enterprises, coupled with the need to raise capital for his California ventures, may have been major factors in his determination, a letter to his father in July provided another explanation for his decision to relocate to New Orleans. "The boys are both at school," he wrote, "and have been since the second day after our arrival in the city—schooling costs nothing here—the expense being entirely paid by the State." General Briscoe, however, was not persuaded by any of these arguments or Andrew's resurgence of self-confidence. "My dear son," he wrote in reply, "you do not acknowledge the rest of my last letter inviting you to bring your family to remain during the sickly season at my house. I am fearful that you may suffer by sickness. I am also fearful that you may not succeed in your line of business to your hopes and expectations. I expect to visit your city in October, when I will have come to a conclusion as regards my future course."[45]

Sadly, his words had no effect. General Briscoe did, indeed, come to New Orleans in October, but he was too late. Andrew Briscoe was a tragic figure who dreamed of greatness but repeatedly fell short, a victim of his own weaknesses. He died of yellow fever October 2, 1849, leaving Mary Jane financially strapped and alone to rear the four surviving children.[46] Her response to his death and to these challenges shaped not only the lives of her children but the way Texans would ultimately remember the Texas Revolution and those who participated in it. A woman of strong will and tremendous physical and mental energy, her influence set the course for her children's lives, most particularly that of the youngest, her baby daughter Adele.

Chapter Two

Early Days in Texas

THE YOUNGEST OF Andrew and Mary Jane Briscoe's children, Adele Lubbock Briscoe was barely twenty months old when her father was buried at his family's home in Claiborne County, Mississippi. Mary Jane's worst fears were now realized, and the burden of Andrew's unsettled business affairs, as well as the responsibility for herself and four small children, fell squarely upon her shoulders. Two weeks after Andrew's death, she wrote to her brother-in-law, James Briscoe, in Richmond, Texas, whom she knew to be the executor of Andrew's will, giving an accounting of the state of Andrew's affairs in New Orleans to the best of her knowledge. With weary resignation she told him that the lawsuit should not be settled without Sidney Sherman paying something. Andrew had always been adamant that Sherman or else the mercantile enterprise of Rice and Nichols would have to pay for the damages to her property. She really was not sure what to do with herself, but if Sherman paid, she wanted to procure a home near some permanent school where, by taking boarders or undertaking some other enterprise, she might contribute to the support of her family. If the lawsuit settlement did not provide enough, she hoped to trade or sell some land toward that purpose. She had no time for grieving, she knew. She must arrange her business in New Orleans immediately and get away from there as quickly as possible. If she had to lose two hundred or three hundred dollars in order to get away, it was certainly better to do so than remain there. Her decision was greatly facilitated by her father-in-law, Gen. Parmenas Briscoe, who arrived in New Orleans as Andrew was on his deathbed. He helped her close up the business and insisted on taking her and the children back with him to his plantation near Port Gibson, Mississippi, where he laid Andrew's remains to rest in the old family cemetery.[1]

Little more than a month after Andrew's death Mary Jane and her young family were settled at the Briscoe plantation in Mississippi, but their future was far from settled. Many decisions were left to be made, and some matters required urgent attention. A large part of the property in Andrew's possession had been held in trust for others, though in some cases there was no documentation of or witness to the fact. To complicate matters further, real estate titles showed property to be absolutely his, when, in fact, he held no honest interest in it. There were 2,214 acres of land in Jefferson County on Cow Bayou, out of a grant to James Dyson; 1,107 acres in Fort Bend County, out of a grant to Brown and Belknap; and 531 acres in the same county, out of a grant to Abner Kuykendall, belonging to the heirs and legatees of John Birdsall. Then there was the judgment against Sidney Sherman for more than five thousand dollars, which was pending in the Texas Supreme Court on a writ of error under the control of attorneys Hadley and Terry.[2] Mrs. William Beaseley of Red Bluff had a claim to a quarter of that sum when it was collected. Thomas Carothers, a cousin of Mary Jane from Pennsylvania who had settled in Walker County, Texas, held an agency to sell Andrew's Winter's Creek land, which he owned jointly with Edward Hall.[3]

Mary Jane knew that Andrew's brother, James, would help her, but he would have to see Andrew's papers before he could get an accurate picture of his business. Adding to the urgency of the situation was Judge John Birdsall's estate. Birdsall had died in 1839, and the heir wanted the estate closed, which could not be done because Andrew had had all the papers with him.The Sherman lawsuit was of particular concern to her as it actually involved her separate property, which she had inherited from her father. She had every right to dictate the mode of settlement. She could keep the proceeds out of the settlement of Andrew's affairs if she wanted to, and James advised her to do so. At least, she thought, she was fortunate that James was executor of Andrew's estate. More important than the purely legal and financial aspects of this business, she and James shared a strong mutual regard and affection for one another. She trusted James. He respected her intelligence, judgment, and competence, which he demonstrated by speaking to her as an intellectual equal. Because of that, she valued his opinion. Now, she wished him to advise her on what to do with herself and her children.[4]

"I am a poor hand to advise," he told her. He had written to his father asking him to offer a definite proposal—to say precisely what he would do as an inducement to keep her and her children in Mississippi. He assumed she would have received letters from her family urging her to come back to Texas, but he felt compelled to point out other considerations: "You know what opportunities there are here for raising children as they ought to be. Where you are is not the best place in the world, but you will be able to make a comparison between that and Texas for yourself. Your children have lost their father and they may find friends wherever they go all over the world but they will never find another father." James also assumed that General Briscoe would want to keep his son's widow and his grandchildren with him. "Where you are," he argued, "they will come nearer finding a father than anywhere else on earth. He will only not be a father because he will be too indulgent probably for their good. You and your children could be a comfort and a blessing to him in his old age."[5]

A part of Mary Jane longed to take the course James advocated. She was tired, and it would be easy to simply accept General Briscoe's hospitality. On the other hand, she was very concerned that her children be well educated. Then, there was Andrew's sister, Emily, and her husband. The Mississippi plantation was also Emily's home. General Briscoe was her father. She did not want to usurp Emily's place in his affections and attention. She feared the friction that might easily develop. More than anything, though, she prized her own independence and ability to govern her own life and make her own decisions with regard to the rearing of her children.

James had a ready rebuttal. "Emily and her husband are there more as company for him than anything else," he countered. "You would be even more agreeable company for him than Emily. You would be under his own especial charge and protection. That would give to him a feeling of responsibility that would be a pleasure. Emily has her husband, and father's attention to her and her children might frequently come between her and her husband so as to make it unpleasant. With you it would be different." In the last analysis, he told her, the choice was hers. He knew every woman considered the welfare of her children, but he urged her to consider her own peace of mind. He would help her whatever she decided. If she could stay there and be perfectly satisfied, she should do it. "But," he cautioned, "it's not right for anyone to sacrifice their peace of mind for any consideration. If father can't place you in a situation that you may have employment that will be useful to him, don't stay at all. I know that a feeling of dependence would render you unhappy to a degree that no woman or man ought to bear. I would not advise you to stay anywhere under any such circumstances." He closed his letter to her with a promise to send her all the information he could get on the morrow.[6]

The next day James wrote to Mary Jane of more recent developments from Houston, where he had visited her brother: "Your brother Clint says you'd better get the Sherman business arranged because there are other interested parties who will appoint their own agents now that Andy is dead. Sherman has paid $1,200 to one of the parties and has a receipt for that amount since the rendition of the judgment." A lawyer had advised him, he told her, that such a separate deal would prevent any award in the higher court for damages in the whole amount. It was a strange rule to him, and he knew it did not make a lot of sense. He would not advance one single step in the business nor give her advice on the subject until he had studied it himself. He assured her he would go to Houston during the next term of the probate court and have Andrew's will probated and recorded on the last Monday of the month.[7]

With the knowledge that any further action on her part must await the probate of Andrew's will, Mary Jane and her children passed Christmas quietly with her husband's family in Port Gibson. It was a brief respite, however, for the new year had hardly begun before she learned that James had heard from Clinton about the Sherman matter. The land that Andrew owned with Edward Hall, if sold, together with the judgment against Sherman, would suffice for her support if properly managed. James told her he would leave the decision about where she wanted to live, Mississippi or Texas, up to her. Obviously, if she lived in Texas, she would not have any monetary support from the Briscoes.[8]

Mary Jane procrastinated, more because of the weight of making such a complex decision than an unwillingness to make it. James's letter gave her a lot more to think about. He sent her a copy of Andrew's will in case she had not seen it and told her that it would be right for her to be there to either accept or remand the will as far as it concerned her, but he did not believe that it was absolutely necessary unless she chose to renounce it. "There are some provisions in it in regard to you that I do not approve of," he told her, "but they are so and we cannot alter them. You should consider the matter well before you determine whether to accept or reject it, and I do not know that you need be in a hurry about it." That was not even the worst of his news. She read on: "Andy's circumstances must be very different now from what they were when he wrote that will as he alludes to the annual revenue of his property. That must have been written before he sold his cattle when there was a prospect for an annual revenue, but now we shall have to sell property and invest in active property before there is any sort of revenue." However, James reassured her, the money that Carothers would get with the amount of the Sherman judgment would give them funds enough to buy some property and probably enough to produce the needed revenue, with economy and good management. If more should be necessary, the Montgomery County land would have to be the source of it. He shared other family business with her and gave her information about his own affairs to pass on to his father. His parting words, though, contained a foreshadowing that would ultimately settle her decision about where to live: "Tell father to forget about going to California. If he can't think of anything but to go to California, he'd be better off to come to Texas."[9]

Unfortunately, General Briscoe found the lure of the frontier irresistible, and by early 1851 he had departed for California. As it turned out, he had been making plans in that regard at least since the summer of 1849. In going through Andrew's papers Mary Jane encountered a letter from his father written that August in which he confided to Andrew that he had a strong notion to go to California and that he planned to start in February: "Do not write to dissuade me, for I wish to have fair play in making up my mind; I am in perfect good health and think I could stand more hardships than many a younger man." A midlife crisis? Perhaps, but Mary Jane knew otherwise. She folded the letter and returned it to the pile of papers. Andrew and his father were cut from the same cloth. In her father-in-law she recognized the same nervous restlessness, yen for adventure, and craving for more that had dogged her husband, and it filled her with foreboding.[10]

Her sense of dread was confirmed when word came late in 1851 that General Briscoe had died in a storm near Acapulco, Mexico, on his way back from California. Sorrowfully, she wrote to James. She had been worried that the general would never return from California. She knew from the moment he informed them of his plans that if he did not, she and her children would no longer have a home. This bereavement was the saddest that could have befallen her family, for it not only obliged them to find another home but also deprived her children of a grandfather. She confided that she was under the impression they would have to leave the next fall, and she thought they had better do so immediately. She hated to leave Andrew's grave but would be obliged to, so she saw no point in putting it off any longer. William, James's younger brother, said she could stay the remainder of that year if she paid her proportion of the expenses, but she didn't know how much that would be and thought she could live anywhere else on the same money and furnish everything but house rent. If her children were doing well she wouldn't leave till fall, but they had not been in school and there was no prospect of having a school in place anytime soon. Even if they got one right away, she would have to withdraw the children halfway through the semester. She would prefer to live in Mississippi or Louisiana but did not think she could afford it. She concluded the only thing she could do was return to Texas—even though she was loath to do so as long as Sidney Sherman was alive, because she did not want to lay eyes on him. She would move to either Houston or Galveston. She did not want to be too near the bayou or the graveyard or any place more than walking distance from a school.[11]

Thus, Mary Jane Briscoe returned to Texas in 1852, partly out of financial necessity and partly to pursue educational opportunities for her children. Although Mary Jane's first thought had been to live in Houston or Galveston, her plan had changed by the time she returned to Texas. Saint Paul's College for boys and girls had been established "on a commanding hill" at Anderson, Texas, by Rev. Charles Gillette of the Episcopal Church. He was one of the leading educators of the time and founded Wharton College in the city of Austin some years later.[12] Mary Jane's desire for higher education for her children was not surprising, considering that the movement to improve educational opportunities for women had begun as early as

1828 in the Northeast, where she had been reared.[13] Gillette offered to the initial student body of forty-three boys instruction in English, geography, history, classical languages, and the sciences. The girls' school, conducted by Gillette's sister, Jeanette, included many of the same subjects taught in the boys' division, as well as French, piano, drawing, painting, and needlework. Saint Paul's, despite its "college" designation, functioned almost exclusively as a secondary school or "academy." Mary Jane's eldest son, Parmenas, was thirteen, and the prospect of sending him to school, combined with the fact that she owned property in that area through her husband's estate, made Grimes County a sensible choice of residence. Mary Jane might almost have felt content had not her brother-in-law James, upon whom she had relied so heavily for help with Andrew's estate and for moral support, died of yellow fever even as she returned to Texas.

Anderson was the seat of Grimes County, northwest of Harris County, where Mary Jane Briscoe's brother, John Birdsall Harris, and his family resided. It boasted a courthouse and jail. There were no railroads and no telegraph lines, but five stagecoaches carried passengers and mail between there and Houston.[14] The Fanthorp Inn attracted distinguished visitors. Situated in a clump of trees, it was a large log house with a rock chimney at each end. In days gone by it had served as a post office for the provincial government of Texas. The inn owed its popularity to its location at a spot where two of the most important stage lines of this section crossed—one running between Houston and Springfield, the fast-growing seat of Limestone County, and the other between Nacogdoches and Austin. The stage stands stood across the road, and there drivers watered or exchanged their teams and made repairs while passengers refreshed themselves at the inn.[15]

The Briscoe family's time in Grimes County was relatively brief. The college failed in 1856, and Mary Jane moved to Galveston, at that time the largest city in Texas. In 1859, at her mother's urging, she returned to Harrisburg with her family. They shared the Harris homestead with her mother. Adele, now ten, was enchanted with her ancestral home. Her mother's dear friends, Francis and Adele Lubbock, owned a ranch on Sims Bayou only about a mile from her grandmother's house. In the summer of 1859, Lubbock agreed to pasture about forty camels, cared for by four or five Arabs, for an Englishwoman who had landed them at Galveston and needed a safe place to hold them until they could be sold.[16]

Although it meant little to a child of ten, the presence of the camels was part of one of the more interesting episodes in Texas history. Camp Verde, a US Army frontier post in southern Kerr County, became the headquarters in 1856 for forty camels sent by Secretary of War Jefferson Davis to be used in a system of overland communications. It seemed like a good idea at the time. Davis reasoned that camels, being likened to ships of the desert, would be better suited than horses, mules, or oxen for use in the desert of the American Southwest. It was from Camp Verde that Albert Sidney Johnston departed in 1857 on his expedition against the Mormons in Utah.[17]

One day, in the company of three other youngsters—Ella Hutchins, John Bringhurst, and Charley Gentry, who had come from Houston—Adele, bursting with curiosity, went to see the camels.[18] They were sorely disappointed when their wish to take a ride on one was denied, as the only gentle one had gone missing from the herd. It was finally discovered mired to its chest in the mud of the bayou, but all efforts to free the animal that day failed. When the camels were brought to Harrisburg, Adele got another chance for her camel ride. One of the beasts was equipped with a strange-looking packsaddle. It was covered with rugs. She rode with one of the gentlemen of their acquaintance on one side of the shelf-like contraption while another gentleman rode on the other side for balance. They rode about three-quarters of a mile led by one of the Arabs, who trotted ahead continually exhorting and encouraging the camel. The camel's strides produced a rough, swinging motion that was rapid and not especially comfortable. When the ride ended, the animal, in obedience to the handler's command, sank suddenly to its knees. Adele and her two fellow riders would have taken a headlong spill had they not come so quickly to level ground. It was a memorably exotic educational experience for a ten-year-old girl.[19] Memorable as such episodes were, Mary Jane's determination to have her children classically educated persisted. That persistence was eventually rewarded, for some of their earliest educational experiences made deep and lasting impressions, especially on the youngest, Adele.

Early in the 1850s the people of Texas had become genuinely interested in the subject of education. The desire to provide educational facilities that would fulfill the dream of the fathers of the Republic of Texas was strong and widespread. The education movement culminated in the passage of the common school law in 1854. The state treasurer was appointed ex officio superintendent of common schools. The judge and commissioners of each county were to constitute a county school board, instructed to divide each county into school districts and see to the election of three trustees in each district. It all sounded grand, but, lacking adequate funding or oversight, it never produced the desired results. The system as finally developed in 1858 was simple in the extreme and apparently acceptable to the main body of the people. Those parents who desired could form a school and could secure their own teacher and receive the state apportionment for their children. Those who wished to patronize one of the existing private schools were permitted the same privilege. The state apportionment was not paid until the close of the year, when the teacher had made a full report of attendance. The patrons were naturally obliged to advance the salary of the teacher throughout the term. At the close of the school the patrons would receive directly from the county treasurer the amount due to them for each child. This paradigm was loose, unsupervised, and lacking in the means to build permanent schools or school spirit. Changes in the law were frequent. People did not have time to familiarize themselves with the operations of the system and formulate plans for the future before some vital change would be made.[20]

The most powerful inducement for the establishment of a state public school system at the time lay in the universal desire to build railroads throughout the state.[21] John Angier, who came to Harrisburg with officials of the first railroad built and operated in Texas, boarded at Jane Harris's home.[22] The railroad was young and the duties of the treasurer light, so, to occupy himself in a literary way, Angier offered to teach Latin to Adele. She was about ten years old and not attending school; his offer was gladly accepted. At Christmas 1860, he presented Adele with a book, *Elements of Character,* as a reward for her patient efforts. It afforded the first serious reading she ever attempted, and she kept and referred to it all her life. Her lessons ended tragically, however, when Angier met with an accident while horseback riding and died after a few weeks. He was buried in the Birdsall-Harris graveyard, later part of Glendale Cemetery at Harrisburg.[23]

In 1860 the citizens of Harrisburg built a schoolhouse and engaged the services of a Professor Reuter, whose name as a prominent Texas educator got him the job. Reuter was a thoroughgoing classical scholar and devoted to higher mathematics but had little regard for discipline. His pupils were entirely untrained, which mattered nothing to him as long as they had learned their lessons. He would forget the regular curriculum while devoting hours to classes in algebra and Latin. At the noon recess he would invite the schoolchildren on a walk through the woods, where they would gather wildflowers to analyze during the afternoon botany class. To the bright pupils he was kind and helpful, but he was very antagonistic and even savage "when confronted with dullness." He soon gained a reputation for having a hot temper, which got him the respect of the unruly older boys. However, he had had a temper tantrum while teaching a large class of "nearly grown" girls in Houston, which proved his undoing. The oldest student failed to respond intelligently to his mathematical query, and he flung the recitation book at her, exclaiming, "You are a perfect Jackass!" She dodged the missile, bit her lip, and walked calmly to her seat. No charges were made against him, but he was replaced the next year. He would learn to temper his behavior in Harrisburg.[24]

Parents were so eager to obtain good teachers that they readily overlooked everything short of brutal physical punishment administered to the pupils, which probably explained their patience with Reuter's behavior. Professor Reuter was of medium height, past middle age, and a bachelor. He boarded, by choice, at the home of a farmer two miles from the schoolhouse and rode back and forth on horseback. The top of his head was perfectly bald, but this defect was concealed by a partial wig called a "scratch." The boys always wished he would ride under a low limb and scrape off his hat and "scratch," but it never happened, and his temper discouraged any pranks. He had been reared among people of culture and could have filled the chair of professor of languages, mathematics, or botany in a college, with credit. But his school in Harrisburg was broken up by the secession of the South.[25]

During the bombardment of the Texas coast by the Federal fleet during the second year of the war, many people fled to Harrisburg. Among them were Rev. Henry Sproul and his family. Sproul was a Scot, a retired minister of the Congregational Church. For years he performed services without much remuneration, preaching on Sundays and teaching during the week. He was learned in ancient languages, but he was advanced in years and his kindly nature prevented him from practicing any coercion, so he was content to lead his students along with gentle voice and persuasive manner. His system of study was said to teach concentration of thought. Pupils studied aloud, creating a kind of hum, at its best like the whispering of leaves in a forest, at its worst a babel of discord. When the din became too great, Reverend Sproul would raise his voice with gentle admonition, "Boys, boys, not so loud, not so loud!" and the babel would subside into a low buzz, which seemed like calm after a storm. Adele attended Professor Reuter's school regularly until it dissolved. The one taught by Reverend Sproul she attended only at intervals when circumstances demanded her temporary absence from Miss Brown's school, which she attended beginning in the fall of 1861.[26]

The absence of public schools in Texas up to this time left the field open to the growth of private and denominational enterprises. A number of religious groups had taken steps to found institutions, and a large number of individual teachers had opened schools and built up a local patronage.[27] Miss Mary B. Brown was a gifted teacher whom Father Augustine, a Roman Catholic priest, had induced to come to Houston to open a school for girls, and it was there that young Adele and her sister were to receive not only a formal academic education but also the manners and decorum that defined a woman of culture and refinement. One day in the summer of 1861 when Texas was mobilizing troops and companies were preparing to march to war, among them Andrew Briscoe's two boys, Parmenas and Andrew Birdsall, Mary Jane learned from a neighbor that a new girls' school was to open on the first of September. The coming of the Civil War had devastated schools, such as they were, in Texas. This news was welcome indeed, as it meant that the girls' educations could continue despite the demise of Professor Reuter's school.[28]

The schoolhouse, situated on Franklin Street between Caroline and San Jacinto, was a frame building of one story. It had a long room with a gallery in front, which at each end was partitioned off to make two small rooms, one of which was fitted with hooks for hanging up bonnets and cloaks, dinner buckets, and baskets, with benches under which overshoes were deposited. The other room was designated as the lunchroom. This building, together with another room in the backyard, was the property of the Roman Catholic

Church, and the church building adjoined it on the corner of Caroline Street. Here, under Miss Brown's tutelage, many of the daughters of the leading families of Houston were educated.[29]

The school opened in September 1861 with about fifty pupils of all ages, and enrollment soon increased to a hundred, a figure that remained stable for the ten years of the school's existence. The course of study was correct spelling, penmanship, grammar, geography, and arithmetic. For the junior classes, small catechisms on Greek, Roman, and Hebrew biography and history opened the door to an immediate interest in the more comprehensive course in ancient geography, history, and mythology, which engaged the attention of the more advanced students. Natural philosophy, chemistry, astronomy, botany, rhetoric, and French completed the senior class studies. Good manners comprised not only proper salutations on entering and leaving the schoolroom but modesty in the position of the feet, both standing and sitting; crossing the legs at the knees was regarded as an almost criminal breach of the etiquette of "good society" and was punishable by the loss of a certain number of merit marks previously gained by good lessons. Regular attendance of the majority of students was noteworthy, many walking through rain and mud over unpaved sidewalks and streets for many sessions, without being absent a day. At eight o'clock the study hour began and at nine a teacher opened the session with prayer, usually followed by the reading of some elegantly worded essay or legend conveying a moral lesson. Daily, students were inculcated with the principles deemed necessary to form character: modesty of demeanor, humility, and obedience to parents. Christianity, not sectarian doctrine, was taught. Adele attended these opening exercises with the whole student body assembled and then joined the other members of the junior class in their own classroom. The school building was painted white with green blinds; the inside walls and ceilings were white also. Lead-colored desks to accommodate six or eight students each had benches of corresponding length without backs. Inkstands were securely set in the desks, each shared by two students. The plank floor was unpainted and required scouring every few days to conform to the required standard of neatness. Students were asked to wear overshoes because of the unpaved sidewalks, but if a student did not have them, she had to bring an old pair of light shoes or slippers to wear in the schoolroom, and this rule was rigidly enforced though it caused a hardship during the war when new shoes were scarce and "good money" hard to get. Miss Brown was Roman Catholic, but she did not proselytize, as most of the students were Protestants or Jews. They had a fifteen-minute "intermission" at ten o'clock, recess from noon to one o'clock, with another ten-minute "intermission" at three o'clock, and dismissal at four-thirty. A salutation was required of each pupil at the doorway, no rushing or scrambling, and the same decorum as would have been observed in a drawing room.[30]

When the war was over, Miss Brown bought half a block at the corner of McKinney and Crawford Streets and erected a two-story frame building, thus enlarging her school to accommodate a limited number of boarders. She also increased the number of assistants to include a music teacher, a teacher of drawing and painting, and a special professor for German and mathematics. The school flourished even though public schools by then offered tuition-free education to impoverished people. Parents preferred to deny themselves for the sake of securing for their daughters the careful training, which years of experience enabled Miss Brown to give them, and the atmosphere of refinement that pervaded her schoolroom. Graduates sent their own children to her. Miss Brown spoke French and was well versed in literature and history. She excelled at reading poetry aloud, and she instilled in young Adele a deep and lasting appreciation for it.[31]

Mary Jane Briscoe's youngest child, Adele, thus spent the war years in school, which was both a blessing and a sacrifice for Mary Jane. Though unable to send any of her children to college, she had succeeded in obtaining for her boys, now twenty-one and nineteen, as good a classical education as could be obtained in antebellum Texas. She intended to do the same for her daughters, but doing so in the midst of the Civil War required significant sacrifice for a family of no great means. Many of the daughters of the leading families of Houston were educated at Miss Brown's school. While Mary Jane Briscoe may not have inherited great wealth, her background assured her elite standing in the community. Education of children, both male and female, was seen as a mark of gentility, signifying the highest type of refinement. Mary Jane Briscoe valued education not only for its own sake but also as a way to maintain class distinctions.[32] Fortunately, living expenses were not a burden since the family shared a home with her mother, Jane Harris, who took in boarders to help pay the bills. Altogether no fewer than thirteen souls resided under the Harris roof: two railroad conductors, each with a wife and child; an Irish chambermaid; Mrs. Harris; Mary Jane Briscoe; and her four children. In 1860, they owned little of value except real estate. In addition, Mary Jane owned two slaves, whom she had brought with her when she returned to Harrisburg. Under the circumstances, cash was scarce and tuition for Miss Brown's school would come very dear.[33]

In 1861, when Texas seceded, Parmenas and Andrew Birdsall immediately enlisted. Parmenas became a sergeant in Company A, Second Battalion, of the infantry of Waul's Texas Legion, known as "Sam Carter's Company," where he was destined to have a role in the Battle of Vicksburg. Birdsall, known to friends and family as "Brits," became a private in Company K of the Eighth Texas Cavalry Regiment, known as Terry's Texas Rangers, destined for Tennessee.[34] As both had been employed, their absence further reduced the revenue stream in the Harris household. Although Birdsall did sustain a battle wound, both remained in active service until the end of the war. In the meantime, their sisters began their studies at Miss Brown's school, and Mary Jane kept up regular correspondence with friends and family. Seeking much-needed funds, she contacted her husband's cousin and agent, Thomas Carothers, in Huntsville, Alabama. "My Dear Lady Friend," he replied, "Times are hard here, but not so hard I cannot respond favorably to your request." He promised to send her a few hundred dollars and sympathized with her in her dismay and despondency over secession and her beloved General Houston's resignation as governor. "The blow was a sad and heavy one," he admitted. He continued:

> I trust you are a better Christian than I and can see behind the cloud of despondency a sun whose rays promise happiness for the future. The present Governor's intercourse and mine has always been pleasant, and sad as my heart has been because of the unfortunate breach between Governor Houston, whom I love so well, and the Convention, yet I, conservative as I have always been, have wearied with the encroachments of the North upon rights I have felt were sacred, and I voted for a connection with a Government who had chosen the noble Mississippian Davis for a Leader, instead of being a subject of Lincoln's. If you should happen to pick up a Lincoln man for a helpmate, then I would think you had made a bad trade, and take this method of letting you know.[35]

In fact, Mary Jane was in a peculiar position as a result of the war, having grown up in New York and having retained deep affection for family members and friends still living there and in Pennsylvania. She kept up a lively correspondence with a good many gentleman friends, too, but was unlikely to find a Lincoln man among them. Even the New York natives among them had cast their fortunes with the South, including William DeVoe, a major in the Confederate Army, who participated in the Red River Campaign and remained to serve as city surveyor in Shreveport, Louisiana, after the war. Mary Jane had a special sensitivity for soldiers. Letters were her way of supporting the troops. She read their accounts of romantic adventures, the "noose" of matrimony, their fears of battle, and the boredom of encampment. In reply she teased them and offered words of wisdom and advice.[36] All the while she worried and carefully monitored her sons and her property, directly when possible and indirectly through acquaintances when necessary. Her longtime friend and neighbor, Francis R. Lubbock, was elected to replace Edward Clark as governor in the fall of 1861. He left his ranch on Sims Bayou in the charge of his stock keeper. His residence he left in the special care of his neighbor, Mary Jane Briscoe.[37] In this way, she passed the difficult years of the war with her family and most of her assets intact.

The outcome could have been much different, however. When Lubbock took office, he called attention to the exposed condition of the Gulf coast. No sooner had he been inaugurated than word came from Galveston that the US blockading vessel *Santee* had set fire to a Confederate vessel in Galveston harbor. Before the end of the year, rumors of the proposed evacuation of Galveston began to circulate. All property, public and private, was being moved from the island; the hospital stores and sick had arrived in Houston, and the *Galveston News* had likewise moved its operations there. The vulnerability of the Texas coastline was exacerbated by the threat of Indian depredations from the northern frontier, which threatened to dilute troop strength and resources. By late January 1862, Col. B. F. Terry of Terry's Texas Rangers was dead and Governor Lubbock's brother, Thomas, had been killed in Kentucky. In May 1862, the evacuation of Galveston began in earnest. When Union forces gained control of the Mississippi River, it began to appear that Texas might be cut off from the rest of the Confederacy. By June, Austin was put under martial law. Before the Texas legislature was to convene on February 2, 1863, Lincoln issued his proclamation freeing all slaves within the Confederacy, and fear of their insurrection immediately spread. In March, Mary Jane wrote to Lubbock worrying what to do about

Adele. Lubbock urged her to keep Adele with her if she could do so without injuring her studies too much.[38]

Adele spent the war maturing into a young lady at Miss Brown's school. She took her studies seriously, as she did most things. In appearance, she most resembled her father. She had his eyes and mouth but lacked the mischievous glint of Andrew's gaze. Whether from life experiences, the influence of her mother, the consequence of being the youngest sibling, or a combination of all those things, her demeanor was far more serious than that of most sixteen-year-old girls. The values emphasized so rigorously by Miss Brown were those that had been impressed upon Adele throughout her youth. They became evident in her words and actions early on and foreshadowed the forces that drove her throughout her adult life, as was clear in her address from the junior class to the senior class in 1864. She acknowledged the advantages that she and her classmates enjoyed and the obligation they bore as a consequence to grow in knowledge and virtue. They had an even more particular obligation to become a credit to their heritage, to Texas, and to their country, which, in 1864, meant the Confederate States. By way of apology for lacking the privileges of those who were educated in the East or in the capitals of Europe, she emphasized the nobility of "fulfilling the duties of our sphere," which had a double meaning—their sphere as Texans and as women.[39]

Two years later, in 1866, with war behind them, Adele delivered the valedictory address to her graduating class. Her love of words was obvious, and again, she struck a note for Texas and homegrown education: "My young companions, let us cherish a generous emulation, and show those friends, whose presence lends such sweet encouragement, that the schools of our own loved Texas can develop talent and nourish virtue. Yes: let us endeavor to prove that diligence and care may win science beneath the lowly shingled roof, as well as in the classic structures of distant lands."[40] It was by no means empty rhetoric. Adele Briscoe's life evidenced just how seriously she followed her own advice. The influences she identified as a young graduate marked all that she did. Miss Brown's school marked the ending of her formal education and the beginning of a lifelong passion for learning and writing.

With her graduation in 1866, a new phase of Adele's education commenced. In August 1869, the indomitable Jane Harris, having established what would become a female dynasty in Harris County, Texas, finally succumbed to the one frontier no one, man or woman, can ever conquer or escape. With her mother's death and the war behind them, Mary Jane Briscoe made up her mind that the time had come to introduce her youngest daughter to her Harris kin. Her brother Lew, like her husband and father-in-law, had been lured to California by the gold rush in 1849. Unlike them, he had survived the adventure and was living in Sacramento.[41] Hoping to recoup money her brother owed her from the Harris estate, she and Adele planned to embark sometime in 1870 on a tour to visit relatives from coast to coast, a journey that would serve the dual purpose of taking care of business and acquainting Adele with the extended Harris family.[42]

Early in 1870, Adele's sister, Jessie, made a trip of her own to visit her brother on Matagorda Bay. Brits had been in Indianola since 1868, where the Indianola Railroad Company had resumed work on a line connecting the port of Indianola with the San Antonio and Mexican Gulf Railroad at Clark Station in Calhoun County. The Morgan steamship line had moved the world's first mechanically refrigerated beef to New Orleans by steamer the summer before, and railroad service was about to commence. Indianola was twelve miles south of Port Lavaca at the eastern end of the road to San Diego, California, the shortest overland route to the Pacific.[43] Before the Civil War, Indianola, originally Indian Point, had been a busy port of entry for German immigrants bound for western Texas. By the end of the Mexican-American War it was beginning to rival Galveston as the principal port on the Texas coast, and in 1870 it was the scene of much energy and activity. It had replaced Port Lavaca as the seat of Calhoun County when Charles Morgan decided to make it the terminus of his New York–based steamship enterprise. The population had swelled to more than five thousand, and the town, known as the "Dream City on the Gulf," boasted four newspapers.[44] The Briscoe sisters kept each other apprised of their respective adventures through regular correspondence. Jessie's letters to "Dell" were filled with parties, clothes, boys, and dancing lessons. Adele's on the other hand tended to be much more substantive.

"Dear Dell," Jessie wrote in reply to a letter from her younger sister in late February, "I received your long and very interesting letter, but you know I am not much on the write and always put off answering until the last moment." In hasty, truncated sentences, she described the society activities of Indianola. "Having a pleasant time; danced until 2:00 a.m. last night, but it was the closing soiree of the dancing school, so probably won't have another party before the middle of next month." Not to seem too self-absorbed, she closed consolingly that she knew Dell had had a good time during Major Looscan's visit.[45]

Mary Jane set out for California with Adele later in the spring. She hated to leave Jessie and "Bub," her pet name for Parmenas, but believed that was best. On the first leg of the trip, they left Harrisburg for New Orleans in late May 1870.[46] Jessie kept up her newsy correspondence to Adele, and it frequently centered on their respective romantic interests. Like most girls in postwar Texas, especially those whose brothers had so recently served the Confederacy, the Briscoe sisters found soldiers particularly attractive. "Dear Dell," Jessie wrote in June, "I like Captain Howe so much better than your admirer. Major Looscan has been twice to see me, making upon both occasions a very short call. The first time I think he came merely to inquire about you. Did he write to you?" She admonished that she expected to get another letter from her little sister the next day and hear how pleased she was with Sacramento. Captain Howe came down from Houston and remained for tea, she teased.[47] By late July, however, Jessie genuinely began to miss her family. From Galveston, she wrote, "Everything's lovely. When are you coming home?" After catching Adele up on family and neighbors, she confided that she would like to buy a house in Houston, which she found so much pleasanter than Harrisburg. "I expect to hear from you every week," she warned, "so don't disappoint me."[48]

Adele made a faithful effort not to disappoint with her letter writing and admonished her mother to write Jessie, too. She found California entertaining. They met a family from Maine with two grown sons, and the mother and sister avidly courted Adele on behalf of one of them, which flattered Adele and provided Mary Jane with much amusement. Mary Jane, however, could not answer Jessie's question about their return. She did not know when they would start home. She had been hoping to get enough money from her brother to get home on, but she was not sure she would get it. Lew, she wrote to Parmenas, had no property in Sacramento. He had lost money in a recent mining scheme. He did have land in Texas, which he would sell and then pay her there. She worried Jessie would have a lonesome time of it; she would have to make it up to her. Maybe if there were no fever in New Orleans, Jessie could join them when they visited in Mississippi. Mary Jane worried about the annual threat of yellow fever, which had taken so much from her. "You and Jessie be careful about the fever," she wrote to Parmenas. "I do wish we were all settled in this healthy country."

This trip represented the longest spell Mary Jane had ever been separated from her children except while Brits and Parmenas were soldiering. Distance, worry, and her brother's circumstances prompted her to reflect on her priorities. "Attend strictly and closely to your business so as to earn a good name at least, and above all things, do be strictly honest and upright," she told Parmenas. "A good name and a clear conscience are inestimable treasures that money cannot buy, and without which, money is of very little value." She was fortunate to have mature, responsible children. "God be thanked, I have never had to blush or mourn over any of my children," she confided. "I am always proud of them." But there were so many causes for worry, from yellow fever epidemics to taxes. "May our Father in Heaven protect you all is the prayer of your Mother," she finished her letter.[49]

After visiting and admiring the healthful climate and beauty of the Pacific coast, Adele and Mary Jane boarded a steamer in San Francisco for the trip to New York. For the first time in her young life, at the age of twenty-one Adele met her New York relatives. In October she wrote from Seneca Falls of going to Penn Yan and Albany, where she had met cousins and friends she liked but couldn't stay long to visit.[50] The Finger Lakes region was on fire with all the splendid flaming colors of autumn. In retrospect, there was a certain cosmic rightness in the fact that the historic "burned over" district, scene of early nineteenth-century religious fervor, had originated the first women's rights convention in American history in the very year of Adele Briscoe's birth and had also been the origins of three generations of women like Jane Birdsall Harris, her daughter and granddaughters—women of such rare courage and determination.

Having been away from Harrisburg for five months, the Briscoe women turned their journey homeward. They would leave western New York before winter set in in earnest and have time to visit the Briscoe cousins in Mississippi before returning to Harrisburg. They were welcomed warmly by Parmenas and Jessie, upon whom the lengthy separation had begun to wear, and truth to tell, Adele and Mary Jane both were glad to be home. Adele, it seemed, had acquired an unexpected souvenir of her trip in the person of an admirer, Mark Kelly, who traveled to visit her after she returned to Texas. This sad episode demonstrated the influence her mother exerted over her and provided perhaps the best glimpse into her personality she ever permitted herself to reveal. Although their affection seemed mutual, her mother's disapproval doomed the relationship. In May 1871, following his visit, Adele wrote to him in strained tones.

She had put off doing so for several days, unable to summon the will or the words to write certain "unpalatable facts," and yet she knew she had to make him understand perfectly the present state of affairs, no matter how painful. She confessed that she had answered some of his letters already simply because she could not make up her mind to acknowledge what a miserable, weak, changeable creature she found herself to be. "My friend, you vainly imagine and hope that I am very happy and enjoying to the fullest extent every amusement with which we are favored," she told him, "but I really have very little enjoyment in any of them." Although she had gone a good deal into society over the winter and had more company than usual, she had really taken very little pleasure in it. "After you left," she wrote, "I was grieved by my mother's sad looks, occasioned by the belief that I thought more of you than of anyone with whom I had before been associated. Knowing as I did how she regarded you and loving her as well as I do, how could this fail to make me unhappy?" She explained that when, after a while, she let herself be persuaded to go to Houston and Galveston to visit some friends and participate, in appearance at least, in the gaieties of the season, she could see that her mother wore a brighter look, and she felt a degree less gloomy to think that she could remove the cloud from her mother's brow. She confessed that though she did at first feel more bitter than she should have allowed herself to be under any circumstances, she had come to look upon her mother's reasoning with a more impartial eye and saw less that was unkind or inconsiderate than she ever thought could be proven to her. The result of all that had been said and hinted left the conviction upon her mind that she could never truly love him and retain the same affection for her mother. Adele had had other suitors, but she recognized that her mother had not ever felt a pang of uneasiness on their account because Mary Jane saw plainly that they occupied her thoughts only very slightly. Steeling herself against painful emotions, Adele admitted, "You doubtless remember the promise I once made you that I would steel my heart against loving anyone else; it was a very useless unnecessary promise for I don't believe I ever shall, and I think now more than ever that I am incapable of loving very deeply."[51] Although their correspondence continued for a short while longer, Adele confined her letters to mundane subjects such as events in the vicinity of Harrisburg—the flooding that had washed away the railroad track on the Galveston road and interrupted the mails, the fair in Houston, and the opera in Galveston. The highlight of an otherwise mundane summer ahead would be a visit to her brother, Brits, at Indianola. Summer was not the ideal season for that location, but Brits had married Anna Francis Payne on the last day of February, and she was anxious to see them. In July, her mother expected to go to the bay. Adele, herself, generally enjoyed a visit there very much.[52] One pleasant feature of Harrisburg at the time was the Literary Association that had been started there some time ago and that was, by July 1871, flourishing. An Irishman and one of the principal citizens, Colonel Mulligan, was the presiding officer. The *Houston Telegraph* reported that the Harris County attorney, Maj. Michael Looscan, delivered the featured address at the Literary Association meeting on July 1. He was, apparently, quite the attraction. "Most of the young gentlemen of the village and many of the beautiful ladies of the place also graced the hall of the association. He was listened to with marked attention, and received hearty applause at the close. The address was elegantly and forcibly written and abounded in historical fact and fine illustrations," reported the *Telegraph*.[53]

Adele's romance with Mark Kelly and her gloomy declaration that she believed herself incapable of loving very deeply may have had weightier implications than they seemed to have at the time. It was an indication of how sensitive she was to her mother's approbation and to the extent of Mary Jane Briscoe's influence over her daughter. It would be another decade before Adele married, and when she did it was to family friend and longtime suitor Michael Looscan. Looscan was a Civil War veteran and served as county attorney of Harris County between 1870 and 1880. He was a native of Ireland who had immigrated to America in March 1855 at the age of seventeen under an indenture and worked for a year on the Erie Canal and in a cotton mill in Utica, New York. From there he migrated south to Mobile, Alabama, where he worked as a press boy at the *Mercury*, the first secession newspaper of the South. Then, he headed west. He came to Harrison County, Texas, in 1859, where he taught school and studied law in the office of Judge Micajah H. Bonner. He had been admitted to the bar only a few weeks before the Civil War broke out. He enlisted in Company A of Capt. Peter Hardeman's Second Texas Mounted Rifles, under the command of Col. John S. "Rip" Ford. He served throughout the Confederate campaign in Arizona, and when Lt. Col. John R. Baylor was appointed military governor of the territory, Looscan was appointed his adjutant and secretary. In 1862, Looscan was made major of a regiment and sent to Arkansas and Missouri, where he won distinction on the field in Gen. Sterling Price's Arkansas campaign of 1864, during which he commanded the Thirty-First Texas Cavalry. Looscan had been in Houston since the spring of 1865 as inspector general on Gen. Samuel Bell Maxey's staff. Although Adele's brothers, Parmenas and Birdsall, also served, both were in different brigades.[54] Looscan had been assisting Mary Jane Briscoe with the Harris estate after her mother's death in 1869 and had been closely associated with the family ever since.

Looscan cut a handsome figure in those days. He had a head of thick dark hair, swept back as though he'd just run his hands through it. His look was dashing and slightly dangerous. He had shown interest in Adele as early as 1870 but shied away from courting her directly. Instead, he courted her family. While Adele and her mother traveled to California, he sought out the company of her brothers and sister and wrote to Mary Jane. In one such letter, he enclosed a copy of the Texas Historical Society proceedings for her and Lew. "Unable to overlook the claims of Miss Della," he wrote, "I send her a copy, too, although I must say—but no other person shall dare say so, and

Michael Looscan, circa 1870s.
Courtesy of the San Jacinto Museum of History.

live—that she is an unworthy daughter of Texas by her desertion, and I will take pains to so record her, provided, however, that she shall return to her natural allegiance within a reasonable time—then I promise to retract what I may have written and to devote in her promise the brightest page of the Texas Historical Society." All at Harrisburg, he assured her, were well.[55]

The decade of the 1870s was a time of growth and change for the landscape and residents along Buffalo Bayou. Charles Morgan bought the Bayou Ship Channel Company in 1874 and within two years had dredged a channel from Galveston Bay to near Houston. The first ocean vessel arrived there September 22, 1876.[56] In 1874, Mary Jane decided to move into Houston from Harrisburg. Houston was just beginning to flourish after the setbacks of the Civil War. That year the first rails for a street railway system were laid, originally to connect Central Station with the International and Great Northern depot.[57] In a city infamous for its muddy streets, the new system was a milestone. With the previous advice and assistance of male relatives and friends like Francis Lubbock, Mary Jane had managed to convert land she had inherited from her father and husband into revenue-producing property sufficient to sustain herself, and Parmenas was now of an age to assist her in managing legal and financial transactions for his siblings, unmarried female relatives, and even distant cousins. Just as Andrew's cousin, Leonly Harrison, had once predicted, she had relied heavily on her eldest ever since Andrew died.[58] In May 1873, the Texas Veterans Association was organized, and Mary Jane, as a daughter of the first class and widow of the second class, took an intense and abiding interest in it. As her mother, Jane Harris, had been before her, she was a communicant of Christ Episcopal Church. Moving into town made participation in these activities much more convenient.

However, especially with the opening of the ship channel, Houston was just as susceptible to seasonal yellow fever epidemics as the bay area. Residents who were able to get out of town did so during summer and fall. Adele, having acquired a fondness for traveling after her 1870 tour, traveled to Botetourt Springs, Virginia, in August 1876 with her sister Jessie and her husband, Capt. Milton Howe, who had married in 1873. They remained in the East long enough to participate in centennial celebrations in Philadelphia in October, and Adele's animated letters recounted their adventures. She wanted to go to Independence Hall; Jessie wanted to go to New York to shop; their trip to Boston didn't work out—but whatever they did, her letters to Mary Jane expressed her concern about the rumors of yellow fever outbreaks in Houston.[59]

While Adele vacationed with her sister, her brother Parmenas, with the help of Michael Looscan, managed the family's real-estate interests. Probate and real estate were Looscan's main areas of legal practice. Even while he served as Harris County attorney, he continued to assist friends and former clients. He shared not only Confederate service but also political views in common with Parmenas Briscoe and Milton Howe that helped to cement their friendship. In 1880, Looscan was a boarder in Jessie and Milton Howe's home at the same time that the Briscoes resided there. During the 1870s, Looscan had created quite a stir in Harris County. He had practiced law successfully with Judge William S. Oldham since 1867. He was elected county attorney of Harris County in 1870 but almost immediately crossed swords with Gov. Edmund J. Davis to such an extent that the law creating the office was repealed, evidently for the purpose of getting rid of Looscan. He was retained by the county commissioners nevertheless. He then filed a bill charging the Harris County sheriff with malfeasance in office, forcing him and the county treasurer to pay nearly $25,000 in currency and scrip. He brought numerous suits on behalf of the county against corrupt officeholders. When the office of county attorney was restored in 1876, he was elected by popular vote and held the office until 1880.[60] In 1881, he and Adele Briscoe married.

Chapter Three

Woman of the Club

The September evening was warm and humid. Were it not for the light breeze, the congenial group gathered at Mary Jane Briscoe's home on Crawford Street in Houston would have been exceedingly uncomfortable in their finery. The air was redolent of flowers adorning the doorways, balustrades, windows, and fireplaces. Adele's dress and veil were elegantly simple. She had purchased the materials for her wedding outfit from W. L. Foley, Fancy & Staple Dry Goods, in Houston for sixty dollars.[1]

Not a giddy young girl but a mature, deliberate woman of thirty-three married Michael Looscan that fall of 1881. For the first time in her life Adele moved out of her mother's household. She moved into a home of her own and fully assumed her role as a Houston matron, a woman of the club. Her marriage reinforced the impression that she was an unusual woman.[2] Eleven years earlier she had written to an ardent suitor, Mark Kelly, that she believed she was incapable of loving very deeply. Perhaps that was true and explained why she waited a decade to marry Michael Looscan, who had been flirting with her at least that long.[3] Perhaps her devotion to her mother accounted for the unusually long courtship; Mary Jane Briscoe was herself far from ordinary, and her attachment to her youngest daughter had always been strong.[4]

Adele's move from under her mother's roof was a metaphor for her move beyond her mother's shadow. That Adele was so singularly devoted to her mother was perhaps understandable considering that Mary Jane Briscoe had been a single parent and, as such, relied on her children emotionally, as well as for help around the house. In that regard, Adele was typical of young American women of her generation. The role of dutiful daughter was clearly defined and urged upon her from her earliest years. It had been among the values taught at Miss Brown's school. Daughters were expected to help mothers in tasks recognized as female, tasks intended to inculcate equally well-recognized feminine virtues. The distinction, if there was one, in Adele's relationship with her mother was Mary Jane's inclusion of advanced education among those virtues. While she appreciated the practical need to possess general information on every subject of daily life, she also believed mathematics, astronomy, and the ancient languages to be just as necessary to her daughters' education as what the editors of *Peterson's Magazine* referred to as "the true relations of life." Adele had been successfully schooled in obedience and self-control, the two virtues society relied upon to protect young girls from those forces that threatened their proper roles—like falling in love. At the same time, Adele's role models, her grandmother and mother, both were independent, self-supporting women who had fended for themselves most of their own lives and all of hers. They set examples for how women might look to men for assistance when they needed it without becoming emotionally, physically, or intellectually dependent on them. As a matter of fact, it was Jane Harris who had made a success of Harris's sawmill, and it was Mary Jane Briscoe who had turned Andrew Briscoe's land in Texas, together with her share of the Harris estate, into sustenance for herself and her children. Only privately did she reveal her vulnerability and her reliance on her youngest daughter. "It is the anniversary of their marriage," she wrote in her journal one September day in 1885. "Four years today. It seems like ten since I had my girl all my own."[5]

With a husband and home of her own, Adele would become a public woman and her own woman; she would also be in a better position to support her mother. Without being consciously aware of it, she would come to represent the transformation of the "True Woman" into the "New Woman." In some ways, she epitomized the southern clubwoman of the era, but in many other ways, as exemplified by her relatively late marriage, she defied any stereotype.[6] Her involvement in the women's club movement shaped her future course, absorbing most of her time and energy from the time of her marriage in 1881 to the end of her life in 1935.

Adele had established a working partnership with Michael Looscan before her marriage. After his term as county attorney ended, Looscan turned his full attention to his private law practice, specializing in debt collection, probate, and real estate matters. He had already advised the Briscoes in their management of the Harris estate and Mary Jane in matters relating to Andrew Briscoe's landholdings. Adele, for her contribution to the family enterprise, assisted as his bookkeeper.[7] As with all her endeavors, she applied herself to her duties seriously and confidently. As Looscan's legal practice expanded and the family's assets grew, the city of Houston itself was growing and changing.

One factor that made it easier for Adele to leave her mother was the arrival of telephone service in Houston in 1880. Although neither woman was given to extravagance, both embraced the new technology as a practical matter. The reality was that Houston was not an easy town to get around in. It richly deserved its reputation as the muddiest town in Texas. In the winter of 1879–80, three months of steady rain made streets so impassable that it was easier just to stay at home. In March 1880, Houston got its first electric-arc streetlight, which did not make the streets any more passable, but at least the deep mud puddles were easier to see and avoid in the evening. Although not all Houstonians embraced electric lighting immediately, by Christmas 1882 merchants and shoppers were coming to appreciate the illumination it provided to the holiday displays at Foley's, Kiam's, and Levy's department stores.[8] The Houston Light

Guards, almost a decade old now, provided some of the best entertainment around with its military drills. Organized the same year as the Texas Veterans Association, it was one of Mary Jane Briscoe's abiding interests. Railroads were flourishing, a bittersweet development for Mary Jane, but they were an undeniable advantage to her family and the family businesses, as well as to Houston. The year after Adele's marriage, in the summer of 1882, property owners came up with the money to pave two blocks of Main Street, and merchants anted up to spread gravel on fifteen blocks of Congress and Franklin Streets. It was not a permanent fix for the mud but definitely a move in the right direction. The city marshal even went out of his way to enforce the stock ordinance downtown and thus rid the district of vagrant cattle. Miss Brown's Young Ladies' Seminary and Day School had survived the Civil War to become more prestigious than ever and was referred to locally as "the Vassar of the South," providing instruction in French, German, English, and mathematics to the daughters of Houston's best families. Increasingly, education was associated with social status and prestige. As such, it became of increasing concern to Houston's growing population.[9]

Education had seen its ups and downs as a civic priority. After attracting a burst of renewed interest in the 1850s, the Houston Lyceum, a men's club, was reorganized to present debates, lectures, and musicales. Harking back to its origins in the Franklin Debating Society of 1837, the group began to hold weekly public debates on such questions as "Are women capable of the same mental improvement as men?" and "Is the light literature of the present day beneficial to the mind?" and the unusually lively topic, "Ought bachelors over thirty years of age to be taxed for the support of old maids?" Secession and war had brought an end to these stimulating activities, but when the private Houston Academy closed in 1876, it left its substantial library collection to the Lyceum, prompting another revival of interest. The Lyceum soon began buying books from local bookstores, and it opened a reading room for its members, still all male. This intellectual exclusivity, given all the other changes taking place in Houston society, seemed certain to be short lived. Moreover, if there were any truth to the observation that Americans of all stripes were prone to forming associations, it seemed inevitable that the women of Houston, eager for self-improvement and community improvement, would organize to assail this male bastion of erudition.[10]

Houston women's propensity for associating had already manifested itself. Mary Jane Briscoe and those contemporaries who were deeply invested in the Texas Revolution had already associated themselves with the Texas Veterans Association from its organization in 1873, gradually taking on the task of commemorating the scenes of sacrifice as well as honoring the veterans themselves. In 1883, they succeeded in persuading the Texas legislature to purchase ten acres of the San Jacinto battleground, and the following spring Mary Jane was elected an honorary member of the veterans group.[11] It was an association she cherished perhaps above all others but family. Not only was it an association born of shared experience, it was also a link to the husband she had loved and lost.

Houston's now brightly lit streets, improved public transportation, and large department stores also welcomed women like Mary Jane and her daughters to participate in an emerging consumer economy. The urban atmosphere encouraged and made possible the development of women's organizations devoted to philanthropic, social, or political causes. It even provided reasons for getting together, from the recognition of sanitation problems or the awareness of working-class women's special needs to the desire for improved cultural and educational opportunities.[12] Mary Jane had been reared a sociable being; she craved constant activity and the company of others. She had been a widow longer than she had been a wife, as had her mother before her, and she had neither inclination nor intention to closet herself at home. In her experience, homes were for entertaining and hospitality. City living and involvement in a variety of organizations fulfilled her needs and gave them purpose.

Among the earliest of women's organizations in Houston were church mission and benevolent societies. Adele, having been confirmed at Christ Episcopal Church, followed her mother into the Ladies' Sewing Circle and the Ladies' Parish Association (LPA). The organization was founded in 1871 to continue the tradition of fundraising that had begun as early as 1848 with the goal of paying the church debts and the rector. The sewing circle raised money to take over an old school building and turn it into a Sunday school. The LPA was specifically founded to take care of needy people in the community at a time when there were no public social service agencies. Mary Jane was very active in both the sewing circle and the LPA, spending many hours each week in church work. Although she did not join the Women's Christian Temperance Union (WCTU), she was quite aware of its existence. WCTU president Frances Willard's visit to Houston in 1880 had generated quite a buzz, and a chapter had been formed at Shearn Methodist Church, to which many of Mary Jane's friends belonged. The chapter concerned itself with the welfare of women generally. Mary Jane would have known from friends and family in New York and Pennsylvania that women's societies there had expanded their activities to include the study of literature and history for self-improvement and had taken on social-reform projects ranging from building libraries to lobbying for better sanitation. Although the women's club movement gained momentum in the South much more slowly, in growing port cities such as Galveston and Houston it spread a bit earlier. Women's clubs were one way for Houston women to move "from the parlor to the public." The desire of the socially ambitious for better education provided impetus for members of church societies like the LPA at Christ Episcopal Church to branch out from benevolence and charity to intellectual matters, such as learning to handle abstractions, deal with contradictory ideas and written assignments, present papers in front of other women, speak in mixed groups, arrange conventions, travel to conventions unaccompanied by male escorts, do committee work, and lead others into the public forum.[13] It was the perfect kind of forum for Mary Jane Briscoe, and, as usual, Adele went with her.

One of Adele's first initiatives, typical of the southern club-woman movement, drew on the impulse to build a free library for Houston. The groundwork had already been laid to an extent by the Lyceum and the women of Christ Episcopal and First Presbyterian Churches. It remained for someone to bring the interested parties together and spearhead the project. By 1884, the Lyceum had nearly thirteen hundred volumes and subscriptions to several periodicals, but they were not accessible to the public in the society's rooms in Market Hall. The time was ripe; 1885 would usher in a new era for the Lyceum and its library.

On the wintry afternoon of Thursday, February 26, 1885, at the instigation of Adele and her school friend, Carrie Ennis Lombardi, several ladies, mostly from the Ladies' Associations of Christ Episcopal and First Presbyterian Churches, assembled at Mary Jane Briscoe's residence in Houston for the purpose of organizing a society intended to create an environment in which women could enjoy both intellectual and social culture, "having for its object pleasure and improvement." Mary Jane was not the only Houston matron who thought it was time to take steps to supply the long-felt need for a common ground on which ladies "having a literary taste might meet." The name Ladies' History Class was adopted; Mary Jane Briscoe was appointed treasurer, and Adele Looscan was appointed president pro tempore. Her husband, the indefatigable major, printed up the record of the first year's program in a pamphlet and distributed it to friends all over the state, which encouraged the formation of similar study clubs.[14]

The formation of the Ladies' History Class represented a milestone not only for Houston women but for Adele herself. Like most aspects of her life, the club reflected her mother's influence, but it nevertheless established Adele as an individual and not simply the youngest daughter of Mary Jane Briscoe. The Ladies' History Class was one of the earliest women's social organizations in Houston outside of the churches, and it appeared only a few years after the organization of the Houston chapter of the WCTU. By April, the twenty-four members had decided to change the name to the Ladies' Reading Club, and they adopted a plan of study. It marked the beginning of the women's club movement in Houston. Before the Ladies' Reading Club, Houston offered few opportunities outside of church groups for women to gather and voice their opinions. More than half the charter members of the club came from the ladies' associations of the two churches. Like the Houston WCTU, the Ladies' Reading Club had a broad interest in the welfare of women. The charter members were a mix of married and single women, some of them teachers, whose attitude redefined the "cult of true womanhood." Middle- and upper-class women like Mary Jane Briscoe and her daughters had been reared with this notion of separate spheres and the cult of domesticity found everywhere in women's magazines, advice books, religious journals, newspapers, and novels. Some challenged the standard. Some, like Mary Jane, Adele, and Jessie, tried to keep the virtues—piety, purity, submissiveness, and domesticity—associated with it but also to enlarge the scope of womanhood. After all, their own experience had not exactly conformed to the standard as promulgated by *Godey's Lady's Book* and *Peterson's Magazine.* Adele, as the Houston club's first president, expressed her expanded vision of the "true" woman. A woman, she said, should be "one whose mind shall be trained to form her own opinions, to organize her own household, and if need be to make her own living."[15] The following April, in 1886, Adele addressed the ladies of the club, revealing much about her own view of the impetus behind the formation of such organizations by women. With her usual poise, in a confident voice strengthened by training and conviction, she spoke to the assembly:

> That it is easier to drift with the tide of society, doing what others do, perhaps thinking what others think without defi-

> nite aims for the true advancement of ourselves or of those who are to come after us is conceded, but should we not aspire much higher than this? A responsive voice in the heart of every true woman answers that we should, and since all our efforts during the past year have been animated by noble aims, I trust no lady will feel herself less fitted to perform the duties of life, by reason of having devoted some of her time to study, as a member of our Club.[16]

That Adele would emerge as a leader among organizers was not surprising. Among the factors distinguishing her and her mother from the typical clubwoman was their relative independence. Although Adele's oldest brother, Parmenas, provided a stable male presence in the household as well as a financial contribution, Mary Jane Briscoe had long been managing her own affairs and traveling alone or with her daughters. By virtue of her late marriage, Adele had matured in the company of an independent, resourceful, and lively mother. Unlike many of the women who joined the club movement, the Briscoes had not come from a plantation background, and both women had received classical educations perhaps exceeding those of many of their contemporaries. They did not have the wealth to be preoccupied with material consumption, but they had the leisure to devote their time to the causes of improving opportunities for women and improving their community. A revealing journal entry in May 1885 confirmed this circumstance: "Mrs. Perle & Mrs. Hill have gone to Europe; Mrs. Sterne & Mrs. Ryan go to New Orleans; everybody can go to the exposition but me: it is right hard to be poor; if I was sure I would not have to spend a few hundred dollars on my tongue, I would go, but I am afraid I would need the money to take care of me."[17]

The women of the Ladies' Reading Club wasted no time expanding their reach beyond their own studious circle. When the Houston Lyceum, desperate for revenue, voted to admit women in 1887, it provided the women with an opening. Their work to reestablish the languishing Lyceum as Houston's public library illustrated how women's organizations evolved from self-education and social reform into political activism. Although women could now join the Lyceum, it was still an exclusive club for members only. More needed to be done if Houston was to have a truly public library. The women wanted to make the Lyceum public, and they wanted to move it to a more accessible location. A few years after the Lyceum opened its membership to women, Adele addressed the Ladies' Reading Club again, on its tenth anniversary, in 1895, and appealed for a "cordial union among all the literary and study clubs" in order to accomplish the objective of providing an adequate location for a public library. She called attention to the fact that the foundation of a public library had been laid in the city forty years before but that help was still needed to put it on a foundation adequate for a city of sixty thousand residents. The location, she said, was one of the greatest drawbacks. The streets were often muddy, and it was hard to reach the rooms. And, too, the location above the market was not suitable. The various study clubs should be petitioned so that they could have a public library through their combined efforts.[18]

By 1898, when Jennie Cunningham Croly published *The History of the Woman's Club Movement in America,* the Woman's Club and the Ladies' Reading Club of Houston had already become charter members of the Texas Federation of Women's Clubs (1897). Within three years' time, with the endorsement of Mayor Sam Brashear, five clubs gathered to form the City Federation of Women's Clubs, organized to advance the work of establishing a free public library for the city. Unfortunately, from Adele's personal standpoint, there could not have been a worse time for promoting such initiatives. Mary Jane, who had sustained a crippling injury in June 1897, took a fall from her crutches the last week in January 1900 that rendered her unable to sit up at all for more than a week. A committee called on Adele at home, where she was confined by the invalidism of her mother, and requested that she act as president of the City Federation of Women's Clubs. She accepted, of course. How could she not? But to Hally Bryan she confided, "Since I have been prevailed upon to accept the Presidency of the Houston Federation of Clubs, contrary to my expectation much attention has been required of me in order to get the organization in working order."[19] Although Adele did not realize it, her comment was prescient. By that time, Adele was already actively involved in at least half a dozen organizations, not only in Houston but in San Antonio, and with the Mount Vernon Ladies' Association in Virginia, with a decided emphasis on study, history, and historical preservation.

In their endeavors, the Houston clubs followed the pattern of emerging women's organizations throughout the nation.[20] Once they united, they immediately realized the need to polish their political skills in order to achieve their goal. Adele had to work from home. She wrote letter after letter to Mayor Brashear and the district judge. These letters were delivered almost daily by a faithful servant, asking that some action be taken in the matter of a public library.[21]

Backed by the club, Adele told the officers of the Lyceum that every member of the Ladies' Reading Club would become a member of the Lyceum and pay $3.00 in dues per year and that the club would also tender $5.00 per month to be applied to the rent, provided the books were moved to a more accessible place. The club's strategy and political instincts demonstrated the nimbleness with which women adapted management of the domestic sphere to the public sphere.[22] Once they gained consent from the members of the Lyceum to relocate the collection, they needed the city council's financial support. At that time women did not go before the council and ask for things; it just wasn't done. So they decided on a bold plan to invite the mayor and aldermen to come to them in the library room as invited guests. Their invitation was accepted. As a result, the women moved the library from the city hall to a room in the Mason Building. They had written Andrew Carnegie for a grant for a public library, and in

October 1899 they were rewarded with the news that Carnegie would give them $50,000, provided the city furnished the site and maintained it at a cost of $4,000 per year. When the new federation had raised $7,880, the city purchased a lot at the corner of McKinney Avenue and Travis Street. The cornerstone was not laid until 1902, and the Houston Carnegie Library did not open until 1904, but thanks to the Ladies' Reading Club the citizens of Houston had their library. Characteristically, Adele directed public gratitude to the women of the club, especially Carrie Ennis Lombardi, and claimed little credit for herself.[23]

Once the women's societies in Houston began collaborating, opportunities for activism and service expanded exponentially. Another of their initiatives was the Woman's Exchange, which they started in downtown Houston in 1887. The Woman's Exchange served as a marketplace for women to earn a livelihood through the sale of their handmade goods, and it became a destination for shoppers seeking high-quality merchandise. The exchange also operated a tearoom serving inexpensive meals, and it included a resource library, where instruction was available in such areas as cooking, sewing, needlework, chair caning, and other domestic arts. Working women could purchase a nourishing meal cheaply, attend classes, play cards, or simply enjoy a quiet place for relaxation and companionship. Adele was chair of the first executive board of the exchange. With Mrs. Horace Baldwin Rice, she organized and conducted a free sewing school, where little girls were taught to cut fabric for and sew dresses. The completed garments were then donated to the children of the Bayland Orphan Home in Houston.[24]

Adele and her sister Jessie were not exactly new to the concept of activism through association. They had been enlisted by Mary Jane to assist the Texas Veterans Association to effect the purchase and designation of the San Jacinto battleground property as a state park. In essence, their Texas heritage was all they had of their father or grandfather, and Mary Jane continually impressed the importance of this heritage upon them. Their association with and advocacy for the Texas Veterans Association lasted until the organization dissolved on April 19, 1907. Associating with the veterans' group was a common way of participating vicariously in the glory of defining battles such as the Battle of San Jacinto. But pride, honoring ancestors, and the commemoration of fallen heroes were only part of the women's motivation. Their interest in and devotion to Texas history was even more personal. It was, in some sense, a way of maintaining a connection with the fathers they had never known. In that respect they needed the Texas Veterans Association even more than the surviving veterans themselves did.[25] Mary Jane had become an honorary member in 1884. She and her daughters continued to write letters and memorials to legislators on behalf of the veterans and the battleground for years.

Adele did not confine her writing to letters. Her interest in Texas history and her writing talents led her to submit articles to newspapers and literary magazines in Houston, Austin, San Antonio, and Dallas. Like many of her peers who found writing a convenient intellectual outlet that could easily be combined with domestic responsibilities, she wrote for pleasure. But unlike those who sometimes wrote for money as well, Adele wrote to inform and educate her audience and to argue her causes. Maybe women did not go before political bodies and ask for things, but they knew most everyone read newspapers. In the 1880s, Houston women found newspapers to be an outlet for their short stories, sketches, poems, and opinions. Because expressing opinions was considered by many to be particularly unladylike, women frequently signed their work with their first names only or "Anonymous" or some other pseudonym. Adele, tellingly, signed her articles "Texan." For these writing women to support each other and further develop their skills, Aurelia Hadley Mohl, a fellow member of the Ladies' Reading Club, organized the Texas Woman's Press Association in 1893, and Adele promptly joined. She wrote articles for the Woman's Exchange magazines—the

Texas Messenger, Ladies' Messenger, and the *Gulf Messenger.* Between April 1887 and October 1888, she contributed no fewer than fourteen articles to the *Ladies' Messenger,* the primary organ of the Woman's Exchange of Houston, which at the time was published by Laura Bibb Foute.[26] The topics spanned a wide range, from historical accounts such as "The First Anniversary Ball of the Battle of San Jacinto," to gender issues such as "Industries for Women," to essays on education such as "The Impolicy of Educating Texas Youth Abroad."[27] On questions of Texas history, "Texan" became the authority. The editors and publishers of these magazines regularly turned to her for advice as well as copy. Her association with so many women and her leadership in so many clubs made her a "go-to" person for assistance of all kinds.

For example, when Adele opened her mail on January 3, 1893, she was greeted with a cordial letter on the stationery of Palestine Public Schools. The correspondent was Anna J. Pennybacker, wife of the superintendent. Pennybacker was writing a Texas history textbook for the public schools and wanted Adele to refer her to sources bearing on the lives of prominent early Texans. Anna Pennybacker was a native of Virginia who had married a native Texan and educator, Percy V. Pennybacker, in 1884. She had graduated in the first class of Sam Houston Normal School in Huntsville, continued her education in Europe, and subsequently taught grammar and high school for fourteen years, including some sessions at the Chautauqua Institution summer assembly. Mrs. Pennybacker wrote and first published *A New History of Texas* in 1888, and the textbook became a staple of Texas classrooms. By 1892 she had become involved in women's clubs, and in 1894 she had founded the Tyler Woman's Club.[28] As a clubwoman, writer, and women's suffrage advocate, she went on to become a tour de force of female activism.

Pennybacker's request was one of many instances in which fellow pen women called on Adele for information, advice, or approval. Adele took the opportunity in May 1894 to call upon Pennybacker's support for the San Jacinto battleground park. After complimenting her as one who had written a history of Texas, Adele wrote, "It has been suggested that the graduates of Sam Houston Normal might respond generously to an appeal of this kind. . . . I notice that to you has been assigned the Alumnae address class of 1879 and 1880." Later in the year, in response to another request for information from Anna Pennybacker regarding her history book, Adele graciously referred her to Betty Ballinger for the data she required. Again in March 1895, in response to an inquiry from Mrs. Pennybacker about the San Jacinto battleground, Adele responded with a detailed, seven-page, handwritten letter.[29]

By the early 1890s, Adele's reputation as a writer and authority on the period of the Texas Revolution and Republic of Texas was well known. A year earlier, on Valentine's Day 1894, she had received a letter from William G. Scarff of Dallas, who, along with Dudley G. Wooten, planned to publish a new history of Texas. He needed a lot of photographs of ladies and gentlemen who were prominent during the days of the revolution and republic, and as the work of securing them was rather tedious, he asked for her help. He needed a chapter, too, and according to Scarff, she had been unanimously nominated to write it. Adele willingly accommodated both of these requests and ultimately contributed three chapters to the complete work, including "A History and Evolution of the Texas Flag," "The Women of Pioneer Days in Texas—Domestic and Social Life in the Period of the Colonies, the Revolution, and the Republic," and "Tombs and Monuments of Noted Texans."[30]

When Sara Hartman had begun editing the *Gulf Messenger* literary magazine, she, too, wrote to Adele pleading for suggestions on suitable topics in Texas history. Another journalist, Dora Fowler Arthur of Austin, presented Adele with not simply a request but a challenge. She asked for a sketch of the life of Mary (Mrs. Anson) Jones but then observed, "How remiss Texas has been in embalming memories of the mothers of Texas for posterity. As ours is a woman's

Adele Looscan in 1898.
Courtesy of the San Jacinto Museum of History.

association, now is the golden opportunity to collect and treasure biographical sketches of our mothers who have borne the burden in war and in peace."[31] Adele unhesitatingly accepted the challenge. In 1898, she produced "Texian Women," which became one of her multiple contributions to Dudley Wooten's *Comprehensive History of Texas,* as Scarff's project came to be titled. In this article she included not only the sketch of Mary Jones but also biographies of some thirteen other women, including her mother and grandmother. "You can never know how you have helped and encouraged me," Dora Arthur wrote in gratitude.[32]

Always generous with her time, Adele endeavored to encourage others in their writing efforts whenever called upon. Such was the case with Isaac Dunbar Affleck, a former Texas Ranger and aspiring Texas historian in Brenham, Texas, who was referred to Adele by their mutual friend, Adina De Zavala. Affleck had pursued his interest in Texas flags and the Spanish missions. His work was nearing completion, and he hoped the Daughters of the Republic of Texas, who were raising money to buy the Alamo at the time, would help him publish it for a share of the profits. He wanted Adele to review his 150,000-word manuscript. "My intention," he explained to her, "has been to concentrate the facts as much as possible in a readable shape and in language that will encourage patriotism in which a love for Texas is paramount to all other considerations." She responded without hesitation and with generous encouragement.[33]

Another such protégé was Mary Saunders, a close personal friend of Adele and operator of the Walnut Grove Ranch guesthouse a few miles from Boerne, Texas. Adele and Michael Looscan were frequent visitors at Walnut Grove in Kendall County, a favorite resort in the Texas hill country near San Antonio and far from the mosquitoes and malarial climate of the Texas coast. In the spring of 1900, Adele retreated to Walnut Grove Ranch after visiting her brother Brits at his home in Floresville. She needed a break from caring for her mother. She had not been feeling well, and the dry air and emerald-hued scenery of the Hill Country provided a pleasant respite from bustling Houston.

Adele and Mary Saunders shared a love of poetry. During the Texas Veterans Association meeting in San Antonio, Adele's visit with Gov. Francis Lubbock and a little German woman, who had also been a neighbor from early days in Harrisburg, inspired her to pen a poem about her father.[34] Mary, too, was an aspiring poet, and Adele encouraged her to submit some of her poetry to newspapers and women's magazines. She spent many hours critiquing and editing Saunders's attempt at epic poetry, a work titled "Texas Kalevala," in the hope that she might, through her connections, get it published. When their efforts failed, Adele sent the manuscript to Adina De Zavala, hoping that the De Zavala Chapter of the DRT would print it. With disappointment, Adina reported that the women insisted they could not sell poetry—people's tastes were not sufficiently cultivated. They would agree to print and circulate it—give it away or sell at cost or a small advance to the few who would buy—if they got Saunders's permission. "I hope you will agree as Mrs. Looscan and I are anxious to see the poem in print," Adina urged. Saunders, however, balked at the DRT terms. Adina patiently explained that printing involved quite an outlay of money and that the Daughters were "rather chary." There was a decided misunderstanding all around. "Everyone imagined that the poem was an out and out gift—and that they could do as they pleased so there is consternation in camp," she explained. Saunders's epic never fulfilled Adele's hopes for it, but both she and her mother remained loyal in their regard for Saunders's talent, and it was to Mary Saunders that Adele turned for a memorial upon Mary Jane's death.[35]

Walnut Grove Ranch's proximity to Austin and San Antonio also facilitated Adele's participation in other organizations to which she was committed, such as the Texas State Historical Association. In late June, she went to Austin for a week. She met Mary De Zavala, Adina's younger sister, at the depot in San Antonio, and they kept company

Mary Saunders of Boerne, Texas.
Courtesy of the San Jacinto Museum of History.

on the trip. When they arrived in the Texas capital, several old friends were waiting. They took in all the attractions afforded by the University of Texas and attended a sermon by Lyman Abbott, the liberal-minded social reformer and former editor of *Harper's Weekly*.[36] On Wednesday Adele attended the meeting of the Texas State Historical Association, and on Friday she went to artist Elisabet Ney's studio to meet Bride Neill Taylor—"one of Austin's history women," she explained to her mother. As she described her day in a letter to Mary Jane, energy infused her words. "Mollie declared she had never heard so much intellectual conversation," she wrote, "and part of the time was spent in looking through the studio where we saw many other interesting objects."[37]

It was the nature of club membership that one association led to another. With their enthusiasm for associations, penchant for history, pride in the revolutionary heritage of the Harrises and the Briscoes, as well as their association with Confederate veterans through their immediate male family members and friends, Adele and her mother, like many other upper- and middle-class southern women, were drawn into the Daughters of the American Revolution (DAR), and the United Daughters of the Confederacy (UDC) when those groups were organized in 1896. When the Lady Washington Chapter of the DAR was organized in Houston in 1899, Adele became chapter historian, but for her both the DAR and UDC were extensions of her Texas heritage. In her memorial to the DAR on the death of her sister Jessie, she pointed out that her ancestors, the Briscoes and Harrises, were pioneers and builders of the Republic of Texas before mentioning those who had participated in the American Revolution.

Adele's involvement with the DAR led to her membership in the Mount Vernon Ladies' Association, of which Ella Hutchins Sydnor, who had started the DAR chapter in Houston, was a regent. Although active in all these organizations, Adele equated service in them to service to Texas. "It is a matter of pride to every Texan that from the very beginning of the organization of the Ladies Mount Vernon Association, one from our State has been a member," she would tell the women of the Alexander Love Chapter of the DAR at its initial meeting in 1923.[38]

Given her husband Michael's involvement in the Dick Dowling Camp of Confederate Veterans in Houston, Adele's association with the United Daughters of the Confederacy when the Texas division was established in 1896 was not surprising. However, women like Adele saw the Confederacy and Confederate veterans as extensions of Texas heroism. Thus, for them, the Lost Cause—like the Alamo—stood as a reminder of the heroic character of Texans, and to them it was a righteous cause primarily because Texans had shed their blood for it. Both chapters of the UDC in Houston, the Robert E. Lee Chapter and the Oran M. Roberts Chapter, established in 1901, made Mary Jane Briscoe an honorary member as much out of respect for her as a patriotic Texan as for her status as the mother of Confederate veterans.[39] The tenor of Adele and Mary Jane's participation illustrated the difference between women of the Texas revolutionary generation and later generations of women who did not have that experience. By contrast, Adelia Dunovant, founder of the Oran M. Roberts Chapter of the UDC, grew up in South Carolina and came to Texas only after the Civil War. She sought to rehabilitate the memory of her father, a plantation and slave owner. Justification for the plantation culture of her youth motivated her, because that was her experience.[40]

Although they may have shared some common goals such as community service, patriotism, preserving American history, and education, Adele Looscan and clubwomen like Adelia Dunovant and Cornelia Branch Stone, as well as younger women like Clara Driscoll, often had very different views and motivations, which eventually produced tension, even schism, among the ladies of the club. In the first decade of the twentieth century, these tensions were famously manifest in an acrimonious split in the Daughters of the Republic of Texas. Adele reacted with confusion to this unexpected hostility.

Adina De Zavala, less naïve about human nature and much less patient, provided an assessment that went directly to the heart of the difference and revealed remarkable insight at a time when the internal friction was especially high. "The whole thing will forever remain in the hands of a clique," she wrote to Adele in late November 1907. "Have you noticed," De Zavala continued, "that it is the same clique that has grabbed all the patriotic societies? It is a well-organized clique—they stand well together. They first took possession of the smaller clubs and societies then widened their influence. A clique gets in power and holds it because in the beginning the others are indifferent—or careless or unsuspecting."[41]

The power motive, however, was not the only difference dividing clubwomen. While many southern women involved in the patriotic hereditary clubs connected to the Confederacy sought a sense of ennobled southern womanhood based on Old South values or extolled the virtues of a past "southern life," Adele Looscan, Adina De Zavala, and women like them tended to see the UDC as another vehicle for improving Texas society and culture and reminding Texans of their obligations and duties as citizens.[42] This difference could be noted in a comparison between Adele's reasons for studying history, which she had presented in her address to the Ladies' Reading Club of Houston in 1890, and Adelia A. Dunovant's address, "The Study of History," delivered to the Lamar Fontaine Chapter of the UDC in Alvin, Texas, in 1899. Adele spoke in broad terms of studying history for personal edification, to bring the individual into "sympathetic relations with the great individual minds that have shaped the form and determined the character of what we call history," to give those who inhabit the present a sense of their place in the great continuum, and to appreciate their position as American women, as well as the benefits they derived from that position. Dunovant's message, on the other hand, differed in tone and emphasis if not in essence. History was, she declared, "a tribute at the feet of our beloved South." By "diving into historic recesses," she assured her listeners, they could rescue the principles of the South "from the grave of oblivion" and glorify them. Her reasons for studying history (which she referred to as "mind work") were its indestructibility, the "regal robe" it drew around the Daughters of the Confederacy, and its utility for inculcating southern principles in younger generations.[43]

Dunovant and others in memorial associations formed across the South in the immediate aftermath of the Civil War were dedicated to the reconstruction of the image of southern white men and southern principles, but many Texas women who joined the UDC remained more dedicated to Texas principles. When the United Daughters of the Confederacy wanted to erect a fountain on the Alamo Plaza, Adina De Zavala wrote to Adele, "The question is whether we should allow [it] without public protest. I think a fountain is all right and a great convenience. However, it is on ground sacred alone to the Heroes of the Alamo. On the square of the old Mission San Antonio de Valero where our men were hemmed up so many days and every inch is watered with their blood. It seems to me that every delicacy of sentiment and feeling would have kept them from this sacred spot. Of course," she acknowledged, "most of us are Daughters of the Confederacy, too, but we did not like the Chapter's actions during last Convention and feel that Societies as well as individuals should have some delicacy of sentiment, and that there are certain spots in San Antonio, the Alamo in particular, that should be left sacred alone to the Daughters of the old Republic."[44]

Adele and Adina were not alone in their sentiments among Texas women who joined the United Daughters of the Confederacy. The Texas Division of the United Daughters of the Confederacy was organized in Victoria, Texas, on May 15, 1896, by Katie Cabell Currie and Ruth Phelps, who seem to have been as influenced by the City Beautiful movement as by the need to connect with Texas's Confederate past. Currie, the Texas Division's first president, had traveled to the World's Columbian Exposition in Chicago in 1893 and returned to Dallas from the World's Fair motivated to create a woman's club dedicated to the "beautification and moral uplifting" of Texas.[45]

Adele expressed this dedication eloquently in an article for the *Silver Cross.*[46] She explained that although Texas possessed "a rich store of interesting and romantic detail in her historic records," the period of "most thrilling interest" was between the years 1821 and 1845, during which the independent Republic of Texas was formed. The Alamo, Goliad, and San Jacinto, she declared, had become synonymous with all that was "patriotic, pathetic, and glorious in warfare." "Because the public's attention had been drawn to more recent wars . . . and there was a danger that the names of the heroes of Texas Independence might be forgotten and the battleground of San Jacinto pass irrevocably beyond the power of the State to possess or control," Adele explained, "the Association of the Daughters of the Republic of Texas (DRT) was formed."[47] Of all the many clubs, organizations, and activities that consumed Adele Looscan's adult life, none was more important or dearer to her heart than the DRT.

Chapter Four

Daughter of the Republic

HOUSTON IN THE LAST DECADE of the nineteenth century was, like the rest of the country, changing rapidly and leaning forward. The neighborhood of the Briscoe home, Quality Hill, evidenced the city's burgeoning prosperity. Great houses with turrets, balconies, ballrooms, and indoor tennis courts buzzed with warm hospitality. The first electric streetcar in the city began operation in 1891, providing much spectacle for curiosity seekers, as well as convenient transportation. Among the most significant changes was the growing influence of big business and out-of-state corporations. "Old Houston" meant families like Adele's that had come during the days of the Republic of Texas or before the Civil War, but well-heeled newcomers were welcomed. Money was not the only criterion for acceptance. Those with good manners, good taste, and eager willingness to engage in community service blended into Old Houston society and soon emerged as civic and social leaders. The turn of the century brought many changes to Adele Looscan's life and set the direction of her future as a historian and a public woman.

The Daughters of the Republic of Texas gave Adele, Jessie, and Mary Jane the opportunity to focus their energies on what made them distinguished members of Old Houston society—their Texas heritage—but the association would change Adele's life in ways she could not have foreseen. That fateful enterprise had begun in the

Front piazza, Mrs. Andrew Briscoe house, 620 Crawford Street.
Left to right: Parmenas Briscoe, Mary Jane Briscoe,
Annie Hume, Columbia Hume.
MSSO248-2139, Houston Public Library, HMRC

spring of 1891 when Betty Ballinger and her cousin, Hally Ballinger Bryan of Galveston, decided to form an organization dedicated to the perpetuation of the memory of the heroes of San Jacinto. Both women traced their lineage to the Jack brothers, Patrick and William, through their mothers, and Hally Bryan was a grandniece of Stephen F. Austin. Betty Ballinger had some organizing experience as a cofounder of the first literary club in Galveston.[1] Their interest in this pursuit was aroused by the recent discovery in an old Galveston cemetery of the neglected graves of two Texas patriots: David G. Burnet, first president of the Republic of Texas, and Sidney Sherman, a veteran of the Battle of San Jacinto. The cousins solicited support from other women of Texas whose husbands or ancestors had helped the republic achieve and maintain its independence. Hally's father, Guy M. Bryan, president of the Texas Veterans Association, introduced her to Mary (Mrs. Anson) Jones, widow of the last president of the Republic of Texas, and to Mary Jane Briscoe. Seventeen women assembled in Mary Jane Briscoe's parlor in Houston on November 6, 1891, to form the Daughters of the Lone Star Republic, renamed Daughters of the Republic of Texas at the first annual meeting. Mary Jones was recognized as president. Mary Jane was elected vice president, and Adele was elected historian. Betty Ballinger was chosen a member of the executive committee, which drew up the organization's constitution and bylaws. She laid out the purpose of the organization in terms of the traditional role of southern women: "The future of Texas is in the hands of her sons [who], dazzled by the splendor of the present have forgotten the heroic deeds and sacrifices of the past. But it is not so with woman. Surrounded by the history of the family life, it is her duty to keep alive the sacred fire of tradition. Let us leave the future of Texas to our brothers, and claim as our province the guarding of her holy past." Her choice of words echoed the sentiments of many clubwomen across the country, particularly in the South, as they tried to balance traditional roles with their desire to enlarge the scope of womanhood.[2] The difference between the Daughters of the Republic of Texas and other groups with similar purposes, such as the United Daughters of the Confederacy, was that the past they venerated was Texas's past, one with which these women uniquely identified. They may have been Daughters of the American Revolution and Daughters of the Confederacy, a sisterhood shared by women all over the nation and the South, but Texas's "holy past" was theirs alone. Even as the Daughters of the Republic of Texas pledged to preserve the memory of the republic, though,

Texas was changing: the revolutionary generation was passing, and Texans were looking toward the future.

A few days after the meeting at Mary Jane Briscoe's house, the Houston women organized a local chapter of the DRT with the specific mission of urging the state to purchase the San Jacinto battleground and erect a monument to its heroes—their husbands and fathers. Adele immediately threw herself into this cause and to gaining support for the DRT. Always a letter writer, she penned dozens of letters urging the daughters of Texas veterans to join. She sometimes met with discouragement, as in the reply of Anna Ehinger of Navasota, who wrote, "Mamma got the little book you sent her in the summer, and spoke of joining; then found the others here with so little enthusiasm, and gave it up. I think it impossible to organize anything here—even a chapter of the 'Daughters of the Republic.'" Testimony to Adele's dedication, patience, and tolerance was evidenced in those who displayed initial reticence but eventually became staunch supporters, like Nettie Houston Bringhurst, who responded less than enthusiastically to her solicitation in late November following that first meeting: "I join hand and heart with you in your patriotic undertaking and hope you and your associates may meet with the success you deserve. In regard to my sisters and myself, we all live very quietly and go little into society, calling more for children and home than for glitter and display, but we might aid you in unobstructive ways." These daughters of Sam Houston seemed perfect models of the ideology of "separate spheres." When Adele urged Nettie Bringhurst and her sisters to attend a meeting, Bringhurst complained that she could not leave home, asking if Adele might not find time to come and visit her instead. "We are very primitive here," she professed, "not a particle of style about us, but we will be glad to see you; and you can look around and see a good deal of interest to thinking people like yourself." Her words were to prove bitterly ironic, but at that moment Bringhurst's letter exhibited the attitude, typical of many, that they might agree to join, but Adele should do the legwork.[3] More often than not, she did.

In contrast, some of her appeals found eager participants. In Austin, Dora Fowler Arthur immediately embraced the new organization. From Marie Bennett Urwitz, writing from Yorktown in DeWitt County between Victoria and San Antonio, she received apologies for not sending the papers in sooner. "I believe few applications will yet have been so fully written out as are mine and if the Secretary finds them too much in her way at present, will you please be so kind as to keep them for me? They will be wanted someday. The regular Application can be filed, and these other papers kept for reference," Urwitz wrote imperiously. Her sisters Anna Bennett Louis, Mrs. Walker, and Mrs. Wofford, she informed Adele, were going to join—Louis in the San Jacinto Chapter and Walker and Wofford in the De Zavala Chapter.[4]

Adele's invitation to Adina De Zavala in San Antonio received a warm response in February 1893. Adina was a granddaughter of Lorenzo de Zavala, who had been ad interim vice president of the Republic of Texas and instrumental in the drafting of the constitution of the republic. With Adina, appearances were deceiving. This daughter of an Irish mother had soft brown hair, blue eyes, and a gentle, friendly manner that belied the strong will and fiery temper packaged in her five-foot, three-inch frame. Adina Emilia De Zavala was the eldest of six children of Augustine and Julia Tyrell De Zavala and was born in Harris County November 18, 1861. The family briefly lived in Galveston, where Adina attended Ursuline Academy from 1871 to 1873. She then attended Sam Houston Normal Institute in Huntsville, Texas, from 1879 to 1881 and afterward attended a school of music in Missouri. Adina was another woman poised on the cusp of tradition and progressivism. She taught school in Terrell, Kaufman County, Texas, from 1884 to 1886, before settling in San Antonio, where she continued her teaching career.[5] De Zavala herself had been active in organizing San Antonio women for patriotic purposes. Her response to Looscan's overture on behalf of the Daughters of the Republic of Texas was filled with enthusiasm. "I shall be obliged if you will have forwarded, as you suggest, a copy of the Constitution and By-laws together with the application blanks of membership," she wrote to Adele. "I think it would be a very easy matter to establish here a branch organization. There must be many descendants of heroes and veterans of Texas living here, and if you wish, I will do what I can in the matter."[6]

Adina De Zavala, though thirteen years Adele's junior, was a kindred spirit, particularly in her desire to preserve Texas cultural heritage and memorialize its heroes. She had organized a group of San Antonio women in 1889 to "discuss" Texas and its heroes; it was one of the first women's societies in the state organized expressly for patriotic purposes. Now, she led this group to establish the De Zavala Chapter of the Daughters of the Republic of Texas. The De Zavala Chapter, like the San Jacinto Chapter, had the preservation of a Texas shrine, the Alamo, as its primary object, and the two women became devoted allies. Adele's friendship with Adina would withstand much in the next forty years, including not only the almost literal fall of the Alamo for a second time but also the rending of the association that had brought the two women together. In the meantime, they dedicated themselves to the preservation and promotion of Texas history.

One of the DRT's first and most successful campaigns involved the ongoing effort to acquire the San Jacinto battleground. In 1894 a committee of veterans, including survivors of the battle, located important sites of the battle events; in 1897 they marked them. The preservation of the battleground as a state historical site became a joint effort of the Texas Veterans Association and the Daughters of the Republic of Texas. It was no easy task. The men were able to approach the governor and legislature. The women, unable to take so direct a route, relentlessly wrote memorials and letters and pamphlets and circulars to garner state support for the battleground and to raise money to purchase more of it.[7] The economic depression that swept the United States in 1893 could be felt even in Texas, so the effort to commemorate the battle in a fitting manner demanded great patience, persistence, and a healthy supply of determined optimism, clearly reflected in Adele's correspondence.

"Doubtless you think I have neglected getting subscriptions for the San Jacinto Bazaar," wrote her friend, Mary Saunders, from Walnut Grove, "but I have tried very hard and everybody tells me that times are so hard and they have no money. I have only been able to collect one dollar and a quarter ($1.25), am almost ashamed to send such a small amount, but thought it would be better than none. Mr. Rachow and our own family are the only contributors."[8]

From Eagle Pass, L. W. Yarrington sent a money order for $38.60 to be added to the San Jacinto Battleground Fund: "Miss Stapp and I as members got up an entertainment to raise money for that purpose; realized $15.00 therefrom; expenses amounted to $4.25. During session of District Court I begged $18.00. Had it not been for the continued illness of my sister, I could have done much better. I also, to save myself trouble, enclose my dues $1.00. Kindly attend to handing it in for me. If I do not do so at this writing, in my multitude of cares it may lay untouched for some time."[9]

Adele, a generous patron of literature and the arts, called upon others like Mary Saunders for support of the San Jacinto fundraising effort. In 1895, San Antonio artist Harry McArdle assured her that in response to her many favors, it would give him great pleasure to contribute to the San Jacinto Chapter "a certain percentage of the art receipts" from the exhibition of his painting of the Battle of San Jacinto.[10] McArdle was a native of Ireland who had studied art before coming to America after the death of his parents. He had been a draftsman for the Confederate Navy during the Civil War and had made topographical maps for Gen. Robert E. Lee. After the war he settled in Independence, Texas, with his wife and taught art at Baylor Female College. McArdle worked with veterans of Hood's Texas

Brigade to research the design for his historical canvas titled *Lee at the Wilderness* (1869–70) and developed a growing interest in Texas history. Word of his abilities spread, and in 1890 the governor commissioned McArdle to paint a full-length portrait of Jefferson Davis to hang in the capitol. When the Baylor college was moved from Independence, McArdle left its employ and set up his own studio in San Antonio. Among the most renowned of his historical canvases were the twin pieces *Dawn at the Alamo* (1905) and *The Battle of San Jacinto,* which he completed in 1898.[11] After years of a variety of fundraising efforts, the Daughters of the Republic of Texas finally managed to raise the money to mark strategic sites at the battleground with granite boulders.

As important as the battleground was, Adele's ambition for the promotion of Texas history extended beyond that project. She knew that remnants of the revolution and republic were scattered about the state in the hands of veterans or their families, and she firmly believed that these relics should be preserved and displayed to educate the public. Never one to hesitate putting ideas into action, she drafted a memorial to the Texas legislature in January 1897 proposing that a room be set aside in the capitol for a Texas museum. In this cause, she found supporters among other DRT members, particularly in Austin. Rebecca J. Fisher, president of the William B. Travis Chapter, was among the first to endorse the museum, though she expressed some hesitancy at including any of the rougher aspects of Texas's checkered past, having experienced some of those elements quite personally. Around 1837, Rebecca's family, the Gillilands, had arrived in Texas and settled in Refugio County. In 1840, Comanches attacked their home, killed her parents, and captured Rebecca and her brother William. The children were rescued by Albert Sidney Johnston and a detachment of Texas soldiers and taken to Victoria. From there they were sent to live with an aunt in Galveston. After attending Rutersville College, Rebecca married Orceneth Fisher and they settled in Austin. Like Adele, Rebecca was a charter member of the Daughters of the Republic of Texas.[12] "Do you think it a very delicate and appropriate thing to call for scalps?" she worried. "It does seem out of place for refined, delicate women to make such an appeal. The heart of mothers and children of Texas Independence almost curdles at the thought." On the other hand, she wrote, "anything pertaining to a heroic man, as you say, should be given a place."[13]

For her project of promoting a Texas museum, Adele also found a like-minded partner in Dora Fowler Arthur, whose father had been a Methodist missionary in the Republic of Texas. Dora was a member of the fledgling William B. Travis Chapter of the DRT in Austin, and she was as devoted to the promotion of Texas women as Adele was to Texas veterans. Their interests coincided when Dora wrote to Adele at the behest of the William B. Travis Chapter to convey clippings from the *Austin Daily Statesman* and the *Weekly Home Corner.*

That letter was followed by regular correspondence from Dora Arthur to keep Adele apprised of the activities of the William B. Travis Chapter, including efforts to further the goal of a museum. "Daily, pictures and sketches, biographic and autobiographic[,] are being donated to the Texas museum which is under the control of the local chapter, Wm. B. Travis, and I, as historian of that chapter, have laboriously solicited these donations," she wrote from Austin.[14] Her idea was to give this historical material and women writers more public notice through a column devoted to the Daughters of the Republic of Texas in a new magazine being published in Austin.

Texas Magazine first appeared in Austin in May 1896. At first the content was primarily historical, with announcements of the beginning of the Texas State Historical Association and the activities of the Daughters of the Republic of Texas and other women's organizations. As the magazine became more literary, it featured more fiction and poetry, as well as a section called "Among Writers and Books." Texas historians C. W. Raines and James Thomas DeShields and poets William Lawrence Crittenden and John Peter Sjolander were among the contributors.[15] Dora Arthur edited the *Texas Magazine.* She saw both the DRT and the magazine as being of benefit to women as well as to the veterans of the Texas Republic. *Texas Magazine,* she argued, would provide the Daughters of Texas with a forum. In return, the Daughters would provide a subscription base for the enterprise. The men of Texas, she argued, "have given the political and military history of colonial Texas and the Republic, but the few women who have essayed anything of state history merely gave a rehash, or a condensation of what the men had already done." Arthur explained that the publisher of the *Texas Magazine,* Robert E. McCleary, offered the Daughters of the Republic of Texas a department of as many pages each month as they wished—as many as she had subject matter to fill—and asked only that the sisterhood throughout the state support his publication in return by individual subscription and by contributions of historical material. It was his hope, when his circulation grew large enough to warrant it, to produce half-tone engravings of faces and homes, thereby giving to the people of Texas a homegrown magazine of good quality suitable for their precious memoirs and reminiscences. Moreover, Arthur explained, the DRT column in the magazine would encourage the donation of pictures and sketches, biographical and autobiographical, and other historical possessions to the DRT. Dora Arthur undertook editorship of the DRT section of the magazine personally. Her correspondence with Adele clearly revealed that the promotion of Texas history had as much if not more to do with the promotion of Texas women as with Texas heroes. She had made a study of literature written by the women of New England and the other former colonies in order to understand what Texas women could do for their own state. "I am an enthusiast in Texas history," she wrote, "and think I see where Texas women can do much with equal grace and ease to enrich our state literature by saving from irrevocable loss the memory of our pioneer women; also the domestic and social history of the colonial and republican periods."[16] Adele agreed and responded to all of Dora's many requests by writing articles, by soliciting articles, photographs, and subscriptions, and even by donating money.

That the magazine never gained much traction spoke volumes about the popular interest in Texas heroes, but it did draw Adele into frequent contact with Dora Arthur and other contributors who shared her interest in preserving and promoting the memory of Texas's revolutionary past. As usual, not all members of the DRT participated with equal enthusiasm or spirit of cooperation. Rebecca Fisher was one who didn't. In January 1897, Dora wrote in exasperation, "In regard to your suggestions regarding Mrs. Jones' and Mrs. A. S. Johnston's pictures for our department, I have to say that a good picture of the latter is in our museum collection but Mrs. Fisher accords one no courtesies whatever."[17]

February brought Adele a new round of requests for favors. Dora needed help with pictures for the public schools, and she needed a shoulder to cry on. She grew hungry for that communicable touch with a live and busy chapter. "In Austin everything falls on three or four when work is to be done," she mourned, complaining that, "otherwise, it is not even submitted to the Chapter for a voice in the matter—a sure way to kill what latent interest there might be."[18] Adele dutifully responded, even though her husband, Michael, had been struck with a mysterious and debilitating illness and thus required her constant attention. Within days Dora Arthur wrote again requesting a contribution to the DRT section of *Texas Magazine* even as she acknowledged Adele's indisposition: "You have my sympathy for your late siege of nursing," she wrote. "Please retain my letter if you can find it in your heart to help our department in the *Texas Magazine*."[19] Adele obliged, a typical response and a tribute to her sense of responsibility regardless of personal inconvenience.

In spite of the dedicated efforts of Adele and Dora, *Texas Magazine* did not prove a successful enterprise for Robert McCleary, who sold it to William G. Scarff of Dallas in August 1897, but it did disseminate articles written by Adele Looscan. With Scarff as editor and publisher and Dudley Goodall Wooten as editorial supervisor, the publication covered a wide range of interests, including literature, current events, women's clubs, and poetry. Adele Looscan's contacts and reputation as a Texas historian had prompted Scarff, as early as 1894, to approach her for help securing articles for his planned new history of Texas, which he published a few years later as Dudley G. Wooten's *Comprehensive History of Texas, 1685–1897.*[20] She also obligingly contributed to Wooten's *Complete History of Texas for Schools.* Her writing for newspapers, literary magazines, and history anthologies such as Wooten's no doubt helped to bring her to the attention of George P. Garrison as he began organizing the Texas State Historical Association in 1897.

It was, as a matter of fact, a fellow member of the Texas Woman's Press Association who directed Garrison to Adele in February 1897. Angelina V. Winkler, the wife of a former Indian fighter, state legislator, and Civil War veteran from Corsicana, had assisted Garrison in the mailing of more than 250 circulars inviting persons known to be especially interested in Texas history to join in forming an association for the collection and preservation of documents for the use of researchers and future historians of Texas. Only a week before Garrison and about twenty other invitees met in a room on the north side of the capitol building and organized the Texas State Historical Association, Angelina Winkler urged him to send circulars to two of her colleagues in the Texas Woman's Press Association: Mrs. L. Talley Gulich and Mrs. Michael Looscan.[21] Angelina Winkler was not the only one to encourage Garrison to involve women in the effort to do something about the steady loss of historical evidence in Texas due to ignorance, disinterest, and neglect. Dudley Wooten, who already had some experience with Texas's women writers, wrote to Garrison even before Winkler, urging him to enlist the women in support of this new enterprise. "The most intelligent, discriminating and active laborers in the collection and preservation of Texas historical materials have been her noble women," he told Garrison, and he named half a dozen whom he personally knew to be peculiarly fitted to take part in the work. Wooten knew that not only were the women experienced writers but they also knew where the kind of material Garrison wanted—letters, diaries, circulars, old books, personal recollections, newspapers, pictures—resided, largely in private hands.[22] He knew that these women had already proven themselves effective organizers who had achieved goals by pursuing them with dogged determination and seemingly boundless energy. Wooten was also aware that the first historical society in Texas, organized at Galveston in 1871 by men, had gotten off to an auspicious start only to see interest dwindle to such an extent that the accumulated archives had been put up for sale in 1885 to pay storage charges. Although the collection had been rescued and the society reorganized in 1894, its primary focus had remained on Galveston.[23] With the support of clubwomen, Wooten reasoned, the organization at the University of Texas might have a better chance of enduring and attracting statewide interest.

Although Adele accepted the invitation to become a charter member of the Texas State Historical Association, she was unable to attend the first meeting in Austin only a few days later, on March 2, 1897. It was not yet her first priority. Even as Adele labored to fulfill all the demands on her time that February, Michael deteriorated from a malady that affected his brain. Anxious to find a way of restoring her husband's health, Adele accompanied him to Mineral Wells in Palo Pinto County near Weatherford in north Texas, hoping the famous waters would have a healing effect. Michael's illness could not have come at a more inopportune time. The San Jacinto Chapter's campaign to garner support from the state legislature for improvements and monuments for the San Jacinto battleground was reaching its climax. Following their entertainment of the legislators at the battleground, the women took up for a second time the plan of persuading the state to purchase the entire battlefield and to make it a state park. Now, with legislation coming to a vote, its chief architect and cheerleader, Adele Looscan, could not be present. Marie Bennett Urwitz, for the San Jacinto delegation, on April 1 sent Adele a letter filled with excitement and sympathy.

"Dear Dellie," she wrote, "Our mind and hearts have been with you today, this eventful day in the existence of the lives of the members of our beloved Chapter. From ten o'clock until quarter past three today a hardly fought battle was raged in the House but victory crowned the efforts of our friends & our bill passed without amendments. We all felt that the presiding genius of our good fortune was absent, though." A few days later, Adele received a letter from Jessie that offered her sister's usual level-headed perspective on events: "Our delegation came home much elated over the passage of the bill, but I am not proposing to turn myself home until after the Governor has time to act, although I hardly think he will use the veto."[24] From Walnut Grove, Mary Saunders wrote to congratulate Adele on the success of the San Jacinto campaign: "I should have written to you before but I did not know whether or not Mineral Wells was a town. I am so very glad to hear your dear husband is better and pray for his complete recovery. I think the bill will pass unless the fact of the Asylum needing an extra appropriation should cause the Governor to veto it. No other state or country on earth has so glorious a history as Texas; no people on earth care for it as little."[25] Her words were prophetic.

To the dismay of the San Jacinto Chapter of the DRT, good fortune did not last. A few weeks later, a letter from Michael Looscan's friend, former governor James S. Hogg, caught up with Adele in Mineral Wells. Hogg begged to excuse himself, for reasons the major could explain to her, from taking the part she had asked of him in trying to have an appropriation passed to purchase the San Jacinto battleground. "If the bill now is to pass at all it must do so over the Governor's veto," he told her. So far he had kept aloof from the legislature and legislation except to speak to the governor in favor of buying the land. "The town is so full of lobbyists of all colors and kinds," he wrote, and he was so averse to such association that he could not take part in such matters.[26]

Hogg's letter was not the only discouraging word. In mid-April, Marie Bennett Urwitz, who was standing in as president of the San Jacinto Chapter in Adele's absence, lamented, "No one among your friends has more truly lamented your absence from Houston at this time than I. Although I have not felt that I had much influence in our dear work for the purchase of San Jacinto, I have greatly enjoyed the whole campaign until I found that caucuses were being held and lobbyists both men and women were daily surrounding the Governor helping to influence him against the bill." Gov. Charles Culberson did veto the hard-won bill. "His action was so cowardly," Urwitz fumed, "and he has sacrificed us to his own ambition. In order more thoroughly to effect our defeat, he waited, withholding either his signature or his veto, until the last moment of grace was gone. Very few even of our best friends thought we would get the bill passed in its original form," she admitted, "but after it was passed and by such a majority, no one thought Culberson would or could afford to veto it." The trouble is, she told Adele, "we have not the sympathy of the people, disguise the fact as you may, and unpleasant as it is, such is the truth. We heard mutterings among ladies, even, while we were at the Capitol; it comes from Galveston; it is here in Houston, and from people who should be in sympathy with every line of that bill—even native Texans and fathers who fought at San Jacinto. I am surprised at the indifference of this city," she confessed.[27] Ultimately, the Daughters of the Republic of Texas achieved at least a partial victory: Culberson approved an appropriation for a little less than half of the twenty-five thousand dollars they had sought for the battlefield.

Not all battles had as successful an outcome. Even as the women of the San Jacinto Chapter struggled to save the battleground and the Texas State Historical Association struggled to establish itself, the De

Zavala Chapter embarked on a campaign to save the storied mission of San Antonio de Valero. In the process, they sparked a monumental struggle within the DRT itself, one with lasting importance for Texas, for the DRT, and for Adele Looscan personally. The second battle of the Alamo was brewing, and Adele, always at the forefront, found herself caught squarely in the crossfire.

The trouble originated even before the Daughters of the Republic of Texas was founded. By the time the De Zavala Chapter of the DRT had come together, the old Spanish mission of San Antonio de Valero, popularly known as the Alamo, had changed hands many times. It had been used for many purposes, including serving as an army depot. Army engineers repaired the two-story stone building known as the *convento* and directed the completion of the roofless church, an effort that included construction of its distinctive arched gable. Other construction efforts during the 1850s obliterated most traces of the outer walls. The mission's south gate, or "Low Barracks," served as a jail before being razed in the late 1860s.[28] Although the army had used the property before and after the Civil War, it actually belonged to the Catholic Church. In 1877, a merchant, Honoré Grenet, purchased the two-story convento (known as the Long Barracks) and added wooden porticoes. The state later bought the mission chapel and placed it in the hands of the city of San Antonio. When Grenet died in 1882, his executor sought a new owner for the convent and in 1886 found one in the Hugo-Schmeltzer Company, a wholesale grocery firm. Commercial success and modernization became the primary focus at the Alamo. Its significance as a historical site ran a distant second.[29]

In 1892, Adina De Zavala extracted a promise from the Hugo-Schmeltzer Company to give her group first chance at buying the property should they decide to sell it. Since 1893, the De Zavala Chapter had been working enthusiastically for the projects of other chapters of the DRT. Adina personally worked tirelessly to raise funds for the organization, and she was one of its most successful fundraisers. In 1897, she and other members of the San Antonio Battle of Flowers Association took advantage of the annual Battle of Flowers event to raise money for the DRT. The Battle of Flowers had originated during the 1891 Fiesta San Jacinto flower parade, conceived by Ellen Maury Slayden, wife of US Rep. James L. Slayden, as an April 21 salute to the heroes of the battles of the Alamo and San Jacinto. A group of San Antonio women formed the Battle of Flowers Association and established an annual event. During the parade, participants in carriages would pelt one another with flowers as they rounded Alamo Plaza. By 1895, an elaborate weeklong celebration surrounded the Battle of Flowers Parade, and the first queen was chosen.[30] In May, Adina reported to Adele, "The Daughters made nearly two hundred dollars of which they gave one hundred to the widow of [a local veteran]. We will have a meeting Tuesday and appropriate ten dollars to help you with pictures for the schools. We will try to give Milam's grave a little attention with the remainder of the money."[31]

The spring of 1897 was encouraging for DRT chapters around the state. It was a difficult and fearful season for Adele, however, even though she kept up with her commitments and her correspondence. Despite her concern for her husband, she took some comfort from them. A letter from Belle Blandini, a high school teacher whom Adele had assisted the previous year, must have brought a slight smile to her face as she read it, even though she had had to decline an invitation to visit the class.[32] Letters like this one, written only to express gratitude, were rare. Most combined thanks with additional requests, and most of her friends, who had only known her to be reliable and accommodating, could not appreciate the burden of fear and worry under which she labored to respond. Despite her prayers, her research and consultation with various physicians and healers, despite the therapeutic waters of Mineral Wells and the wholesome air of Walnut Grove, despite everything she could humanly do to effect a cure for Michael, his condition continued to worsen. William

Scarff and Dora Arthur, intent on the success of their own projects, barely acknowledged her indisposition. "Your letter received, for which I return my thanks," Dora wrote on June 2. "The delay was unaccountable to me except there must be illness in your family." Then, without pause, she continued her account of the latest developments regarding publication of *Texas Magazine*.[33]

If Michael Looscan's decline were not burden enough, Mary Jane took a bad fall on the steps of her house in late July, prompting Adele to rush back to Houston to care for her, too. Jessie could be of no help. She was in Canada, seeking a change of air and scene for her own husband, Captain Howe, who was also ailing. "It is certainly a trying situation our troubles have come in a lump," Jessie mourned. "If there was any one here that we knew I would not mind so much leaving Captain Howe but it does seem so far from all the world."[34] What could be done? Brits's daughter Carrie had come from Goliad and was helping out. "Do you think Carrie P. is a good nurse?" Jessie worried. She ran through the list of female relatives they might call upon to tend their mother, but in the end there had been nothing for it but that Adele return to Houston.[35]

Undertaking the care of two patients demanded Adele's full attention as the summer of 1897 wore long, but the added burdens did nothing to stem the steady stream of demands on her time, talent, and energy. She was vice president of the Ladies' Reading Club that year. In mid-August 1897, Norma Bonner wrote from Tyler asking for assistance with the course of study as she prepared for the reopening of clubs in the fall. "Each of the committee is anxious this year's work should be doubly interesting and instructive," she explained.[36] Two weeks later she wrote to graciously thank Adele for her prompt response. "Many thanks to you for your kindness. Should your time not be too occupied with your dear invalids, I should like very much the name of gift books used in the University when your friends send them."[37]

Adele's time was preoccupied with her invalids. Just days before

Norma Bonner's letter arrived, on September 7, Michael Looscan died, placing new burdens upon her shoulders as she settled his estate, business, and legal affairs, paid delinquent taxes on his properties, and assumed the full responsibility of caring for his ill and indigent sister, Winnefred, and her husband, John McAran, in Philadelphia.

Adele seemingly took all these responsibilities in stride. Hardly a month later, George Garrison communicated from Austin. "My dear Madam," he wrote, "Could you not find leisure some time to write an article for the Quarterly of the Texas State Historical Association? The Publication Committee would be glad to have something from you. The association is unable to pay for contributions to the Quarterly, but, in spite of this, we have every hope of making it a very high-class magazine."[38] Adele put him off for the time being by assuring him she was working on several articles.

In December he wrote again, pleading with her to attend the midwinter meeting of the Texas State Historical Association in San Antonio, and to bring with her "as many from Houston as possible." In closing, he apologized for pressuring her, explaining "that none of our members in Houston would be more likely to respond favorably to such an appeal." Garrison knew that her sense of duty, whether to Texas, to education, or to the organizations to which she had committed herself, generally overrode her own comfort. As her mother once observed in her journal, "Adele is more kindhearted and generous than most of us."[39]

All her many friends and associates in the numerous organizations she served seemed to expect nothing less of Adele than her usual level of energy and involvement, despite her bereavement and her mother's disability. She continued to fulfill her duties in the various offices she held. She kept up her correspondence. She continued to write articles for newspapers, magazines, and the Texas State Historical Association *Quarterly.* She rented out her house on Capitol Street and moved back into her mother's house on Crawford

Street to assume her nursing duties full time. To her friends and family, she was still Dell, the dynamo. But within her secret self, she suffered and grieved and turned for consolation to her and her late husband's old friend, Mary Saunders of Walnut Grove.

Mary knew Adele as probably no other person did, perhaps because of her poet's sensitivity or because, as an immigrant herself, she had a unique connection with Michael Looscan. "You know the sympathy between us was very strong," she confided to Adele shortly after his death. "When we spoke of beautiful or heroic scenes or deeds, thought met thought almost before it was spoken." Perhaps it was simply because Mary was outside Adele's circle of family and friends and thus did not have the expectations of Adele that others did. Whatever the reason, she became Adele's confidant, comforter, and, after Michael, her muse. "My dear friend," Mary wrote in late November,

> Yes, I know eternity does appear far off and time slow, but in reality the time left you is very short. You have so much to do, so much work for a fitting monument to him who yet lives in you, whose name and influence you, more than all the world, can cover with honor. You have told me that he awoke your patriotism. Unite with your love for your state your love for your dead so that the two are inseparable and every flower you lay on the altar of Texas will blossom on his grave. I cannot think that with death we are separated from our loved. The best part of them is still living, and though invisible, is near, especially when we are doing what they would have us to do. Such love as yours and your husband's may have its roots on earth but its branches reach to heaven, and there shall its richest fruitage be. Take as your motto "For his sake" and you will find life yet a full rich sweet possession.[40]

Looscan home on Capitol Street. Michael Looscan, Adele Looscan, and Annie Hume on the porch.
Courtesy of the San Jacinto Museum of History.

Mary went on to remind Adele about the cause that Major Looscan had championed for three decades: "Pardon me my friend if I am persistent, but you did not answer my last letter; some of those veterans are very poor, all are very old, and if anything is done for them, it must be done speedily. If you have my last letter yet, refer to it and see if you can do what is suggested."[41]

Adele, however, remained dispirited. She went about her work under a gloomy cloud and even considered giving up. She wrote as much to Mary. In early January, a reply came. "Now, in answer to your letter," Mary wrote, "you must not undervalue yourself. Your very letter proves you to be a many sided woman. Nurse, housekeeper, interested in procuring an artist for a magazine, companion to an invalid, minding to business, planning to help a poor poet, etc., etc. You do not bury the talents bestowed on you so lavishly; do not deny nor underestimate them." As further encouragement, she enclosed a letter from an admirer of her poetry. "She quotes from my poem, 'Foreign Born Americans,' inspired by and dedicated to Major Looscan," she pointed out. "I mention this to show you how the good he has done lives after him. It must be a delightful thought to you that you can give additional honor to his name and link it with your noblest work. It is impossible for me to tell you what you have been to me, you two," she went on. "You will notice that my best work has been done since we met."[42]

Michael Looscan's sister, Winnefred, reinforced Mary's admonition. "The Patriotic society you belong to is often mentioned in the Houston Post," she wrote. "I think it would be unwise for you to give it up as it will be a means of occupying part of your time and will give you pleasure in performing a duty that your husband took such great pride in. It is well known that he was always brave and fearless and was never daunted when duty called him to action," she reminded Adele. "So go on in the good work you have undertaken and God will give you strength to accomplish what is grand and laudable."[43]

Although her sadness lingered, Adele took their advice and encouragement to heart. She threw herself into her many projects with renewed determination, if not joy. She joined the Robert E. Lee Chapter of the United Daughters of the Confederacy that had been organized in Houston in December 1897. She continued writing and soliciting others to write for William Scarff's publications, she prepared articles for the Texas State Historical Association *Quarterly,* and she continued her active role in the Ladies' Reading Club, but her greatest efforts were reserved for the Daughters of the Republic of Texas.

Chapter Five

Disillusionment and Change

Adele's writing and her devotion to collecting relics and information about the Texas Revolution and the Republic of Texas were all parts of her effort to raise awareness and generate interest in the history of Texas and the Daughters of the Republic of Texas. In her article for the *Silver Cross*, Adele had recounted the history of the DRT. She noted the accomplishments of the San Jacinto Chapter in obtaining appropriations from the Texas legislature for the purchase of and improvements to the San Jacinto battleground. "But the special object of the society," she explained, "is placing statues of Austin and Houston in Statuary Hall in Washington, and the collection of relics of early Texas for preservation in the State capitol in Austin." She closed by referencing the Spanish-American War, in which the nation was engaged, to give currency to the Texas Revolution. "Let us hope the horrors and hardships of the present war may remind the public of what is due the early Texans for rescuing so fair a land from the hands of a government as despotic, as cruel, as inhuman as that against which we are contending," she wrote.[1]

Adina De Zavala heartily supported these efforts to educate the public about the DRT and its work. She firmly believed that the Daughters should be a statewide organization and not a collection of loosely associated regional chapters. In her view, organizing on a statewide basis was a way to get more support for her own preservation projects. "We claim here that the Daughters of the Republic of Texas is the Landmark Club of Texas and is it not?" she wrote to Adele. "It has done and is doing all it can to preserve our historic places. Were not the Daughters the first in Houston to raise a voice for the protection of historic buildings? Because they ask aid of other societies is no reason they cannot claim this work. Of course, we shall need plenty of money," she noted. "If you refer to the subject again kindly refer to our work," she wrote a few days later. "I am really 'jealous' for the Daughters of the Republic. I am afraid we are all too modest and timid. Many ideas and good deeds originate with us, yet others claim them and get the credit. We, heretofore, have been satisfied if the thing is accomplished. I have come to the conclusion that we should have the name too."[2]

Indeed, for years all the chapters of the DRT had been engaged in efforts to remind the public about the early Texans. Adele firmly believed that the state's schools were key. She embraced Adina De Zavala's proposal to name schools after Texas's revolutionary heroes and to put framed pictures of them in classrooms. As Adina pointed out, "It is a grand idea, for by teaching love of country and patriotism to the children, we are sure the grown people of the future will be well informed and loyal patriots, and we have also arrived at the surest way of reaching their parents."[3]

By 1902, Adina De Zavala had earned herself a place on the executive committee of the DRT. She proposed that the Daughters ask the state to transfer control of the Alamo to the DRT. The group decided to leave the matter with the mayor of San Antonio, with the request that a member of the De Zavala Chapter be placed on the committee to appoint a custodian for the property.[4] Adina felt strongly about preserving the historical accuracy of the Alamo's remains, and being both a San Antonio resident and a Tejana, she viewed that history in a much broader context than did many of the Daughters. Hers was a view that appealed to Adele's sensibilities but that would soon uncover divergent interests within the DRT that had long existed. There the situation stood when Clara Driscoll returned from Europe and joined the De Zavala Chapter of the DRT in 1903. Although none of the women realized it at the time, the arrival of Clara Driscoll in their midst was to mark a fateful turning point in their lives, in the life of the organization, and in the future of the Alamo itself.

As fate would have it, commercial interests in the East had expressed interest in acquiring the Hugo-Schmeltzer property early in 1903, and it seemed likely they would do so. The DRT had not been able to raise enough money to purchase the property, and their option was about to expire. San Antonio sculptor Pompeo Coppini learned of the plans for the Alamo property from a local architect. He hoped to receive a commission for a sculpture to be placed in the foyer of a new hotel in San Antonio, but when he realized the proposed location of the hotel was the Alamo property, he alerted Adina De Zavala, a friend of his wife. From the owners of the Menger Hotel on Alamo Plaza, the two learned that Clara Driscoll was in town. She was the daughter of a wealthy, elite Corpus Christi family whose eligibility for membership in the DRT derived from the service of her grandfather, Daniel O'Driscoll, in the Battle of San Jacinto. Clara was a beautiful woman with red hair and a hot temper to match. Like Adina De Zavala, she possessed a strong will, although at twenty-two she was still young enough to be impulsive. She had not been involved with any of the mission preservation projects, but she had previously expressed dismay at the condition of the Alamo; thus there seemed reason to believe she might be persuaded to help. De Zavala and Coppini decided to enlist her aid by appealing not so much to Driscoll's patriotism as to her ego, explaining "how she could become famous all over the nation by saving that sacred spot."[5]

The pitch seemed to have worked. In mid-March, De Zavala and Driscoll went together to meet with Charles Hugo, who owned the property in question, which lay adjacent to the Alamo chapel where the mission of San Antonio de Valero had once stood. After some negotiation, Clara Driscoll agreed to pay Hugo five hundred dollars to extend the DRT's option on the property for thirty days. The DRT had its work cut out for it, and Adina knew it. She wrote to Adele a few weeks later, "We must be careful of our acts and reputation, and not let lesser matters usurp the places of the greater or more important." Of developments on the Alamo project, she confided, "Things took a turn quite unexpected to me, and I think Miss Driscoll has more than she bargained for. She is a brave girl. Has paid $500 and stands ready to pay the $4,500 out of her pocket. I think she is very brave and we must do all we can to help her. I am afraid she has gone too far to retrace. She must go forward or lose! It is equally perilous to retract and being of brave mould she chooses the forward!"[6]

The pressure was on the Daughters of the Republic to protect both the Alamo and Clara Driscoll's investment, but even as Adina De Zavala and Clara Driscoll bargained for the Alamo, Adele Looscan suffered another great loss. Mary Jane Briscoe, champion of Texas veterans, driving force behind the enshrining of the erstwhile republic in the public memory, family matriarch, and the single greatest influence in Adele's life, died on March 8, 1903. Adele was grief stricken. As before, when plunged into grief, she turned to Mary Saunders, who composed a fitting elegy. The funeral took place at Christ Episcopal Church on the afternoon of March 11. Adele had assumed much of the responsibility for managing family business affairs a half dozen years earlier, after her mother's debilitating fall. Now, with her mother's death, she managed not only her own business affairs but her mother's and those of her mother's former servant, Carrie Phelps, as well as those of her husband's family. And as before, expressions of sympathy were swiftly followed with requests for her attention. By July, she had published a memorial biography of her mother in the *Quarterly of the Texas State Historical Association* and bestowed gifts of the memorial booklet to all the organizations of which Mary Jane had been a part. She promised to secure the rem-

Jessie B. Howe (left) and Adele B. Looscan (right), taken at Walnut Grove Ranch, 1903. *Courtesy of the San Jacinto Museum of History.*

iniscences of Texas pioneer Dilue Rose Harris for the *Quarterly*, and she pledged to help Adina De Zavala save the Alamo.

All chapters of the DRT entered into the effort to protect Clara Driscoll's investment and raise the funds to pay the forty-five hundred dollars Hugo required for extending the option on the Alamo for another year, but none worked harder than the De Zavala Chapter. Even the dreaded "yellow jack" (yellow fever) did not deter them from their fundraising endeavors. "Our Fair went right ahead," Adina informed Adele in late October, noting, "of course, after the quarantine no one could come in but the 'Daughters' Restaurant' did a good business. I worked hard early and late [and] so did Miss Driscoll. She made an expert and beautiful waitress. All the men and women fell in love with her."[7]

Adina made public speeches to solicit support and conceived the idea of selling commemorative spoons to raise money and patriotic sentiment for the Alamo. As the February 1904 deadline approached, the women of the De Zavala Chapter took to the streets, knocking on doors. Adina reported in January, "We have districted the city and the house to house canvass by our ladies begins tomorrow. Two ladies are appointed in each ward. They select their committees and subdivide the district, thus making it accessible in a short time."[8] The chapter held a tea at the Menger Hotel and sold tickets. Schoolchildren gave a benefit at a theatre, The Grand, on a Saturday night. Despite all the energy and effort expended, however, February 10, 1904, arrived to find the Daughters of the Republic of Texas far short of their twenty-thousand-dollar goal. The DRT was about to lose the Texas republic's most precious shrine, and Clara Driscoll was about to lose her investment.

A few days later Adele received a letter from Adina De Zavala with the news that Clara Driscoll had made the twenty-thousand-dollar payment and had guaranteed the payments of all the other notes standing between the DRT and Hugo—a total of fifty thousand dollars in annual payments of ten thousand dollars plus interest at 6 percent per annum—and would hold the Alamo as security until she was paid. "Her father was a lamb—a perfect dear," Adina confided. "He says I ought to have taken the guarantee with me to Houston—but, of course, Clara wasn't sure until he arrived and could make no positive statement. Now, she gives us unlimited time to pay her. We deal with her exclusively. She deals with Hugo but with the understanding that it is for the Daughters of the Republic of Texas. . . . Of course, I believed Miss Driscoll would eventually do it. Now, we must get money to pay the loan instantly—Your bankers will now have to come forward heavily likewise the Galveston people who promised under a guarantee."[9]

Clara Driscoll, Adina De Zavala, and the DRT were now committed more deeply than ever to the Alamo. Fundraising, obviously, would have to continue. The most significant portent of the future in Adina's letter was the postscript, which hinted that all might not be well. "The deed is dreadfully garbled," she wrote, "but our lawyer, McGown, contends that the statement for use as a park doesn't make a particle of difference." Evidently, Adina's misgivings about the language had not been completely allayed, for she continued, "Please ask Mr. Ball. It all originated in a mistaken idea of Hugo's and Miss Driscoll as to my and our wishes in the matter as she really was not a legalized member when we took it up together. I fought against it in the deed but McGown said Hugo did not want to sign any way, he was so disappointed—and as it did not make any difference we had better not delay to get another deed made. Please get several opinions as soon as possible in writing if you can."[10]

In fact, the "park" Adina De Zavala worried over in the deed made quite a lot of difference. Mention of it in the deed hinted at the difference between Clara's and Adina's perspectives on the Alamo. Clara Driscoll had a flair for the dramatic, and she loved an audience. She wrote a musical comedy titled *Mexicana* that she paid to have produced in a New York theatre in 1905. The same year she published a novel, *The Girl of La Gloria.* The following year, she published a collection of short stories, *In the Shadow of the Alamo.* Both books were unabashedly sentimental and romantic, and they revealed their milieu, a context very different from that of Adina De Zavala. In Driscoll's stories, the past was not a complex tapestry woven from all previous occurrences but a single event representing all previous occurrences. Her stories also revealed her attitude toward Mexicans, whom she invariably depicted as flawed, incomplete characters. Thus, her perception of the social and cultural implications of the

Alamo and the events of 1836 was incomplete or dismissive. She saw the Alamo as a place in which to legitimize the new social and economic order.[11] Her vision for the preservation of the shrine focused primarily on the revolutionary battle and considered the church to be the main feature of the site, which could be better emphasized if the convent were removed.

Adina De Zavala, on the other hand, sought to restore the unity of experience and vision that animated her grandfather's generation, to reestablish a link with a past in which heroes were identified as neither Mexican nor American but "the whole people of her beloved Texas land," a social and cultural world now rapidly disappearing in the midst of industrialization and economic development. She envisioned preserving the Alamo as it stood in its mission days and also as a landmark to the heroes of the 1836 battle. She hoped to emphasize its mission background by restoring the main building (convent) to its original arcaded appearance.[12]

This fundamental difference of perspective on what, exactly, the DRT wanted to accomplish with the Alamo soon divided the membership. In 1904, the task at hand was reimbursing Clara Driscoll. Despairing of raising the full amount themselves, leaders of the DRT decided to lobby the Texas legislature to purchase the Alamo. In that effort, they were able to remain united, and so for a year they campaigned to persuade the Texas legislature to purchase the remaining Alamo property, including the enclosed convent. Foreshadowing of divergent visions appeared during that year. In a pamphlet designed to help the DRT raise money in April 1904, Adina De Zavala explained that although the chapel of the mission was the property of the state, the scene of the greater part of the memorable battle had taken place in the part of the Alamo property previously owned by Hugo-Schmeltzer.[13] She repeated this clarification with emphasis in a magazine article a short time later. The chief struggle of 1836 took place in the monastery, and "it was long one of my dreams," she wrote, "to restore the Alamo and make of it a Texas Hall of Fame and a Museum of Historic Art, Relics and Literature."[14] Adele, drawing upon the authority of her position as historian general of the DRT, sought more pointedly to correct the "unfortunate and inexcusable ignorance in regard to the scene of the struggle in the Alamo" in an article published in the *Quarterly of the Texas State Historical Association* in July 1904. The chapel has been "accepted by many who ought to know better as the whole and only theatre of the siege, defense, and holocaust," she chided. "Just because it makes the story of the assault more thrilling to point out the exact spot where this one fell, and that one made a stand, this grand old pile has been made the medium for the perpetration of false accounts, until people who do not read history accept such teaching as true, and point to the tablets that have been hung in the old chapel, to contradict authentic historical statements recorded soon after the revolution."[15]

Clara Driscoll, meanwhile, expressed her conception of the Alamo in a newspaper article as the new year of 1905 dawned. She opined that Texans during the battle defended the outer walls before retreating to the monastery and finally to the chapel.[16] The first volley of the second battle of the Alamo had been fired and was soon returned. After a meeting with DRT leadership, Driscoll told a reporter for the *San Antonio Express*, "While no definite plan has been outlined, the idea of the Daughters is to beautify the place . . . to lend more prominence to the chapel, which, of course, is the main feature in the Alamo mission."[17]

The annual state meeting of the DRT was to be held in La Grange in April 1905, with Clara Driscoll now a member of the executive committee. Adina De Zavala remained cheerfully optimistic that plans for the Alamo could be worked out to their mutual satisfaction when she wrote to Adele in February:

> Of course, the Executive Committee will appoint De Zavala Chapter Custodian or rather to take charge as was agreed years ago when we spoke of getting control of the Church

> and I begged the Association to take it up with us. De Zavala Chapter will retain Miss Driscoll as Chairman and Treasurer of the Alamo Mission Fund—and I believe she is now willing to be "Chairman" since she has seen that the Legislative Heads are chairmen—for in her last communication to the Express she called herself "Chairman" of the "Alamo Mission Fund." I will have a little talk with her as soon as I can—I believe everything will move on now harmoniously.[18]

Doubts, however, were beginning to creep in. A few weeks later, Adina wrote that she was still waiting for the attorney general's ruling on the title to the Alamo property that would allow the De Zavala Chapter to take custody of it. She vowed to see the attorney general in person when she went to Austin in March for the Texas State Historical Association meeting. "These pretended friends make me so angry," she fumed. "I'd much rather have a straight out enemy; then you know what you are doing." She pointed out that many details, such as the official designation of the De Zavala Chapter of the DRT as the custodian of the Alamo, the amount the DRT paid for the property, and the fact that they had ever paid anything, had been scrupulously omitted from the last deed. "It is made entirely personal. The men think we are entirely silly," she wrote, "and without business acumen. The deed does not show the real history of the case, which proves again how little we can depend on even documents of the past for history unless we know the inside facts."[19]

As the date of the annual meeting of the DRT drew closer, other signs of friction among chapters showed up in tangential matters. In March, a misunderstanding arose over an order of commemorative spoons the Daughters were selling to raise money for the Alamo Mission Fund. Adina wrote to Adele in consternation. "Miss Banks is counting on arousing petty jealousy and dividing the DRT into sides," she fretted. "I'm loyal and expect the DRT to be and do not

Photograph taken April 21, 1905, at the annual convention of the Daughters of the Republic of Texas on Monument Hill, La Grange, Texas, the site of the memorial for the Dawson Massacre. Seated on the bench, left to right, are Milvern Harrell, Asa C. Hill, Stephen F. Sparks, Mrs. George Lee Sings, Francis R. Lubbock, and John W. Darlington. *Courtesy of the San Jacinto Museum of History.*

think of taking the spoons out of the Chapter's hands. I have tried to divine her scheme and that is all I can make of it."[20]

The annual meeting of the state membership in La Grange in April 1905 revealed further fissures within the organization. Although support for the Alamo project seemed virtually unanimous, the authors of the De Zavala Chapter's report went out of their way to emphasize that the Alamo Mission Fund originated with the De Zavala Chapter and that, while Clara Driscoll deserved gratitude for her financial support, it was Adina De Zavala who had been the animating force behind it. The day before, Adele had made a motion to make the De Zavala Chapter the agent, and the executive committee had approved. The convention voted in the morning session to accept the executive committee's report appointing the De Zavala Chapter to serve as the DRT's agent in charge of the Alamo for one year. But that same afternoon they voted to "reconsider the action of the convention in accepting the report of the executive committee in full." Leading this revolt were Adele's erstwhile friends, Cornelia Branch Stone and Marie Bennett Urwitz, joined by Emma Burleson. Although she had not yet been admitted to DRT membership, Emma Burleson voted in the convention and moved to delay the matter of custody until after the property title had been transferred to the state.[21]

Adele, meanwhile, attended to family business, grieved for her beloved Governor Lubbock, who had died in Austin, and tried to be of assistance to George Garrison with the Texas State Historical Association. The spring and summer of 1905 proved to be a challenging time for him and for the association as well, for not only did Francis R. Lubbock depart life in late June but the president of the University of Texas, William L. Prather, died suddenly and prematurely of heart failure only one month later. "The suggestion of help from the Daughters is most welcome," Garrison wrote in late April, "and I trust they will be able to extend it. I can guarantee that every dollar they may find it possible to raise to assist in carrying on the historical work we are doing either in the regular university courses or through the Historical Association will be well spent."[22] Nor was Adele any less attentive to the mail she routinely received from aspiring historians such as I. D. Affleck, with whom she had been corresponding every few weeks all summer regarding an article he was writing on the history of Texas flags. He had condensed his article to some seventy pages and hoped that, being "more familiar than anyone else in Texas" with the subject, she would peruse and critique it for him, which she did within a fortnight.[23]

In late August, the title to the Alamo property was finally transferred to the state, and Clara Driscoll, amid preparations to travel out of state, contacted Mary (Mrs. Anson) Jones requesting temporary control of the Alamo until the executive committee of the DRT could meet again. She received an immediate reply from the executive committee granting her request. She promptly appointed Florence Eager custodian, to be installed by Mrs. H. P. Drought as her personal representative, though neither was an official member of the DRT. With that accomplished, Clara Driscoll departed for New York on September 2.[24]

Certainly the maneuver was a blow to the De Zavala Chapter. Not to be outdone, however, Adina De Zavala acted quickly to persuade the mayor of San Antonio to turn over to her the keys of the chapel less than a week after Driscoll's departure. As the *San Antonio Express* reported, the state had transferred custodianship of the Alamo property to the DRT on October 4, and the De Zavala Chapter women took charge of the chapel. The friends of Clara Driscoll "attempted to gain possession on her behalf, and finding opposition, they sought to gain their ends by strategy," namely to change the lock, but "Miss Dezavala soon arrived upon the scene, relieved the locksmith of his lock and tools and put him ignominiously to flight."[25]

The gauntlet had been thrown down. On November 3, the DRT filed a petition for a restraining order, naming Adina De Zavala defendant, stating that she took illegal possession of the church, and expressing fear that she might dismantle the church's relics. The petition sought to restrain De Zavala from further retention of the property or interfering with the control of it.[26] She filed an answer denying all the allegations, and, on November 8, the De Zavala chapter intervened, asserting that three persons had claimed possession of the Alamo on Driscoll's behalf and asking the court to determine who was entitled to take possession of the property, thus relieving the chapter of responsibility for delivering the property to someone not lawfully entitled to possession.[27]

Adele, who had been traveling in Mexico during September and had retreated to Walnut Grove Ranch to wait out the heat, got her first inkling that real trouble was brewing in a letter from Mary De Zavala in mid-October. "I do not like the way the Daughters are acting about the Alamo," she wrote.

> Adina has had definite plans for the Alamo for many years and has been building to a purpose. I do not mind complimenting Clara Driscoll any way in the world they want it, but it does not look much like gratitude to me to hurt someone else's feelings and overthrow the weary work of years to gratify a whim of hers. Mrs. Urwitz wrote Adina that Clara D. asked to be allowed to appoint a custodian in return for what she had done. People do not need to be given everything they ask for. She also wrote Adina to "be satisfied with the laurels she had won" or something to that effect. Adina has not been working for "laurels." I did not like her letter at all.[28]

Less than a week later a letter arrived from Adina. "I have received a note from Mrs. Stone calling a meeting of Executive Committee for Mrs. Urwitz on Thursday Oct. 26th," she informed

Adele. "This is unusual; heretofore, when I am teaching they have always called it on Saturday to save me unnecessary expense. I shall go down of course, leaving here Wednesday morning on the 'Sunset' unless stopped by a telegram or otherwise."[29]

By the time another week had passed, Adina was writing a letter almost every day, and if Adele had hoped to remain above the developing fray, she was to be disappointed. Her loyalty, to Adina and to Texas, would not allow her to demur. By November 10, Adina was appealing to her for help. "I want you to find out for me the following," she began with little preamble. "Did Mrs. Milby ever affix the seal of the society to any statement or resolution intended for use in this suit? If so, find out exactly what the resolution or paper states. There must surely be a duplicate. Did she refuse to affix the seal to a resolution presented to her by Mrs. Stone? (Do your best on this.) Be as diplomatic as you can, but find out positively for me and get copies of any papers to which the society affixed its seal."[30]

The following day the suit was dismissed, but the matter clearly was not settled. The *San Antonio Express* captured the implications:

> [Clara Driscoll] was feted and made much of in all quarters of the United States. She quite eclipsed Miss Dezavala and other members of the Daughters . . . and in her sudden rise their long efforts seemed forgotten. They had worked when obstacles were many and when recognition of their plans was slow. They felt they had made Miss Driscoll's somewhat meteoric success possible.
>
> Unquestionably there was some resentment of Miss Driscoll's success, but the Daughters put it behind them for the glory of the cause. Then came the resolution of the executive committee to make Miss Driscoll custodian of the building for one year, and on top of that, the statement is made, Miss Driscoll, instead of sacrificing her New York

> work and pleasures for the honor, attempted to turn it over to her friend, Miss Eagers [sic]. This was too much—the last straw.[31]

Adina confirmed the accuracy of the *Express*'s analysis in her letter to Adele. "I fear we did wrong to settle out of court," she fretted. "My reason was to save the Daughters any more publicity . . . for I did not and did not wish other people to believe that the opinion and acts of three or four jealous women were the opinions and acts of the General Association. I am willing to be more than generous! But is it right to myself or any Chapter? I do not know!" What Adina did know was that those women were going to work and pull strings to defeat the De Zavala Chapter in the General Convention. "They will have everything fixed to perpetuate themselves in the Committee," she wrote, and so she and Adele must be better prepared than they had been at the 1905 convention. "Be talking up Mrs. Willrich of La Grange to Mrs. McKeever and Mrs. Milby under the head of spreading it out—new chapters and new ideas—and we must try and find others for the other two vacancies," she urged Adele.[32]

Adina De Zavala was not the only one seeking Adele's assistance that November. A letter from Julia Ideson at the Houston Public Library begged her attention. "I always turn to you where 'Texas publications' are concerned," she wrote. The Library of Congress was looking for two Texas serials, and she thought she would ask Adele if she knew whether the publications were available. The serials she wanted were the reports of the first and second annual meetings of the Daughters of the Republic of Texas. Ideson wanted a complete file of these for the library, as well as proceedings of the Texas Veterans Association. She knew nowhere else to turn.[33]

Adele dutifully set about trying to satisfy both requests and, perhaps, in the process defuse the growing tension within the DRT. To that end, in December she wrote to Cornelia Branch Stone, but the reply she received was not all she might have hoped for. "In reply to the subject of your letter," Cornelia Stone responded, "I will say that my dominant feeling has been that the DRT should recognize the great service done us in carrying out the purpose of our organization, and to our state, by Miss Driscoll and that feeling was shared by others." She felt Adina De Zavala did not agree in this view of the case, "which," she continued with a tinge of smugness, "has been unfortunate for her." With the controversy now created, she thought it difficult to see the outcome. "I would be very sorry to forfeit your good will and confidence," she wrote, "a feeling, that dates back to the days of Maj. Looscan's presence in your home—and in which I always felt that he shared." She expressed regret that they were on opposing sides. "It is all regrettable," she conceded, "but under the circumstances, seems unavoidable."[34] It was not an encouraging note on which to end the year.

The new year, 1906, brought a flood of letters to be answered, including a request from Dora Fowler Arthur for an outline of the work Adele had done with the history committee of the Texas State Historical Association. Adele's dedication to the cause of Texas history was never far from her consciousness no matter what other demands claimed her attention. When, in her usual perusings of the Houston and San Antonio newspapers one Sunday morning in early February, she encountered an error-filled article in the *San Antonio Express* based on an interview with Thomas Rabb, she was quick to send a correction. "As San Antonio is one of the oldest towns in Texas, if not the oldest," she wrote the article's author, Charles Barnes, "people who are not students of history are liable to adopt newspaper articles from that city as authentic." Adele, though characteristically kind and even self-effacing, minced no words when it came to her history. "I have no objection to the participators in Indian fights making them as desperate and bloody as the wildest imagination can conceive, but do object to the members of our first Convention being changed to suit the taste of belated aspirants for political honors. I have read many of your sketches of historical characters with pleasure, but warn you that it is not safe to accept the statement of every Indian fighter, except as to his own deeds of prowess."[35]

Not all her correspondence concerned historical pursuits. Michael Looscan's niece, Mary, wrote to thank Adele for her Christmas gift and to seek her assistance in checking on her other aunt, Winnefred Looscan McAran, about whom she was concerned. She expressed sympathy for the persistence of the pain Adele suffered in her hip and leg that necessitated her use of a cane. When that problem had first appeared, Adele hoped that treatment would clear it up, but after several years it seemed likely that she would be coping with chronic pain. It kept her from being as mobile as she would have liked, what with so much to do in preparation for the DRT annual convention, and, of course, chasing down recalcitrant relatives. She was compelled to seek help from family members living in the San Antonio area. Her cousin, Gwynn Briscoe, obligingly visited the Alamo chapel in early March and reported to Adele on the contents, enumerating pictures, books, historical sketches, and, of particular note, a picture of Clara Driscoll hanging on the wall.[36]

As the date of the DRT state convention drew near, the De Zavala Chapter marshaled forces to make certain that the chapter was not underrepresented, as it had been in 1905. Others in the organization sought to strengthen their current position with respect to custodianship of the Alamo as well. Nettie Houston Bringhurst sought to enlist Adele in this effort. "Several people have tried to get me to take some action in regard to raising a fund from the different Chapters for paying the custodian of the Alamo," she wrote, "and I wish you who are so capable would help solve this problem."[37]

When the De Zavala Chapter met in April, a majority of the chapter members thwarted the Driscoll supporters, who then retaliated by seceding from the chapter and forming a new chapter, the Alamo Mission Chapter, which was swiftly adopted by the executive committee of the state organization. Some disgusted members of the De Zavala Chapter simply withdrew altogether. With the formation of the new chapter, the division of the DRT into distinct factions became obvious, as did the attempt to undermine the De Zavala Chapter in San Antonio, particularly its claim to custody of the Alamo. Driscoll supporters controlled the executive committee of the DRT. Any hope the De Zavala Chapter had of retaining the custodianship of the Alamo lay in its ability to gain the support of the general association, which met in Goliad, Texas, April 20–21, 1906.

The results were mixed. The first clash arose when Adina De Zavala moved to reject portions of the executive committee report relating to the Alamo, specifically the purchase of a portrait of David Crockett to hang in the Alamo chapel and the election of three members of the executive committee by the executive committee itself. She opposed the purchase of the Crockett portrait, arguing that the thousand dollars it cost should be spent on restoration of the building. Clara Driscoll, who arrived late to her first state meeting, threw a little fuel on the fire by announcing that if the association failed to ratify the executive committee's purchase of the portrait, she would buy it herself and present it to the Alamo. Despite this grand gesture, the De Zavala Chapter won the vote on the motion to amend the executive committee's report.[38]

The second round belonged to the De Zavala forces as well. A motion was made to give custody of the Alamo to the De Zavala Chapter under the jurisdiction of the general association on November 13, 1906. An amendment substituting the name of Clara Driscoll as custodian was defeated. Pandemonium ensued. The recording of the minutes was rudely interrupted. When the dust finally settled, the minutes resumed with Adina De Zavala's motion that Clara Driscoll be given custodianship of the Alamo until November 13, 1906. Clara Driscoll, for her part, announced that she was being "thrust" out of the custodianship of the Alamo. She metaphorically stormed out by literally resigning custodianship of the Alamo and membership in the organization. Her resignation was not accepted, but the motion to give the De Zavala Chapter custodianship of the Alamo was, with six of nine executive committee members and the first vice president, Rebecca Fisher, opposed.[39]

Thinking ahead, members of the De Zavala Chapter then sought to strengthen their position for the future by proposing half a dozen amendments to the DRT constitution. The first switched the election of executive committee members from the committee itself to the general association in annual convention, thus dissolving the cliquishness of the executive committee. The second required the resignation of any executive committee member who missed two consecutive meetings. It was not so subtly aimed directly at Clara Driscoll, who had seldom attended executive meetings since her election to the committee in 1904. One other proposal was critical. It asserted that where monuments or buildings of historic character exist in the same locality with a chapter, that chapter should have charge of such monuments or buildings. Each proposal was voted on separately. The first passed unanimously, and the proposal concerning monuments and historic buildings passed by a healthy majority. It seemed that the De Zavala Chapter would institutionalize most of its agenda in the constitution.[40]

One final item remained: the election of officers. Cornelia Stone, second vice president, presiding, reminded the assembly that Mary (Mrs. Anson) Jones (who had thrown her support to the Driscoll faction) had been elected president for life but was reelected each year as a courtesy. Mary Jones, however, advanced in age, had been too feeble to attend annual meetings for a long time. The de facto head of the organization, entitled to preside over annual meetings, was the first vice president, Rebecca Fisher, who, for reasons of her own, declined to do so. Cornelia Branch Stone, the second vice president, chaired in her stead. Adina De Zavala was nominated for first vice president, but she declined, possibly as a conciliatory gesture, and

Rebecca Fisher was reelected. It was a strategic error of major proportions.

Adele, in her usual quiet way, had supported the De Zavala Chapter throughout the meeting. She now proposed the election of three executive committee members, since the recent election of three members by the committee had been rendered invalid by the amended constitution. Rebecca Fisher, however, a devotee of Clara Driscoll, ruled that the three elected by the executive committee were legally elected for six years. Technically, she was incorrect, but Cornelia Stone ruled that the amendments to the constitution would not take effect until after the official minutes were published. Despite Adele's repeated demand that three executive committee offices be filled during the meeting, Stone ruled that the three original members had been elected legally.[41]

The triumph enjoyed by the De Zavala Chapter lasted barely a week. "The enemy is hard at work," Adina wrote Adele on April 27. "They threaten us with the 'Governor and the next Legislature'—they will leave no stone unturned to take it away from the DRT because we have the Alamo, but I am not afraid." Adina seemed confident that her network of spies in San Antonio would keep her up to date on the maneuvers of the Alamo Mission Chapter, but, she noted, "All the papers here were silent as to the convention except what was on Sunday's Express and the Gazette by accident and what the Alamo Mission chapter sent in. The fun part of it is," she chortled, "that nearly all the reporters and all the men in the business offices of the papers are ardent friends of ours and they are so disgusted! But," she admitted, "of course bread and butter has to be considered and they are powerless. We can put in anything; that is, I am sure I could do it—but if our silence is to be misconstrued—if the silence of our home papers is to be used against us—something ought to be done—but what? Please get advice of Mr. [J. W.] Campbell and let me know—he is farther removed and can look on calmly."[42]

Adele read Adina's long, manic letter but did not respond immediately. She was not feeling well, and her brother, Parmenas, was ill as well. A week later she was alerted to the executive committee's actions in another frantic letter from Adina. "I do hope you are not ill," she wrote, "but I am afraid you are! I am keeping up but the condition of affairs is unbelievable! And unbearable! Absolutely traitorous actions! Those women betray the society and sacrifice it to whims. They are writing to all the Chapters and trying to turn them against us, they are 'working' the old Veterans, too." According to Adina, Clara Driscoll had broadcast articles over the state that were false. "I know it to be a fact that money is being spent like water," she told Adele. "I was told that the articles in the Gazette and Express were paid for at a cost of several hundred dollars. The latest," Adina wrote, "is that three men are going to all the merchants and businessmen in Commerce Street and San Antonio and telling how she was insulted and asking them to join in demanding her re-instatement as Custodian. Miss Eager is sorry she offered her services free and is trying to get pay. Urwitz, McKeever, Dibrell and Drought et al., think they can turn down the Constitution of the D.R.T. and still rule."[43]

At Adina's panicked urging, Adele wrote to J. W. Campbell, her business and legal adviser, a few days later, enclosing for his inspection the two letters and clipping from the *San Antonio Express* that Adina had sent her. She called his attention especially to a letter from Judge Clarence Martin, who had participated in the campaign for the state's purchase of the Alamo. "I suppose this is the point Mrs. McKeever tried to make about the amendment being contrary to the State Constitution," she wrote. "She alluded only to Section I of Article Y but Judge Martin evidently includes all. If his opinion is correct, then all the amendments ever made to the Constitution are illegal. A meeting of the Executive Committee has been called by Miss [sic] Stone as Secretary of the Committee for May 17th. Miss Adina has been notified to attend."[44]

The executive committee, without Adina De Zavala, met in Houston on May 17, less than a month after the general association meeting, and nullified everything the Driscoll group had found objectionable. The committee went further, by proclaiming that all the amendments to the DRT constitution were "illegal," and it divested the De Zavala Chapter of custodianship of the Alamo by claiming the actions of the state convention conflicted with the act of the Texas legislature that gave care and custody of the Alamo to the general association of the DRT "with no power to transfer same to any local Chapter." The executive committee then proceeded to transfer custodianship of the Alamo to Florence Eager, who would earn a salary of forty-five dollars per month in that role. Apparently, thinking to avoid being found out too quickly, the executive committee departed from the usual practice of printing the annual report promptly following the state convention and did not distribute it until shortly before the April 1907 meeting in Austin a year later.[45] Confusion and misinformation among members of the association resulted.

In June, Katie Daffan, from the La Bahia Chapter, wrote to Adele seeking some understanding of what was going on. "I am so anxious to learn something in regard to the Ex-committees actions to know if they really can declare the Goliad Convention 'null and void,'" she wrote. "I notice there has been no change made in the officers that were elected here." Her letter expressed the dismay that was rapidly spreading among the chapters as the members realized that something was very wrong. "My interest in the welfare of the organization for right increases, but if those few women are to run the Society their way, I feel discouraged. Do you know whether the proceedings of the Convention are to be published or not? Could it not be sent direct to the Editors?" She thanked Adele for the manuscript she had sent her. "I have had different ones read it, and we understand why it was not published—that the other side wished we Goliad people to appear in the wrong and discourteous to Miss Driscoll. Do you think if we were to write to Mrs. Stone and ask some questions it would benefit us any or do us harm, which?"[46]

The infighting continued through the summer but without Clara Driscoll, who spent the season in New York, where she married Henry Hulme (Hal) Sevier, former Texas legislator, newspaper journalist, and diplomat, on July 31, 1906. Another new dimension was added in June when T. L. Galloway of Saint Louis secured an option to purchase property behind the Alamo, where he planned to build a "winter theater and auditorium." In August, Adina received a letter from a Charles Reeves of Saint Louis informing her that "hotel interests" had purchased the north half of the property and wanted to put a hotel on it, with assurances that the Hugo-Schmeltzer warehouse would be razed and replaced with a park. It was his understanding, he told Adina, that either the State of Texas or the DRT had agreed to this plan. His clients were ready to go ahead with the plans and "materially assist" the DRT in carrying out the work. Adina responded, explaining that the convent site occupied by Hugo-Schmeltzer was part of the Alamo and that it had always been the intention of the Daughters to make this sacred spot a hall of fame, a place that would be the most attractive in America while retaining the blood-stained walls where the Alamo heroes actually fell. Reeves's answer did not sit well with Adina. His associates were not interested in contributing to a hall of fame, and he threatened that if the Hugo-Schmeltzer building were not torn down, they would sell the property and invest elsewhere.[47]

Adina reported the goings-on in detail to Adele in a long, chatty letter dripping with genteel venom. "What effect will 'dear Clara's' marriage have on the situation think you?" she wrote. "Some think he told her he wouldn't help her anymore if she didn't have him. He is handsome and bright and the only one of her suitors that could have been thought of even for a moment. They certainly make a handsome couple and I am sure he is deeply in love. I certainly congratulate him. He is many years her junior they say—but what matters that?—she has been so well taken care of and will be that she will always be young and beautiful."[48]

Meanwhile, the DRT's executive committee members had stayed busy with plans of their own and had appointed Nettie Houston Bringhurst to be Adele's successor as historian general of the DRT. "I suppose you saw about Mrs. Bringhurst in Sunday's Express," Adina wrote to Adele. "You still take the Express do you not? The poem to Cornelia Stone—pretty 'cute' I think—nicely brought in—but dear me—she does not think it—how can she write poetry about her! I suppose it is the honors thrust upon her of Historian—and the important Committee of placing the placards in Alamo. You see how artfully worded the article—that she succeeded you."[49]

Only a few days later, a letter arrived for Adele from Nettie Bringhurst herself. She was obviously quite sensitive to the fact that she had betrayed an erstwhile friend, but the temptation had been too great for her to overcome, and so she sought absolution. "Before receiving your previous letter I told Miss De Z– what you had written and she expressed herself as eager to put you right in regard to my attitude," she wrote defensively. "I think she has made many mistakes and done many things to drive away her friends and I shall tell her so erelong, but I do not intend to take sides against her, nor speak ill of her, although Mrs. Sevier and I are very good friends. By the way I received the belated wedding cards from N. Y. today. With best wishes for your brother and sister, and love from us all to yourself."[50] If her letter had been calculated to smooth ruffled feathers, it was not particularly effective. Resentment was beginning to build despite Adele's best efforts to reject such uncharitable feelings. She was perhaps more vulnerable than usual anyway, having felt poorly for most of the summer and, on top of that, having tended to Parmenas as his health declined. Adina had written that she believed the trio of McKeever, Urwitz, and Stone was behind the movement, if such there was, to demand that the state take custody of the Alamo from the DRT. "If they find there will be no chance in next Convention to rule—they will be willing to ruin their society," she warned.[51] There simply was no good news.

As summer turned into fall, the news did not get any better. John McAran had died in Philadelphia, leaving Michael Looscan's sister, Winnefred, alone as well as debilitated. Arrangements would have to be made for her care. Parmenas was growing weaker. Adele's hip had been tormenting her, too, but she still somehow found the will and the energy to attend to the needs of the others. Somehow, amid all the other demands on her time, she managed to submit an article for the Texas State Historical Association *Quarterly*.[52] Every day brought, along with gratitude, new requests for her attention. Her cousin Kate wrote asking financial help for her brother Hal, who was struggling with alcoholism. "I know Hal can make a success of his work if he will keep sober," she told Adele. "I will leave the outcome to God. . . . Thanks to you, dear Della, I am enabled to hold out my hand to him in this crisis." Only a week later, Adele received another letter from Kate. She feared her brother's wife, Fannie, intended to ask Adele for more money. "I can't help being discouraged and distressed and all the savor is gone out of my life because of it. My heart aches so for Fannie and her children and also for my poor weak brother," she confided.[53]

Adina De Zavala, too, had been sick most of the summer. Having been out of touch for several weeks, Adina wrote to Adele the second week of September. "I hope you are not ill, and that Mr. Parmenas is about well again, likewise, all the family," she wrote, unaware that the opposite was true. She reported hearing from La Grange that Hal Sevier intended putting in a bill asking the legislature to reimburse Clara Driscoll for all she had paid into the Alamo project. "I knew something was brewing," Adina noted, "as Clarence Martin, just before the gavel fell at the Democratic Convention, entered a resolution thanking Mrs. Hal Sevier nee Clara Driscoll for her generous donations, unremitting work and labor in saving the Alamo." She had seen it in a newspaper clipping. "It was extravagant and not once mentioned the Daughters of the Republic of Texas," Adina fumed. "The DRT were not in it! I wonder if she knew Judge Martin better than we did and was right in her estimate and assertions about him!"[54]

One month later, Adele's brother Parmenas died. Once again, Adele had to bury a member of her family and assume the burden of the responsibilities he had carried and to do so with little help. Her brother Andrew, in San Antonio, acknowledged as much, even as he assuaged his own guilt. He apologized for leaving her to manage "Bub's" estate but thought he would only be in her way since she had so ably managed her own affairs for so long already.[55] Adina De Zavala was among the first to offer condolences. "My dear Friend," she wrote, "Carrie just telephoned this evening to my mother the sad news of Mr. Parmenas' death and burial. How I grieve with you! . . . You know, I had no intimation of the nature of the disease until your last letter and it is such a shock! Was it sudden! Give my love to Mrs. Howe and the other members of the family and tell them that my mother sends heartfelt condolences. We all mourn with you, dear friend, in your new sorrow."[56]

Amid the sorrow, the condolences, and the settling of her brother's estate, Adele did not neglect the matter of the Alamo. Two weeks after laying Parmenas to rest she wrote to Adina, thanking her for her sympathy and briefly touching on her plans. She would remain in the house all winter, at least, and she would pass many lonely hours. "I suppose I shall have to get some crochet or knitting for one cannot read or write all of the time," she mused. But, then, she shook off her melancholy tone and abruptly switched to a businesslike one. "Please receive my thanks for your efforts in behalf of securing accurate information regarding the purchase of the Alamo Church. I have had access to the Journals of the 18th Legislature, and a very kind letter from Wm. R. Kleburg, to whom I wrote for information." She believed the facts about the Alamo could be made not only readable but interesting and was anxious to complete the whole article she had been working on and publish that winter. However, she could provide no new information about the DRT. "There seems to be no prospect for the publication of the Annual Report of D.R.T," she reported. She supposed the chapters would have to write to Maggie (Mrs. Charles H.) Milby, the secretary, and inquire as to the cause of the unusual delay. "I have not been well and am not now," she confessed. "Hope to recover soon." With that she closed her lengthy letter.[57]

A little more than a week later came Adina's reply. "I disliked to write without giving you the promised information," she began, hence the delay. She did, however, have other news to report. Marie Urwitz and her sister were in San Antonio. Adina surmised that their appearance had something to do with the realization that the day upon which the convention had ordered the De Zavala Chapter to take custody of the Alamo had almost arrived. "And she may be here on mischief of her own brew," Adina warned. She had found out about the woman's visit accidentally when she went to the Alamo to look for a friend who had gone over to the property. "I was amazed to see one of our Chapter [letter]heads with my design of the flags and church, on which was printed 'Clara Driscoll, Pres. and Treas., Alamo Fund Organization,' in the case of relics." Adina explained that she had called Florence Eager's attention to it and asked her to trim the chapter logo or fold it under. "She said she would when she got time," Adina reported, but "she did not get time so I turned it under for her." The Alamo chapel was apparently teeming with busy supporters of Clara Driscoll Sevier. According to Adina, "Mrs. Urwitz was standing under the Crockett picture catching all the men and doing all the talking she could." Mrs. McKeever et al. were working with the hotel property developers to get the Daughters removed as custodians and have custodianship placed in the hands of a city commission. Adina reported that Mrs. T. D. Cobbs, of Houston, was a strong advocate of the movement just as her husband, a Houston lawyer, had been against the De Zavala position. Mrs. Cobbs, Mrs. B. Fort Smith, and Mrs. O. T. Holt were getting promises from various officials to take the Alamo out of the Daughters' hands. "Not that they love Mrs. McKeever so, or think the other side right," Adina complained, "not at all—each has her own motive—they were on our side, in the fight, so they say, but 'women can't run anything' and they 'want it put in men's hands.'" The Sunday newspapers contained a direct reply to this argument—citing Mrs. Hetty Green, Mrs. Russell Sage, and Mrs. Walker—under the caption, "Women the Great Financiers." In addition, Adina pointed out, "The Mother Superiors of the institutions here are noted managers managing houses in many states. I told Mrs. B. Fort Smith and Cobbs that they ought to be ashamed to malign their sex."[58]

Adina observed that the list of senators and representatives for the upcoming legislative session had been published recently and wondered if she and Adele had better write to the clubwomen of each district and ask them to see their representatives and urge them to stand by the Daughters of the Republic. "I went to see Mr. Houston about it, but did not get him," she advised. "Of course, we have to be careful—do not let them know that we know what they are doing. There is likely to be another split on that. It will certainly hurt the Pres. of the Daughters of the Confederacy and any woman aspirant for power and honors to say to the Legislature that women are incapable of managing anything. I hardly think Mrs. Dibrell's hate will lead her that far though it was her threat if you remember. She was not then Pres. of the Daughters of the Confederacy. Mrs. McKeever threatened first," Adina reminded Adele, "and a good while before the Executive Board meeting in April."[59]

As pressing as the situation with the Alamo was, Adele simply could not give it all her attention as the year drew to a close. December was always a busy time, and that year was no different, both despite family losses and because of them. Adele found herself weary and stressed as the holidays arrived. Not one to confide often in others or to seek sympathy, Adele was nevertheless comforted to receive a letter from her friend, Nellie Steadman Cox, a fellow member of the Texas Woman's Press Association and Texas State Historical Association.

"My dear Miss Dellie," she began, "If I could sit in your 'turn about chair' and talk awhile, what happiness it would give me! I could almost give you a little touch of 'jim jams' with my chattering and laughter, and we could discuss various matters including the DRT with as much real venosity as the President did the colored brother at Brownsville!" she wrote.[60]

"It's a shame that modern women have such mean, niggardly tendencies to run over and crush the 'underdog' in the fight. We used to talk about this condition," she reminisced, "and I remember you always took the side of the 'poor dog.' Your letter gave me the first inkling of the disgraceful affair," she continued, directly addressing the situation with the DRT and assuring Adele of her support. "If Mrs. Urwitz or any other of the 400 were to attempt to circumscribe my action, the result would resemble 'Maude He Haw.' I appreciate the position of Miss De Zavalla, and assure you that I am enlisted with you both on the side of right. The whole affair appears to be a case of persecution which can never amount to anything but envy." Her cheery closing words warmed Adele's heavy heart: "If I can step in, write, make speeches, or be of any use to either of you let me know and I will take the next train! In the meantime dearie, 'cuddle doon!'"[61]

Unfortunately, Adele had no time to "cuddle doon." Family and business matters pressed upon her. Among the most pressing was the settlement of Parmenas's estate and the management of family properties that he had previously handled for all of them. Brits had overseen the family property in south Texas, but he did not share Adele's intensity. His letters invariably began with an apology for not responding to her "businesslike" correspondence. He would write enthusiastically about his latest presentation to the Confederate veterans and catch her up on the activities of various members of the family (both Briscoe and Harris), knowing her interest in family history. Only when other subjects had been exhausted would he get around to whatever business she had asked about, but his opinions, such as his recommendation in January not to sell off timber on Greens Bayou without a guarantee of sale and removal of the whole, were valuable.[62]

Family was not the only claim on her time that January. Adele, as usual, took time for friends as well. Her young friend and fellow clubwoman, Katie Daffan, lost her father at the end of the month. Adele understood well that sense of loss, and Lawrence Daffan, a railroad man, Confederate veteran, and a charter member of the Houston Elks Lodge, had been a living tie both to her brother Parmenas and to Michael Looscan. Adele had been quick to reach out. "My dear Mrs. Looscan," the younger woman replied, "I appreciate deeply your thought of me in this hour of severest affliction and trial; your sweet letter helped and strengthened me as your presence has often helped me, and in this sorrow and sadness I feel near to you and that I have your genuine sympathy." Her friend continued, "Your nature is strong and true and the sorrows and heart-aches which have visited you, have not left the cruel scars that are left upon the heart and lives of those less noble and unselfish, but you go on with courage and Faith, your life more sweet instead of embittered by heart-ache and separations."[63]

Meanwhile, the Alamo controversy only worsened in 1907, with plans for the destruction versus preservation of the Hugo-Schmeltzer property deepening the divide within the DRT into two genuinely hostile camps. "You can see how these forces are uniting with any force or plot against us," Adina wrote to Adele early in January. "They feel that if we are out, there may be a chance for them," she surmised, "but with us in charge there is absolutely no chance for any graft or pull of favoritism. They are certain of that."[64]

Word was abroad that the business and professional people of San Antonio favored the notion of razing the Hugo-Schmeltzer building and creating a park. Some even went so far as to advocate tearing down all the buildings, creating a park, and erecting a monument for the sake of improving the looks of Alamo Plaza. "A good many old citizens had the 'Alamo Monument' craze—which does not mean as it meant to us—the Alamo building restored—but a tall shaft," Adina wrote Adele in January.[65] A similar story appeared a few weeks later in the *Houston Post.* Reportedly, a group of San Antonio businessmen was preparing to petition the state legislature for the demolition of the Alamo walls.

In response, Adina De Zavala called an urgent meeting of her adherents and took to writing articles in the press to explain her version of the history of the Alamo and differences within the DRT. She wrote lengthy updates to Adele nearly every day. All the publicity dampened the enthusiasm of the Saint Louis group of hotel developers. It seemed that any development of the Alamo Plaza would have to be undertaken locally. A committee was formed in San Antonio to oversee the work, but it soon became apparent that there were various conceptions of what the project would entail.

The constant agitation took its toll on Adina. Adele, with typical pragmatism, tried to advise and calm her, with only temporary success. "I realize now, since you have shown me the other side that I was wrong in treating the charges so lightly," Adina wrote in mid-January, "but I felt so indignant and felt sure that they knew it was not true when they (Mrs. McKeever, Urwitz, Eager, Stone etc.) were plotting over the matter. I do not think they believed what they tried to prove at Goliad—it was just maliciousness and the thought that [they] could worry me and make me uncomfortable—It did neither—but I can well see now that when these tales pass from their authors or malicious abettors to innocent ears—the latter may believe and it may work me a great injury."[66] Adina took the entire conflict very personally, and thus the rejection of her chapter's vision for the preservation of the Alamo was not only a painful disappointment but a personal slight.

Adele, because of her own dedication to Texas history and because of her loyalty to Adina, was supportive and sympathetic, but she never had the luxury of becoming self-absorbed or of focusing solely on the Alamo fight. The first week in March she went to Austin with a crowded schedule that included the Texas State Historical Association meeting and meetings of the UDC and Texas Woman's Press Association, as well as the DRT. On Wednesday, she attended the meeting of the William B. Travis Chapter of the DRT. The chapter president, Rebecca Fisher, informed her in advance in no uncertain terms, Adele recounted to Jessie the next day, that she would not allow the Alamo or De Zavala to be mentioned to her; it made her so nervous. So, of course, although Adina was in Austin, she was not invited to the DRT meeting. It seemed that after the last meeting in Goliad, Emma Burleson had spread gossip and some "exaggerated talk," prejudiced against Adina, and there were only two present at the Austin meeting who ventured to take Adina's part. One of them came to Adele after the meeting, walked with her, and asked to hear the other side, "which I told her," Adele reported to Jessie. The snub by the Travis chapter was blatant, but Adele could really do no more about it. She had promised to visit Mrs. Lou Lubbock and to accompany another friend on a trip to the country to visit acquaintances. While Adele passed time with Adina at the UDC meeting room in Austin, however, the two overheard someone say that Cornelia Stone was in town to attend a meeting of the executive board of the "Press Association." "I am sure she has other business on hand and will try to use every influence to take the Alamo out of the hands of DRT," Adele told Jessie. "Well, if this is to be, I am at least glad they have not disgraced themselves beforehand by conceding to the scheme of the Hotel Company."[67]

In San Antonio, the effort to clearly define a plan for the Alamo made little headway, in part because the meaning of "original walls" remained murky. Marie Urwitz finally attempted to publicly articulate the DRT executive committee's "official" concept in mid-April: "The preservation of the old walls, even the foundation of the Presidio, is the keynote to all efforts of the society today—not the destruction of any part. But the idea of remodeling on those foundations a monastery is entirely impracticable and chimerical. Those walls are gone and their stones forgotten . . . a new monastery, its stones set with this same rare mortar, could not hold the sacredness which will attach to the ruined walls."[68] Her effort to clarify was not entirely successful.

The sniping in the press between the two opposing factions continued in the run-up to the annual meeting of the DRT. Adina wrote to Adele from San Antonio that she no longer knew her friends from her enemies. Accusations that dated back at least two years involving the alleged mishandling of DRT funds related to the sale of commemorative spoons were revived and circulated in the newspapers, primarily, it seemed, for the purpose of casting aspersions on Adina and on her supporters by association. Adina held her fire on the advice of her attorney, A. J. Houston, who thought the "villainous charges" would only help her cause, but she wrote to Adele, "Will you write down every accusation of any kind, that you or Mrs. Howe or any lady, who heard (or man either), can make affidavit to and we will frighten these people out of their little bootees. A married woman is just as liable in this case as a widow or single one."[69]

A few days later, the annual convention opened in the state senate chamber in Austin. Newspaper reporters attempting to explain the proceedings to their readers seemed not unlike spectators at a tennis match. The De Zavala group opposed tearing down the walls of the Hugo-Schmeltzer building and argued that making the Alamo into a park for the purpose of erecting a hotel nearby would invite commercialism "to desecrate the historic spot to business greed."[70] On the other hand, the executive committee wanted the walls retained but claimed the idea of constructing a museum around them was "a desecration of them and that they should be opened to the free use by the people as before the present structure on the property was erected," the position favored by Clara Driscoll Sevier.[71]

The bickering continued back and forth all morning but came to a head over procedural disputes in the afternoon. In the perennial absence of their president, Mary (Mrs. Anson) Jones, Rebecca Fisher, the first vice president, surrendered the gavel to Lida Alford. The De Zavala group protested, and Adina herself rose to read from the constitution, which specified that vice presidents should preside according to their number in the absence or disability of the president.[72] The meeting descended from there to the ridiculous. Mrs. Dibrell moved to "pin badges on all new daughters, no matter what sex"; a motion to adjourn was drowned out by the noise; and Rebecca Fisher, reclaiming the gavel, ruled that the meeting was adjourned *sine die*, in effect indefinitely, at which point forty-six of the sixty-seven women in attendance walked out.[73]

Those remaining proceeded to elect state officers, with Mary Jones as their president and Adina De Zavala as chair of a new executive committee. They presumed themselves to be the legally constituted DRT by virtue of the walkout by their opposition. Trouble was sure to follow when the newly elected officers began exercising their prerogatives, including notifying several banks where DRT funds were deposited to honor only checks written by their officers.

The Driscoll faction, meanwhile, reconvened themselves at the Driskill Hotel and voted to put the Alamo property in the hands of the "executive committee" at the urging of Clara Driscoll Sevier. The women agreed to pursue her aim to create a park on the Alamo property. "We do not build museums over graves," Cornelia Branch Stone pontificated, "we plant flowers." After a brief meeting with the governor at the hotel, this executive committee requested and received from the attorney general a ruling designating the Driscollites the legitimate authority of the DRT.[74]

The Daughters of the Republic of Texas were now irrevocably rent asunder. Brits wrote from San Antonio reassuring Adele that he would keep her apprised of what was happening with the Alamo property. Mary Jones curtly refused to be associated with the De Zavala group. Mrs. Tuttle, an old friend of Adele from Fayette County, wrote to express her dismay and disgust with the situation. "Isn't it a mixture of truth and poetry," she wrote, "your dear Milby makes out as if no one objected to Mrs. Fisher's course but you and Adina. They are nice ladies? If you all had listened to me," she reminded Adele, "this humiliation might have been avoided." The whole idea of electing Mary Jones as president of the DRT was foolish make-believe anyway, she fumed. "The woman is too old to serve. I have no adverse feeling for the old lady; but she is dead to all intents and purposes, and to treat her as if alive gives unscrupulous persons license to stab us in the back." And, it seemed, the mischief having been made, the mischief makers had all left town. Mrs. Alford, Mrs. Tuttle informed Adele, had summoned her old husband and gone off to Connecticut; Mrs. Stone had left for Virginia. "Mrs. Anna Bradshaw and daughter Mabel went to California to spend the summer," she confided. "In former time I could have used their name at discretion, but not now they got so disgusted with the way things turned out."[75]

A week later the Driscollites, with Urwitz and McKeever in the lead, sought an injunction in Harris County against the De Zavalans, and it threatened to impeach not only the reputations of some of Texas's most prominent women but some of the most respected members of the bench and bar as well.[76] Adele began to hear from worried Daughters almost immediately as the word spread. "I have been so anxious to hear from you or Miss Adina in regard to our affairs and to my great surprise yesterday I had papers served on me to appear at Houston Court Saturday morning," Celicia Redding wrote in distress. "Such a thing never happened to me before." She said she had been told it was believed in Houston that Judge Norman Kittrell of the Sixty-First Judicial District (1903–13) had been the legal adviser of the Driscollite executive board. Redding's lawyer told her if that could be proved, it would disqualify him from presiding as judge. She wondered if Adele thought it absolutely necessary for her to appear. "All the testimony I could give would be in regard to the conventions of '06 and '07 and what I have gleaned from the papers," she worried. A cohort, Mrs. Bates, had apparently already written her about raising money for their legal expenses, and she told Adele she had sent from their chapter five dollars, through the Bank of Goliad. "You have no idea how I am worried over this thing," she wrote. "I know you are busy and worried, but I know of no one else to turn to for advice." She was wrong about that; Adele knew very well how worried she was. Adele was worried, too.[77]

A little more than a week later Adele penned a letter to her erstwhile friend and successor as historian general of the DRT, Nettie Houston Bringhurst. "My dear Mrs. Bringhurst," she began.

> When I wrote you about the fifteenth of April in regard to the papers of the Daughters of the Republic of Texas in my charge as Historian General, I expected to meet you in a few days at the Annual Meeting of the Society, and deliver the papers to you in person but had no opportunity to carry out my wishes and intentions. Having failed to turn them over in the manner which seemed to me best, viz in person, I now send them to you through the Alamo National Bank of San Antonio. Please go there, look over the papers, and accompanying list, sign the list as receipt to me, and receive the papers from the Bank.[78]

Adele noted that she had published on behalf of the DRT all the papers in her possession in the *Quarterly of the Texas State Historical Association* except a letter from Albert Sidney Johnston and a pamphlet on the Travis Guards. She apologized for the delay, expressed, not for the first time, her gratitude that Nettie Bringhurst had accepted the position of historian general, and proffered her willingness to turn over the remaining items in her possession to her successor. Before the letter had even been mailed, however, Adele learned from the Alamo National Bank that they had received notice from "other sides of this unfortunate controversy among D. R. T." not to deliver the papers; they could not turn them over to Nettie Bringhurst. "So I am unable to do anything in the matter, which I regret very much indeed," she concluded in a postscript.[79]

Adele found herself writing many such humiliating letters in regard to the DRT. She had accepted a number of historic relics on behalf of the Daughters, and she felt compelled to apprise the donors of the status of their gifts in the face of the well-publicized fracture. Within two weeks of her letter to Nettie Bringhurst, she wrote to the donor of a snuffbox alleged to have belonged to Santa Anna. "You doubtless remember that about two years ago you came to my house for the purpose of bringing a snuff box said to have belonged to Santa Anna and presenting it to the San Jacinto Chapter of the Daughters of the Republic of Texas," she reminded Mrs. Huber, a distant relative. As she wrote, a hint of resentment crept in:

> Since that time grave dissensions have arisen in the Society, chiefly from a desire on the part of the officers of the General Society to override the rights of the Chapters. In this connection they have brought suit against me for the possessing of this snuff box, which I have been ready at any time to deliver to the Chapter.
>
> You may remember, although it came through my family, I requested that it should be given to the San Jacinto

> Chapter. I retained it in my possession only at their earnest request and at no time thought that the officers of the General organization could assume to have anything to do with it.[80]

Her letter was a warning, she explained to Mrs. Huber. On other occasions when officers of the general society had tried to get possession of relics that had been donated to chapters, they had written to the donors to procure statements that they had given the relic to the Daughters of the Republic of Texas. "In many cases," Adele explained, "donors have not been aware of the trick practiced and have unintentionally fallen into their trap. It is for this reason that I am writing, to put you on your guard, should such a letter be addressed to you."[81]

Nothing got easier as the summer wore on. Adele determinedly applied herself to her commitments. She had managed, despite all obstacles, to submit an article to the *Quarterly*.[82] It was hard to tell whether the distractions of business and family were a blessing or a curse. Winnefred Looscan McAran, despite being at death's door on several occasions, seemed to be getting along since her husband's death in 1906, but Adele received a rambling letter from Mary Looscan in late August informing her that Michael Looscan's nephew and namesake, Mike, had been sick ever since her last letter and had worked only one month since January. "He has not improved much looks very thin and bad," she told Adele, and of course that was a great worry to her because she had thought he was getting along very well. She thanked Adele for handling her money for her.[83] She said she was getting more of it, felt it was safe, and never worried about it. She worried about what would become of Mike, though, if something happened to her. "You know I am all alone in the world, no one to ask advice from. I feel that I can write this way to you and ask you things that I would not think of asking others about," she confided. "Mike has never said one word to me about the money, and he don't [sic] know how much I have. I never talk with my friends about those things, so that is the reason I ask you about it. You have always been so sweet and kind to me that I hate to say one word that would hurt or offend you." She wanted Adele to look out for her money if anything happened to her. Mike was the nearest relative, and she wanted him to have it if she should die first, but she did not believe he was capable of managing it himself.[84]

Not all letters demanding her attention were as flattering. As the DRT lawsuit dragged on, even those to whom Adele owed nothing excoriated her personally, hurt her feelings, and strained her patience. To one such individual, she responded indignantly:

> Your letter has been received and read both by my sister and myself. First, I will remind you that some years ago when there was a difference between my cousin Kate and yourself, we did not take up her quarrel but continued to treat you in the same friendly manner that we had always shown towards you, although Kate filled the place of a sister to us. This much to remind you that we are not quick to enter into a quarrel.
>
> As to the affairs of the Daughters of the Republic of Texas, I claim to have far better opportunities for knowing the truth about them than you have ever had or can possibly have now, or ever can have. Since you chose to align yourself with those who were, in my opinion, injuring the Association, I naturally concluded you did not value my friendship. As I never injured you by word or deed, I can only regret that your sense of duty has required you to take such steps, could have had no other purpose or situation than to cast discredit upon me, as well as upon others associated with me. I have been treated with such discourtesy in the San Jacinto Chapter as to excite the indignation of comparative strangers who were present, yet such treatment to

> me and other members of my family has evidently met with your approval.[85]

Adele's hurt was evident.

Thus absorbed with family members asking for financial advice and assistance and buffeted by questions and insults over the trouble with the DRT, Adele passed the fall of 1907. On New Year's Eve, she picked up her pen and wrote a note to Adina. "A Post reporter has just phoned that he wants to get a sketch of Mrs. Jones's life, which was published in the Texas Messenger. It was written by me in 1897. I sent it to him with the request that it be accredited to me."[86] An era had passed and, with it, another milestone for the DRT.

The death of Mary Jones and the ascension of Rebecca Fisher to the presidency of the general society of the DRT seemed to energize the loyal opposition even as the whole DRT controversy was taking its toll on Adina and Adele. Mary De Zavala wrote worriedly to Adele in January, "Adina has certainly more on her mind and heart than any mere human ought to be burdened with. I fear her health will be completely ruined as it is impossible to continue always on such a strain. I hope the Daughters 'case' may be called as soon as possible and that it will all be over. I do nothing and can do nothing but the whole affair is such a worry. Emma Burleson and Mrs. Alford—a most unscrupulous pair! I am sure it is no honor to belong to an Association boasting such women. I do not know who our friends are."[87]

Adele was not so sure who her friends were either. If attacks came from unexpected quarters, so did support. Betty Ballinger, whose inspiration and insistence had given birth to the Daughters of the Republic of Texas in Mary Jane Briscoe's parlor but who had been absent for a number of years, sent a letter of encouragement and support. "Like you I have felt convinced that she [Mary Jones] was a tool in the hands of others unscrupulous for themselves and for her," she wrote. "Long ago I became persuaded from things happening in our own chapter, that Mrs. Stone cared only for her own personal advancement and would stoop to actions which I could not countenance," she confided. "I have done all I could for some time without an open issue, to defeat her plans so far as the honor of the organization was concerned. I wish now that I had made a bolder fight when she insulted and drove from our work one of our best members, Mrs. Carrie Hemp," Ballinger wrote regretfully.[88]

Ballinger then observed that if Cornelia Stone had indeed asked last summer "what the Daughters of the Republic are fussing about," she most assuredly professed no such ignorance any longer. Stone was "laying her plans with untiring energy and all the skill she possesses to insure her election to succeed Mrs. Jones," Ballinger assured Adele. She promised to influence her sisters to prevent the Galveston chapter from supporting Stone for president of the DRT and to go to Beaumont and lend their efforts to save the organization.[89]

Ballinger went on to mention other members from Galveston who had expressed revulsion at the coarseness of manner and morals of the Driscoll supporters in Galveston. "Mrs. Randall wrote last summer that Mrs. Gresham's bearing towards Miss De Zavala was beyond belief for one who had not been at the meeting. My own face grows hot when I think of her language to me when I went to see her after Goliad. Mrs. Griggs would be even worse if she became involved," she asserted, "and you know Mrs. Stone manages both of them." She went on to name several besides herself and Mrs. Randall whom she believed would stand up for the De Zavala position. Although the idea of holding office did not appeal to her, she was willing to stand for election if Adele thought it would help.[90]

The constant stress took its toll on Adele's health. Her hip pained her constantly. She could not walk even a short distance without her cane or other support, but she did her best to take it in stride, and by early February she was feeling improved and a little stronger. "I am glad you feel as you do about it," Mary Looscan wrote her. "So many others would feel very bitter over all the trouble you have had and it sounded very good to me to hear you say you felt thankful that you can get around alone. When I read [your letter] I felt how much I had to be thankful for good health and how little I ought to complain."[91]

Adele's improved health and spirits, however, were in for another blow. The airing of the DRT dirty laundry in public had been bad enough, but it had subsided somewhat with the passing of Mary Jones and subsequent memorials celebrating her life. The respite was short lived, for Adina's agitation had been steadily increasing. It culminated in her rashest actions to date and catapulted her name to the front page of every newspaper in the state. The second week in February, Adele opened a letter from Adina that began, "In the Alamo! In the Alamo!—not the buck and wing dancers, but the De Zavala Chapter. The lease expires today, I thought and still believe, this morning, but I hear that the Hugo-Schmeltzer people say that it expires at twelve o'clock tonight. I also had rumors that the other people were going to capture the Alamo, so to make sure, I walked in and captured it myself. I do not know what they will do, and I don't care much. I am in possession, and they will have trouble in ousting me—either the firm or the enemy."[92]

With two deputies posted outside to thwart Adina's access to food and water, the standoff was resolved within a few days. She surrendered the building to the state superintendent of public buildings on February 13. The Driscoll executive committee (Fisher, Stone, McKeever, et al.) downplayed the incident by publishing its own version of events, claiming that the building Adina occupied was "the old Hugo-Schmeltzer warehouse, a dilapidated wooden structure in no sense a part of the Alamo or of the old Mission de Valero."[93] The *San Antonio Light*, in summing up the situation, revealed the implications for the DRT and Adele's future in it: "Erstwhile friends have become sworn enemies and those who formerly drank tea and exchanged small talk together are arrayed in a warfare quite as determined as the defense of the Alamo."[94]

Of course, in denying that any part of the Hugo-Schmeltzer building belonged to the original structure of the Alamo mission, the Driscoll faction had committed an about-face from its earlier position, a fact that did not go unnoticed by Adina De Zavala. The court ignored her arguments, however, and found in favor of the complaining Driscoll executive committee. The members of the De Zavala Chapter and its supporters continued to plot and plan throughout the year but got nowhere.

Adele had fared slightly better in the lawsuit filed against her over the snuffbox and other relics. Her reputation as a preeminent Texas historian remained intact. Historic artifacts from old Texas families continued to arrive at her door. The toll that the schism in the DRT had exacted was evident, though, in her communication with the donors. In late July 1908, while the DRT appeal was still pending, she replied to an inquiry by Mrs. Huber on behalf of another donor: "I am very sorry that the Daughters of the Republic of Texas are not in a position to receive and care for relics as there is a lawsuit still pending to decide who are the real officers. There is no telling when the controversy may be finally settled. Such a state of things will inevitably destroy the prestige of the Society and endanger the preservation of anything placed in its charge." For that reason, she recommended that a Mexican fan offered to Mrs. Huber for placement with the DRT be given instead to the "Historical Department of the State of Texas." That way, she explained, it would be placed in a glass case in the Department of History in the magnificent capitol building visited by nearly everyone who traveled to Austin. She then wrote,

> I will write on a card of suitable size the history of the Fan as given by you and will see that a suitable record is made of it in the books of the State Department of History and also in the Quarterly of the Texas State Historical Association, published at Austin.
>
> I regret very much to feel obliged to tell you of the trou-

> bles that prevail in an organization of which for many years I was very proud, but my experience has taught me that a few zealous unscrupulous women can in a short time destroy the prestige of the most worthy organization and their malicious tongues blacken the most spotless reputation."[95]

Adele was not yet ready to give up on the DRT altogether, but she had turned a corner. She and Jessie, along with cousin Annie Hume and niece Mary Briscoe, took a vacation to the mountains of Mexico for rest, relaxation, and respite from the heat of the Houston summer. In the meantime, Adina continued the battle to save the Alamo Long Barracks in the face of the court ruling setback, as the stated plans of the Driscollites now appeared to be total destruction of everything except the chapel building.

Adele was not alone in her desire not to sever all ties with the DRT. Betty Ballinger wrote to her in March, saying that she had attended a meeting of the Galveston Chapter and most everyone had been nice to her. "I tell you all this to show that there is no antagonism visible to the naked eye—that dreadful feeling, those harsh, unloving words, those ruptured friendships of which our bad conduct is supposed to be the wicked cause," she wrote. Apropos of this last point, she noted,

> As I came through Houston on my way home from Beaumont, I met Mrs. Rosine Ryan on the street, and she plunged at once into the thick of the fight. I refused her challenge and gave her no sympathy when she drew a picture of herself going along the street in tears, sobbing as if her heart would break because "Delly Briscoe" had refused to shake hands with her. I merely accepted the fact that you had found it necessary to cut her, remarking that I should really dislike to have a woman of Mrs. Looscan's high character refuse to take my hand.[96]

Hostilities erupted during the annual Battle of Flowers in San Antonio in May. Brits reported to Adele on the incident with exasperation at the missed opportunity to expose their opponents. Adina, he said, had made a call on the old "Native Texians" at their club room on the Saturday following the parade. She told them that on Wednesday, the day of the event, she and others had been rudely assaulted by Will Tobin, who tore their picture of the Alamo from its frame, broke the staff of the Texas flag, threw them into an adjoining yard, and then ordered that their float or carriage should not appear in the parade. "None of us had heard of this outrage even though three days had passed," Brits noted. Of course, they rallied to Adina's support and accompanied her to the office of Judge Bliss but could not understand why she "chewed the rag" so long before she sought help. "I don't believe she can give utterance to an entirely natural emotion," Brits observed. "She missed the greatest chance in her Alamo fight by not screaming for the Police and fainting and falling from her Carriage, a great opportunity lost," he mourned.[97]

Not surprisingly, Adele attempted to further the De Zavalans' case in the court of civil appeals by turning to Texas archives for historical documentation. She called on George Garrison to help her locate plans of the Alamo that someone had told her were given to the Texas State Historical Association. He responded that the correspondence she sought must have been given to the State Historical Society at Galveston, because no such papers had been given to the association in Austin.[98]

In spite of Adele's best efforts and the efforts of her supporters in the DRT, the appeals court upheld the district court decision in November 1909, and the victors declared the De Zavala Chapter of the DRT "out of existence." The victorious cabal took possession of the Alamo in March 1910. Betty Ballinger, Lucy Mills, and others reported that efforts were afoot to exclude them from the Galveston Chapter. Adina was not ready to give up the fight, but the emphasis now would be entirely on saving the old walls from total demolition.

The DRT was beyond the control of the De Zavala Chapter and its supporters.

While Adina plotted her strategy, Adele called upon her influence as a respected historian and turned to old friends she thought could be trusted to see reason. In July 1911, she appealed to Oscar Branch Colquitt, by then governor of Texas. "I was very much gratified a few days ago, to learn that you had been to San Antonio for the purpose of examining the two story building which constitutes the most important part of the Alamo now standing," she began. "While the agitation for the destruction of this building has been going for years, and especially since 1905, when interested parties thought they saw a fine opportunity to accomplish their purpose, I have never felt that the building was in danger because I did not believe any Governor of the State of Texas would consent to its destruction." Where Adina had expressed her emotions with actions, Adele poured hers into words. "The most thrilling part of the history of Texas is embraced within so brief a period that no citizen of the State should be ignorant of the events comprising it," she told Colquitt. "To me it has seemed simply impossible that a Park, which any city can have, should occupy the space of this most historic barrack, the scene of such heroic conflict as has never been surpassed in the world's history."[99] She had every faith that Colquitt, who was known to be sympathetic to historic preservation, would listen to reason and be persuaded by evidence.

It did seem that these appeals were gaining some traction. The legislature appropriated some money for the improvement of the Alamo grounds under the governor's supervision. Colquitt called a meeting of all interested parties in San Antonio in December 1911, where he made it clear that he believed no part of the Alamo complex still standing before the battle in 1836 should be destroyed. But the executive committee of the DRT refused to accept the governor's plans for the building, stating that they considered his "interference" a usurpation of their authority, and they even threatened to go to court over it. Colquitt fought back and began his project. During the restoration effort in 1912, workers discovered foundation work that verified Adina De Zavala's instincts that the structure had indeed been an original part of the Alamo, but that revelation had no effect on the DRT position. Work progressed despite the opposition until the appropriation ran out, at which point the DRT executive committee managed to thwart a renewal of it by court injunction. While Colquitt was out of the state, the lieutenant governor allowed San Antonio officials to tear down the walls of the upper story of the Hugo-Schmeltzer building. All that remained of the restoration work was the east wall; all that remained of the original convent was the lower story of the south and west walls.[100] And all that remained of the DRT? Adele's sentiment was summed up succinctly in a letter from Mrs. Tuttle in late July. "I am too old to make up with them," she wrote. "They hurt my feelings too sorely[;] people that can act so dishonest will never again be trusted by me."[101]

Chapter Six

Madame President

THE BETRAYALS, politicization, demagoguery, and cynicism of the Daughters of the Republic of Texas, more than the Alamo issue itself, drove Adele to become a thoroughly disaffected Daughter by 1914, and she never again associated with the organization she had helped to found. Other members of the San Jacinto Chapter, as well as of the De Zavala Chapter, resumed their association with the DRT; among them was Adele's sister, Jessie Howe. Although Adele never did, her dedication to Texas history was in no way diminished by the bitter experience. In the aftermath of the appellate court's ruling, neither she nor Adina abandoned their interest in the Alamo. She continued her work with the patriotic societies, federated women's clubs, historic preservation efforts, the Texas Folklore Society, and the Texas State Historical Association, whose mission combined her interests in history, preservation, and education.

From the inception of the TSHA in 1897, George P. Garrison had drawn freely upon Adele's experience with the Texas legislature and her connections with other pioneer families and various organizations such as the DRT and the Texas Woman's Press Association to find new members and good contributors to the *Quarterly.* He respected her judgment. In 1898, he had communicated to her that the president of the association, Dudley G. Wooten, had appointed her to a committee to devise and execute a plan for securing state recognition for the association in the legislature. All the other committee members had been men—Judge Beauregard Bryan, Gov. Francis Lubbock, Prof. Robert L. Batts, and Judge C. W. Raines. "I earnestly hope that you will be able to act on this Committee," Garrison had written. "Your help will be invaluable; for I know from what I have observed that the ladies often succeed with such things as this where men fail."[1] And, typically, Adele had assured him, "Any service I can render the Association as a member of this committee, will be cheerfully given."[2] She agreed, finally, to her election as a Fellow of the association in 1900.[3] Throughout that most difficult decade of turmoil in the DRT, Adele had contributed at least one article a year, sometimes more, to the *Quarterly*. From the establishment of TSHA until her death, she contributed more than a dozen articles. Her first two contributions, "The Old Mexican Fort at Velasco" and "The Old Fort at Anahuac," were gracefully written and clearly well researched but not footnoted. However, in the second article, on Anahuac, she had included the full quotes of several of her sources in the text and listed references after the last paragraph. In 1901, she contributed an article titled "The Old Fort on San Saba River," in which she took the opportunity to emphasize the importance of historical landmarks and the work of the Daughters of the Republic of Texas to preserve them. In this piece, she again made reference to her sources in the text but did not include notes. It set her articles apart from those written by students, such as Brownie Ponton and Bates McFarland ("Alvar Nuñez Cabeza de Vaca: A Preliminary Report on His Wanderings in Texas," published in January 1898), and professionally trained historians, such as Lilia Casis, who had received her bachelor's and master's degrees at the University of Texas and had begun teaching there in 1897.[4] Adele's other contributions were chiefly biographical sketches, about half of which centered on her family and other pioneers, such as Micajah Autry, John R. Fenn, Miles Bennett, Joseph Daniels, Dugald McFarlane, and John Birdsall. She secured and edited the reminiscences of Dilue Rose Harris, one of the finest firsthand accounts of early Anglo Texas available. Dilue Rose and her family had arrived in Texas in April 1833 at Harrisburg before settling at Stafford's Point in Fort Bend County in December of that year. Her father, a former US Army surgeon, hired a teacher for his children and ten others studying in a one-room schoolhouse. During the Texas Revolution, Dilue made bullets for men going to the Alamo, and she took part in the Runaway Scrape in 1836, when settlers and their slaves fled east from Santa Anna's army, which was pillaging homes and mills as it advanced across Texas. When the war of Texas independence ended, the Rose family moved to the area of Bray's Bayou five miles outside of Houston. In 1839, Dilue married Ira A. Harris, an emigrant from New York who had arrived in 1836 and served with the Texas Rangers. When Adele persuaded Dilue to allow her memoirs to be published, the pioneer woman was seventy-four and widowed and had been living in Columbus, Texas, since 1845.[5] The project was a major undertaking and was published in three installments in 1900 and 1903.

In 1904, Adele contributed her article "The Work of the Daughters of the Republic of Texas on Behalf of the Alamo," in which she laid out the evidence in support of her and Adina's interpretation of the Alamo's history as a plea for support. As was her habit, her sources were included in the text.[6] Up to that time, in every byline she formally included her title, "Historian, Daughters of the Republic of Texas," following her name. All of her contributions after July 1904 simply bore her name as author.

That members of the DRT had not been more engaged in the work of the TSHA, especially with regard to contributions to the *Quarterly*, had always been a source of consternation to Adele. In hindsight, perhaps that had been a foreshadowing of divergent interests within the DRT. She had been frequently disappointed by other Daughters of the Republic who had not shared her devotion to Texas history even then. She expressed this frustration to Garrison on occasion. "Don't feel troubled over the lack of interest shown by the Daughters in the *Quarterly*," he consoled her. "They will be drawn to it in the course of time."[7] In fact, just the opposite had turned out to be true. Although several other women contributed articles to the *Quarterly*, only a few of them, such as Dora Fowler Arthur and Marie Urwitz, were affiliated with the DRT. Between the inception of the *Quarterly* and 1935, when Adele Looscan died, an average of 42 percent of the articles in the *Quarterly* were submitted by women. Several members of the Daughters of the Republic of Texas eventually served on the executive council, but most, including Anna J. Pennybacker and Cornelia Branch Stone, did not write for the *Quarterly*.

Despite the distress caused by the rupture within the DRT and the amount of time consumed by her efforts to preserve the Alamo, Adele had remained actively engaged in the affairs of the TSHA and with all aspects of Texas history and culture. When John Avery Lomax organized the Texas Folklore Society in 1909, she took an immediate interest. Like the Texas State Historical Association, the folklore group's membership consisted primarily of men. Through her involvement with the TSHA, she knew many of the founders and leaders. When John Lomax asked her for a contribution to the folklore journal, she obliged by sending an account of Negro superstitions she had encountered.[8] The following year, when Adina De Zavala reorganized the Texas Historical and Landmarks Association, Adele enthusiastically lent her support to that as well.

The schism within the DRT resulted in the loss of a number of female members from TSHA, and the supplanting of Anna Pennybacker's *New History of Texas for Schools* with a new textbook by Eugene C. Barker, Charles Ramsdell, and Charles S. Potts contributed to the exodus.[9] Anna Pennybacker had been elected a Fellow of the Texas State Historical Association along with four other women in the association's first year, 1897, but she never served on the executive board. When she had asked for a review of her textbook in the early 1890s, Adele had been graciously complimentary. Their approaches to Texas history were not that different. Both women emphasized great historical figures and used biography as their primary organizing principle. In Pennybacker's teaching, great men and women were to serve as exemplars for students, and the study of their lives was relevant for guidance in living one's own. She viewed history as drama, with historical figures as key elements. Settings and plot were secondary to the human interest and action.[10] Although their sympathetic treatment of pioneers and heroes was much the same, Adele's adherence to documentation, as well as the training she had received from Professor Garrison, prevented her from taking the dramatic license in her own writing that was so prevalent in Pennybacker's textbook. Anna Pennybacker approached history from a typical nineteenth-century view—as a teacher, not a historian. She was a nineteenth-century romanticist who saw history as a vehicle for teaching moral lessons. Adele was a historian, not a teacher. She saw history as imparting practical lessons—to bring the individual into "sympathetic relations with the great individual minds that have shaped the form and determined the character of what we call history," to give those who inhabit the present a sense of their place in the great continuum—as much for herself as for future generations.[11]

As early as 1891 a review in the *San Antonio Express* had severely criticized Pennybacker's textbook, as well as her qualifications as a writer. The reviewer listed incorrect details in the textbook.[12] While making revisions to the book in 1903, Pennybacker wrote Adele for information concerning the Daughters of the Republic of Texas to supplement what she already had. Adele obliged but at the same time drew attention to several errors in the textbook.[13] In 1912, Eugene C. Barker, Charles Ramsdell, and Charles S. Potts produced their own textbook on Texas history that competed with Pennybacker's book, which, by then, had been a staple in Texas public schools for more than twenty years. By this time, Pennybacker had gained many contacts as a result of her prominence in women's clubs, at both the state and the national levels, and she urged these contacts to pressure their husbands, school trustees, superintendents, and teachers to write recommendations for her book. According to her biographer, "Some supporters acknowledged that their reason[s] for writing recommendations were related to their association with Mrs. Pennybacker and her past support rather than the merits of the book itself."[14] When the new text by Barker, Ramsdell, and Potts was adopted, Anna Pennybacker quit the TSHA and retaliated by openly criticizing it.[15]

With the drop in membership, Adele put her mind and energy toward attracting new members and subscribers to the *Quarterly.* Through her work with libraries and schools, she had become attuned to the reality of changing audiences. Since the deaths of her husband and brother, both active Confederate veterans, her own historical interests had expanded to include the Civil War and its heroes. "I regret that no method for increasing the number of subscribers occurs to me," she wrote to Prof. Eugene C. Barker in May 1914. "I have heard it remarked that the Quarterly deals with no subjects less than 'one or two hundred years old' and those of our people who read books in the spaces between newspaper issues usually turn to fiction, or history of the Civil War period." An avid follower of the *Atlantic Monthly*, she noted, "Confederate portraits by Gamaliel Bradford in last year's Atlantic were so fine that I wish some writer equally capable would contribute a similar series to the Quarterly. It would undoubtedly create an interest not heretofore manifested."[16] Despite this advice, she never published any articles on Civil War Texas herself.

When Barker, who had succeeded Professor Garrison as TSHA president in 1910, asked for help in building an endowment for the association, Adele did her best to oblige. Certainly, she had gained valuable experience asking men for money during the San Jacinto battleground campaigns of years past, but having been directly engaged in business through the management of the estates of her mother, husband, and brother, she had become more attuned to the forces that swayed them. "I cannot give a very satisfactory reply in regard to the probability of finding ten men who would be willing to contribute $250.00 each toward establishing an endowment fund for the Society. The best I can do at present," she told Barker in August 1914, "is to enclose a list of names of such as are financially able to do so. The immediate present seems rather full of threatened panic, financial depression and other drawbacks to the enlistment of interest in the preservation of the past. A personal appeal is usually much more effective than the usual plan of mailing circulars."[17] She provided him with a list of names in Houston, but she was perceptive enough to realize that her overtures to this same group for various causes in recent years might lessen their enthusiasm for appeals from her now. "You may have observed," she warned him, "that, usually, those who have been successful in accumulating anything more than a competency are oblivious to all claims upon their purses, except those urgent demands for charity which are constantly thrust before them." She agreed to approach a few of her closest friends, such as Col. Guy M. Bryan and Will Hogg, but she urged Barker to make a personal visit to appeal to others, man to man. As he had asked her for a suggestion, she recommended that in late September or early October he write a personal letter to everyone on the list of contacts she had given him and any others he might know and then follow up with a visit. "I need hardly tell you that I should be glad to see the establishment of an endowment fund," she assured him, "and you may count upon me for a contribution of the amount."[18]

One of Adele's assets was her ability to see the correlation between soliciting contributors and subscribers to the TSHA. Her suggestion that the *Quarterly* seek to appeal to a more modern audience by including more articles on the Confederacy and Confederate veterans coincided with efforts by the United Daughters of the Confederacy to memorialize Confederate veterans. Her many affiliations and obligations prevented her from being as actively engaged with the UDC as she might have been, but her work with the TSHA put her in a position to take note of the fact that comparatively little had been written about Texas's Confederates in the *Quarterly*. In her mind they were Texas heroes and, therefore, noteworthy, but she also saw this lack of attention as an opportunity. Knowing Barker's editorial fastidiousness, she persisted in her letter to him, "I trust that you may have developed some patriotic writers in the University, who may take up a few biographical sketches of Texas leaders in the war between the States."[19]

Adele's willing participation in all aspects of the operation of the TSHA did not escape notice. In 1915, Judge Zachary T. Fulmore, who had served as president of TSHA for two terms, declined to stand for reelection, leaving Barker with the task of securing reliable leadership for the organization. Still feeling the loss of so many female members, he set out to find a woman for the job. He had approached Bride Neill Taylor and Hally Bryan Perry a few years earlier, without success. It was now the first week of March, and the pressure was on. Barker turned to Adele Looscan. "Judge Fulmore did not want to be re-elected," he explained. "In looking over the membership list, he and I could find no one who had taken more effective interest in the Association than you. I think you deserve it by all odds."[20] Who exactly was the greatest beneficiary of this honor might have been open to question; certainly, its bestowal contained an element of condescension, but Adele did not turn him down, which was virtually impossible anyway since she had learned of her appointment ex post facto through the announcement of it in the *San Antonio Express*.[21] Adele's personal knowledge of so many early families was an asset to Barker, as it had been to Garrison, in the accumulation of primary sources of Texas history, in identifying potential members, and in the verification of purportedly historical accounts. "It would keep many rapid writers busy every day in the year to correct fanciful writers' newspapers articles," she reminded him on occasion.[22] Interestingly enough, in an apparent effort to cover all bases, Barker recruited Cornelia Branch Stone to serve as a vice president that same year.

Cornelia Branch Stone, like Adele, was the offspring of a pioneer Texas family. She was born in 1841, in Nacogdoches, daughter of Judge Edward T. Branch. She married H. C. Stone when she was barely sixteen. "Nellie" Stone had served as acting president of the DRT for Mary Jones (1891–1907) and for Rebecca J. Fisher (1907–15) and had been the direct cause of much of the friction within the DRT that had alienated Adele. Although she served on the executive committee of the TSHA from 1915 through 1918, the position seems to have been titular. No hint of their former animosity appeared during her tenure on the council; the TSHA was clearly not a priority of hers. A biography written for an anniversary of the federated women's clubs listed her leadership in the DRT, the United Daughters of the Confederacy, Texas Federation of Women's Clubs, Texas Woman's Press Association, and her directorship of Texas War Relief Work during World War I but made no mention of her association with the Texas State Historical Association.[23]

Adele never thought of herself as simply a figurehead. As president of TSHA, she became involved in every aspect of the association. Within a month of her acceptance of the office in 1915, Barker sent her TSHA stationery and envelopes and outlined his immediate wish list. "If you can get a number of Libraries to subscribe and buy files of the Quarterly, it will help greatly," he began. "In the matter of personal subscriptions anything is welcome, of course, but life memberships are much more lucrative."[24] He said he had adopted the practice of devoting life membership fees to the endowment, and so far he had held to that. He suggested she use this information with those she approached on the subject as an argument of more or less appeal.

She applied her pen immediately to these tasks. In May 1915, she received a reply from Claudia Norvell in Beaumont, who was busy spearheading the documentation of historic Texas trails but took time to congratulate Adele on her new role. "It is now my intention to get you some members," Norvell wrote. "I will see if I can interest some friends to become life members. I want to become a life member as soon as I am relieved of some of the expense of this trail work," she added. On the subject of the *Quarterly*, she regretfully reported that they had no public library in Beaumont, though a movement for one had begun. She promised to ask the Woman's Reading Club about a subscription to the *Quarterly*, and "I'll let you know about my friends," she promised.[25] In June, Adele was able to report that the chair of the history committee of the Texas Federation of Women's Clubs at Paris, Texas, had promised to interest the library there in the purchase of a full set of the *Quarterly*. Adele never seemed to weary of the effort or to allow other activities to distract her from TSHA goals. A year later she reported that a bulletin had gone out to superintendents of city and county schools recommending the *Quarterly* for high school libraries, and she indicated her intent to visit Rice Institute personally to place a complete set of the *Quarterly* in the library there.[26]

That Adele's involvement in other activities never abated in the slightest once she became TSHA president in many ways advanced the interests of the association. Through these other pursuits she made and sustained contacts on every level, from local to national. She continued to be active in the women's work of Christ Church in Houston, to which her mother had been devoted. The mayor of Houston, Ben Campbell, appointed her to a committee that included F. Charles Hume, Judge Edwin P. Hamblen, former mayor John T. Browne, Mrs. Gentry Waldo (Corinne Abercrombie), and Mrs. Charles Stewart to select a design for a flag for the city of Houston.[27] She frequently capitalized on her association with the United Daughters of the Confederacy, as most of the members were the daughters or wives of the most influential men in Texas. She also demonstrated the savvy she had acquired through years of business dealings and experience in women's clubs. She suggested to Dr. Barker that the convention of the UDC in Austin in December 1915 would afford a fine opportunity for pressing the interests of the TSHA, while to half a dozen of her friends in the UDC she indicated that it was the intention of the editorial managers of the *Quarterly* to publish more matter relating to the period of the Civil War, as well as the period immediately preceding and succeeding it, than had hitherto been done. "The January number will contain a sketch of General John A. Wharton, whose gallant career is a matter of pride to all Texans," she promised, even though the editorial board members—progressive historians and the interim president of the University of Texas, who was a classics professor—were far more inclined toward the Spanish colonial period, post-Reconstruction, and the Southwest than to Civil War Texas.[28]

With her work on the flag selection committee barely completed, Adele agreed (or at least did not decline) in January 1916 to serve on a Sam Houston monument committee, which was charged with "the entire program of raising the funds, selection of site, location and in fact everything connected with this undertaking."[29] As historian general of a chapter of the Daughters of the American Revolution, Adele was tasked by the national society later that year with obtaining old cemetery inscriptions; town, county, and family histories; family records; biographies; and other books and manuscripts on the deaths of older inhabitants of Texas that the DAR wanted to preserve, a project that improved her grasp of primary sources of Texas history. Her continued active affiliation with the press associations also presented opportunities to further the goals of the TSHA. In the spring, she reminded Charles Ramsdell, TSHA treasurer, of these opportunities. "It seems to me," she wrote him, "the Association is not sufficiently noticed in the Press of the State." The approaching meeting of press members at Austin, she suggested, would be a very favorable opportunity to place the merits of the association before them. "You and Dr. Barker with the cooperation of Mr. Mayes, the head of the School of Journalism[,] could, I am sure, forward the interests of the Quarterly if you have the time to devote to it." Apparently, the pace she set had not yet worn them out. When the TSHA annual meeting rolled around in the spring of 1916, there seemed no question that she would continue as president.[30]

As the TSHA approached its twentieth anniversary, Adele's knowledge not only of old Texas families but in many cases of the disposition of their family papers became even more valuable, especially considering the dual commitments of the association to education and to the development of an archive of Texas history. When Charles Ramsdell inquired about the papers of Judge Peter W. Gray, Adele responded immediately with a thorough report. Any newspapers or documents of historical interest relating to him had long since been deposited with the Grand Lodge of Masons. While she understood that the collection of his papers was undertaken and preserved for the purpose of promoting the writing of an authoritative history of Texas, she had never been told that Gray's will provided that it "should be given to a State Historical Society," as Ramsdell seemed to think, but if that were the case, she intended to pursue the matter. She also knew about rare copies of old newspapers that State Librarian Ernest Winkler had inquired about. She knew that they had at one time been kept in the law offices of Baker, Botts, and Baker in Houston but had been given to the Houston Light Guards Armory and subsequently tossed out with the trash. She advised Ramsdell, "Tell Mr. Winkler that the bound volumes were rescued and deposited in the Carnegie Library, here."[31]

Years of experience in women's clubs had honed Adele's organizational skills. She made arrangements for annual meetings, solicited papers for the sessions, and helped set the program agenda, but always in the back of her mind was a whisper of self-doubt, an echo of the ideology of "woman's sphere." She understood perfectly well that the critical needs of the TSHA were financial support and political support, mostly but not always in that order. "I am interested in doing all I can to forward the interests of the Association; have done a little, in a small way, all along, but a man of wide influence could do a hundred percent more with the same effort," she told Ramsdell.[32] In truth, the men who had preceded her had done no better. The problems of membership and funding persisted. Attendance at the annual meetings was generally poor. She considered taking the association to potential audiences. However, additional costs would be involved that the association could ill afford, and Zachary Fulmore's attempt to hold the annual meeting in Brenham in 1914 had been a failure. Nevertheless, Adele thought the twentieth anniversary of TSHA might be an opportune time for another try. She wrote as much to Barker, suggesting they hold the March meeting in Houston and advertise aggressively to attract additional members. Thus, the Houston Chamber of Commerce approached Charles Ramsdell in January 1917 about having the annual meeting in Houston. The first week of February Adele received a letter from Louis J. Hennessey, manager of the Houston chamber, asking her as president to make suggestions as to how to further their effort to have the next meeting of the historical association in Houston.[33] In promoting Houston as the site for the annual meeting in 1917, she wrote Ramsdell that she expected to "work up an audience among the teachers in the schools, Rice Institute, and the Women's Clubs, and [am] making fair progress along those lines. How long," she inquired, "has it been since a meeting has been held elsewhere than at the University?"[34] At least there might be a chance of stirring up some interest. Unfortunately, she had less success in stirring Barker's interest. Even after she had canvassed all her contacts and purchased advertisements in the Houston newspapers, he decided to hold the meeting in Austin. Adele was chagrined but undeterred.[35]

The twentieth anniversary of the TSHA prompted Adele to bring up another initiative that she felt strongly about. "I am anxious to see an index volume for the first twenty years of the *Quarterly*," she informed Barker. She knew from Ernest Winkler that Elizabeth West had worked on indexing the first fifteen volumes. He thought the remaining five could be completed in a short time if someone could be found to work on the project. Adele pledged to contribute liberally to this project, provided the compilation and publication could be accomplished within the limits of her resources. When she unhappily acquiesced to the cancellation of her plan for the association to meet in Houston, she reiterated to Charles Ramsdell her determination to see the index completed. "I shall try to attend the meeting at Austin, where I shall recommend the adoption of steps to provide an index for the *Quarterly*," she warned.[36]

Her insistence on the indexing of the *Quarterly* dated back several years. She saw the publication and distribution of the journal as the most effective means of disseminating Texas history, increasing membership, and raising money, and she believed that an index was key to that effort. Elizabeth West had abruptly resigned in 1915, and her departure not only slowed completion of the index but heralded other troubles on the horizon.

In 1911, when Elizabeth West had begun working as an archivist at the Texas State Library, Maj. George W. Littlefield, a highly successful rancher and businessman and a Confederate veteran, was appointed to the University of Texas Board of Regents. At first, Barker saw Littlefield's preoccupation with the southern history presented in textbooks as an opportunity to garner support for his own goal of developing a collection of archival material at the University of Texas to further historical research, and their discussions bore fruit in the establishment of the Littlefield Southern History Collection in 1914. But Littlefield's challenging of the teaching staff at the university did not bode well for TSHA. In 1915, a resolution was introduced in the Texas legislature about pro-northern sympathies among the university faculty, and Joseph W. Bailey, a former US senator and conservative firebrand, declared that "socialist doctrines are finding lodgement in the university of this State." At the other end of the political spectrum was Adele's longtime friend Will C.

Hogg, a business progressive. Both Littlefield and Hogg were firm believers in academic freedom and represented a strong-willed brand of politician who would rather see the university shut down than endure the suppression of opinions advanced by good scholarship.[37] Into this sensitive situation entered James E. Ferguson, sworn in as governor in 1915. With a great sense of self-importance and a view that state employees, which included the regents and faculty of the University of Texas, owed him deference, it was not long before he clashed with Barker and others such as William J. Battle, a member of the *Quarterly's* editorial staff. Ferguson removed Ernest Winkler as state librarian in 1915. In protest, Barker resigned as chair of the Texas Library and Historical Commission, and with that, Elizabeth West left her job as state archivist. It was a crippling blow to progress on the *Quarterly* index. It did not help TSHA's membership and fundraising efforts either. Ferguson, who fancied himself a Progressive reformer but who also insisted on the personal loyalty of all state employees, was not finished wreaking havoc on the association. That spring and summer of 1917, as Adele and Ramsdell corresponded furiously in their effort to come up with a successful strategy to address the TSHA's financial needs, two gigantic obstacles loomed over them. The governor ramped up his attacks on the university and its faculty. The conflict between Ferguson and the regents became increasingly intense and public. William J. Battle was among the casualties. At the same time, the nation moved toward war with Germany, and R. E. Vinson, by then president of the university, recommended firing all Germans associated with the institution who were not naturalized citizens, a policy that the regents expanded to include all aliens of whatever origin.[38]

This constant war of innuendo and outrageous accusations severely undermined the public's trust of the University of Texas and everyone associated with it. Nevertheless, opportunities presented themselves. In March, Ramsdell informed Adele that the association had a chance to get some good securities promising a 7 percent return if they could come up with a thousand dollars to invest, but they were three hundred dollars short. "In soliciting contributions to an endowment fund, it is of the utmost importance that contributors may feel assured of the safe investment of their contributions and that strict business methods are followed in the conduct of all money matters," she replied. "Why would not a committee comprising [Judge Torres], yourself, Dr. Barker, and two others to be selected by those named, be a better working committee than the whole council and consult Judge Torres about the matter[?]." She sent Ramsdell her personal check for the three hundred dollars needed to complete the investment, but as for the two prospective donors she had been cultivating, she told him she would have to see whether they were willing to contribute cash or only pledge contingent upon TSHA raising the five- or ten-thousand-dollar amount of the endowment as originally contemplated. "So many changes can take place in a short time, and rumors of war tend to make people extremely careful about expenditures," she reminded him.[39]

War abroad and wars in Austin also hindered efforts to increase membership in the association. This problem weighed heavily upon Adele as she felt, correctly, that she had been appointed president primarily for the purpose of gaining new members, as well as to collect for the state "archives corner" the primary sources of Texas history then held by individuals and families. She sent names to Ramsdell on a regular basis, urging him to send out membership applications. However, Adele's inclination was to conflate these two objectives. She approached prospects for membership in the association based on their probable interest in Texas history and saw them as not only potential members but as sources of historical material. She would write to Ramsdell saying this person is in the Moses Austin family and that one's grandfather fought in the Battle of San Jacinto, and so forth, but he and Barker, the only full-time staff in the association, could not keep up correspondence at the same rate she seemed able to, and some of her contacts never received the promised membership information. The association had only to notify them of their election, and they would send the two-dollar subscription, she told Ramsdell in exasperation. At times this scenario was humiliating, and Adele became more cautious herself. "I have lately received an interesting manuscript of Confederate history matters, but I will not forward it to the Association until I am assured that it will be promptly acknowledged," she told Ramsdell.[40]

Adele was also able to conflate impact of the wars, World War I without and Ferguson's war on the University of Texas within on the progress of the association and its objectives. "The war is deplorable and the departure of our young men for service brings it in a manner to our very doors. But, our University seems to have become the theatre for an irrepressible conflict, which from late accounts has become more and more bitter, and no promise of a truce," she lamented to Ramsdell.[41]

Despite the war clouds gathering all around, Adele continued her effort to promote an index for the *Quarterly.* Ramsdell had suggested a subscription drive to help underwrite the cost. Adele, as usual, threw herself into it, seeking subscriptions from libraries, schools, clubs, and individuals. These were discouraging times, though, for educational endeavors. The general public, never as supportive of historic preservation or education as Adele would have liked to believe, was more distracted than usual in the spring and summer of 1917. The woman suffragists, led by Alice Paul, were grabbing headlines in Washington, DC. Revolution had broken out in Russia. Labor disputes had ignited race riots in Illinois and lynchings in Texas and Tennessee. Farmers in Oklahoma were rioting against the conscription that had been implemented in June in preparation for war. Charles Ramsdell reported in mid-July that he had received only forty orders for the index so far. "We will wait a while and then make another effort," he advised Adele. "If we do not get a satisfactory number of orders it will then be necessary for us to determine whether we shall go ahead and print the index or whether we shall wait until some more favorable opportunity presents itself. It may be just as well to print it and trust to future sales to bring us out even," he suggested, "but I should like to have the opinion of yourself and the other members of the Council before taking that step." In the meantime, political mischief continued to hamper prospects for support from the University of Texas. "You have no doubt read all about the meeting of the Board of Regents in Galveston yesterday and this morning, and know the humiliating story of their action. There seems no help for the University except through the action of the people and I do not know how that can be obtained," Ramsdell lamented.[42]

Despite such obstacles, Adele continued to press for the completion of the index. When the Texas Library Association planned its annual meeting for Houston in late November, Adele saw it as a prime opportunity to present the index feature of the *Quarterly* to a receptive audience, but she realized that she would need specific information to give them. Ernest Winkler had promised to complete the work of indexing, but she did not have an estimate of the cost of printing. "Our Quarterly without an index will be virtually a sealed book to students, and I am anxious to proceed as far as we possibly can toward furnishing a key to the mass of valuable material contained in the first twenty volumes," she wrote to Ramsdell, adding, "Please write me soon and oblige."[43] She received a reply in a remarkably short time. Ramsdell informed her that she should tell the Texas Library Association that the TSHA hoped to get the index out toward the close of the coming winter or during the spring. He explained that Winkler wanted to go over the whole mass of references compiled by Elizabeth West for the sake of verification and would then compile the references for the last five volumes (volumes 16–20). "We expect to include along with the index proper a complete table of contents for the whole twenty volumes arranged by periods and subjects—i.e. 'The Revolution,' 'Annexation,' 'Biography,' and the like," which he thought would be especially helpful to teachers who wanted information of a special kind. "Many of them would not know where to turn in an index," he explained. "We believe this feature would make the volume very useful to the schools." The price, he reminded her, would be five dollars. Ramsdell expressed confidence that the index would be well done but much less confidence that it would be done within the time frame mentioned. Winkler was busy, and in the fall of 1917 nothing much was certain.[44]

Providing an index to the *Quarterly* was not Adele's only concern. Other matters that needed to be addressed, in her opinion, included the Texas State Library and Archives and a state museum. The library had experienced many ups and downs. After an ignominious start, it had begun to flourish under the charge of Valentine King, state librarian from 1877 to 1880. However, a devastating fire at the capitol in 1881 destroyed most of it, and so the state library remained for the next decade "without a habitation and almost without a name." When James Hogg had come to the office of governor in 1891, he had taken preservation of the history of Texas as one of his missions and appointed C. W. Raines the task of reviving the library. Hogg and Raines decided to make the Texas State Library a Texana collection supplemented by reference works of history and literature.[45]

By 1901 there were twenty-five thousand volumes in the library, bound and in pamphlet form, four-fifths of which were government documents. The library also began collecting early Texas newspapers. In 1902, the Texas Federation of Women's Clubs had helped organize the Texas Library Association, and it spearheaded legislation, passed in 1909, for the organization of the Texas State Library and Historical Commission. It was this commission, of which George P. Garrison had been a member, that appointed Ernest Winkler as state librarian. Winkler worked "to realize his idea of making the State Library 'the treasure house of information relating to Texas and the Southwest' and to 'permit nothing relating to Texas to escape.'"[46] Gov. Jim Ferguson, of course, had put an end to that effort. Adele had been deeply concerned about conditions in the library, not only the preservation of state archival records but the lack of calendaring for them. What good were archival documents if they could not be found when needed? Feeling frustrated, she wondered if, with Ferguson out of the picture, Ernest Winkler might be persuaded to return as state librarian.[47] After his run-in with Ferguson, Winkler had become reference librarian and curator of Texas books at the University of Texas library and, along with Barker, had been developing the Littlefield Southern History Collection. Adele regarded him as the most qualified person to right the wrongs at the Texas State Library, so she floated the idea with Charles Ramsdell. "I have often wondered whether Mr. Winkler would like to have the appointment of State Librarian, or does he prefer the position he now fills at the University," she mused casually in a letter in early February 1918. Ramsdell required no time to ponder before responding. He knew that Winkler was emphatic that he did not care to go back to the Texas State Library. One experience of the political sort was quite enough for him. However, Ramsdell offered an alternative. "What would you think of having the historical manuscripts transferred from the State Library to the University Library?" he proposed. "Dr. Barker, Mr. Goodwin, and Mr. Winkler all think it's the best thing to do. The Legislative Reference Library should remain at the Capitol, and probably the books of the State Library could stay there," he continued, "but it is really necessary to any serious research in Texas history that the manuscripts be more available than they are now." Ramsdell pointed out that Winkler could manage those materials at the university, where he could get more done anyway, with the help of university archivist Mattie Austin Hatcher and others. The only disadvantage, he worried, was that the university library was becoming crowded, but he was optimistic that in five years they would probably have a considerable extension built. "Besides, these manuscripts are so important that we'll make room for them," he assured Adele. "The prime consideration is to make useful and available the rich historical material which now lies unused and practically useless in the State Library and several Departments. It would be a great step forward for the whole field of Texas history."[48]

Adele was disappointed but not ready to let the archives issue drop. "The other matter of grave importance, which will require legislation to accomplish, would have my approval," she wrote Ramsdell, "for I realize how inaccessible are historical manuscripts unless calendared and arranged systematically." She had read the legislative committee's report on the library and library commission, and it seemed to carry a strong recommendation that each state department should attend to all the historical manuscripts in its hands. This she saw as a problem. A few years back, she had engaged a copyist in Austin to go over certain papers in the comptroller's office pertaining to Harris County in the early days. The woman reported that these papers had been subjected to the ravages of insects to such an extent that the figures could be deciphered only partially and only by the aid of a powerful magnifying glass. "I believe many resolutions have been passed at different sessions of the Legislature for saving manuscripts from the dampness of the basements where they are stored," she told Ramsdell, "but the bills introduced do not seem to be framed in a manner to insure action, and become dead letters. In case there should be legislation favoring the removal of Historical Mss to the University, might it not also include others besides those in the State Library?"[49]

Very little escaped Adele's notice, and as her lifelong habit had been to read newspapers from all over Texas and elsewhere, she was already aware that George Littlefield had given the University of Texas the John Henry Wrenn collection of rare books, which could perhaps be turned into an opportunity to rescue the state's archives. The acquisition would undoubtedly require the university to have a larger library, one adequate for all library uses. "I hope when the war is over," she wrote Ramsdell, "we may have [a library] large and imposing, an ornament to the State." When the historical association met, they would pass suitable resolutions of appreciation for Littlefield's gift. Ramsdell agreed. Any patronage that could be bent to serve the ends of the association was worth encouraging, even if it was not of immediate assistance to history. Knowing of Major Littlefield's intense interest in southern history, Adele suggested that perhaps he could be persuaded to help underwrite the cost of publishing the *Quarterly* if more articles on the Civil War era were included. In reply, Ramsdell expressed his own idea to start a series under a title such as Littlefield Publications in Southern History, but he did not know whether the association could do that with the present supply of funds. He was hesitant to ask the major for more. "I agree with you that more material should be published in the *Quarterly* on the War of Secession," he told Adele, but "the difficulty is that there are few mature students who are doing work in that field."[50]

As for the state archives, Ramsdell told her, the chief difficulty in handling them at the capitol location was the persistent lack of sufficient expert help. When Ernest Winkler and Elizabeth West were there, the work proceeded more slowly than was desirable, and there was little hope in the foreseeable future that the state would have the services of such experts. "If the archives could be transferred to the University where expert supervision may be had," Ramsdell confided, "I believe they could be arranged and made available in one-fourth of the time that it will take at the Capitol and the work will be better done."[51]

These were matters that Adele intended to pursue at the annual meeting, but due to her own indisposition on March 2 and Barker's absence during the week of March 6, that would have to be postponed until San Jacinto Day. Adele's continued involvement in so many organizations meant inevitable conflict. In order to attend the TSHA meeting, she would have to miss the Texas Historical and Landmarks Association meeting in San Antonio on April 18, at which she was to report on the state of historic preservation in her region of Texas. A written report would have to suffice.

She reported that the world war crisis had prevented the organization of a chapter of the landmarks association in Houston, "but the spirit of the fathers of Texas lives in the hearts of their descendants, and inspires many a soldier on the fighting line in Europe to deeds of heroic adventure. The lessons of the Alamo, Goliad, and San Jacinto, have become household words to our whole nation, and Texans take their stand in the front ranks everywhere." The San Jacinto battleground was being well kept by the state, she assured the preservationists. A keeper's residence had been recently erected through an appropriation made by the legislature, and a retaining wall would be built to prevent erosion of the banks of the San Jacinto River. She also included a word of appreciation for Adina, for her publication of "History and Legends of the Alamo and Other Missions in and around San Antonio," and for her many contributions to the *San Antonio Express* on historical subjects of great importance that were not well known to the general public. "The work of the Historic Landmarks Association," she wrote, "is being felt throughout the State in a way which will encourage the marking of historic sites, so that, in time, our history may be read by those who pass by, in tablets of stone and bronze." Adele's report reflected the many ways she continued to promote Texas history despite her advancing age and the demands of business and family. "My efforts in forwarding Texas patriotism have been expended mostly for the Texas State Historical Association, which is devoted to this cause," she wrote, as amply shown in the pages of the *Southwestern Historical Quarterly* (formerly the *Quarterly of the Texas State Historical Association*) published at Austin. "I have assisted Mrs. Lipscomb Norvell, Chairman of the Old Trails Committee of the DAR," she reported, "in establishing and marking the line of the Old San Antonio Road or 'Camino Real' across the State of Texas. This summer will probably witness the consummation of this meritorious undertaking." Finally, she pointed out, "It is an encouraging sign of the times that the Women's Clubs throughout the State generally devote two or three days, and some of them yearly programs to Texas features. I sometimes assist in these programs, as well as those of local patriotic organizations to which I belong."[52]

Adele sincerely did regret not being able to attend the landmarks association meeting in San Antonio, but the historical association meeting in Austin was an important one. In addition to the perennial concerns of money, membership, and contributions for the *Quarterly*, she still wished to promote the idea of a state museum and archives and a published index for the journal. There was also the election of new officers to see accomplished. Adele, increasingly doubtful of her own efficacy as president and hoping to tie Major Littlefield's interests to the interests of the TSHA, nominated him as her successor. Barker and Ramsdell, however, thought differently. After talking over her suggestion, they concluded that while Littlefield had considerable interest in Texas and southern history, he was not the one to help actively in the work the association was doing. "Such advantages as his elevation to the presidency would give us might be obtained by making him one of the vice presidents," Ramsdell explained. "Certainly if you can find it possible to accept, we much prefer that you remain president another year."[53] Adele was seventy years old; her hip and leg gave her so much trouble that there were times she could not even walk with the help of a cane, but resignedly she accepted.

At Adele's urging, George Littlefield and Lewis R. Bryan were installed as vice presidents, replacing Cornelia Stone and Katie Daffan. For the first time since Adele had become president, all of the association vice presidents were male. All of them, along with Ramsdell, shared her interest in Civil War history, but none provided significant assistance when it came to alleviating the association's most persistent problems. At times her efforts at promotion seemed solitary. When issues of the *Quarterly* were published, she tried to publicize them by sending reviews of the contents to the newspapers, and sometimes getting cooperation even in that was frustrating.

Failing to receive any reviews of the contents of the July 1918 *Quarterly*, she asked Ramsdell what had become of the obliging and gifted writers who habitually furnished these notices to the public. These reviews were not only beneficial but necessary, and as the newspapers were more interested in them soon after the release of the *Quarterly* than at a later date, getting them out in a timely manner was critical. She also regularly tried to sell copies of the *Quarterly* herself to contacts in Houston and elsewhere, such as the Mount Vernon society, so she requested copies of the July number. Her exasperation was evident in her request: "If not taxing you too much, please give me the address of the writer, Wm. Lytle Schurz, author of 'Acapulco and the Manila Galleon.' The article is of unusual interest, and deals charmingly with the old customs in Mexico during the Spanish dominion. The July *Quarterly* is packed with good matter, and the public ought to be told of it."[54]

Part of Adele's irritation arose simply from her own busy schedule. She planned a trip to California in August to visit her cousins there and needed to tie up loose ends in Houston before leaving town. Moreover, business matters demanded attention. Even as she prepared to return from her relatively brief trip to California, she received a letter from her attorney in McLennan County urging her, as she was to pass through Crawford on her way home, to stop off and visit the farm she owned there. "It will give you an idea as to its value and you will have the benefit of a personal interview with [the tenant] Mr. Abney," he wrote.[55]

She had barely returned from her trip when the flu epidemic that had broken out in Kansas in January reached Texas. Reports of the spread of the disease started appearing in newspapers by September 12. By September 23, state officials were reporting the presence of influenza in Williamson County, Kaufman County, and Bosque County. By October 4, thirty-five counties had reported influenza. By the end of October, 106,978 cases and 2,181 deaths had been reported in the state's urban centers alone.[56]

On October 2, Adele sat down to write to her nephew, Birdsall, who was serving in Europe. She got business out of the way first, assuring him that she had checked on deposits at the South Texas Commercial National Bank for which he wanted verification and that she had received the bonds of the second Liberty Loan he had purchased. She promised to place these with the other one she had in safekeeping. She admonished him to take care of himself so as not to be any more vulnerable than he already was by virtue of being on the battle line. By the first week in December, her focus had shifted from perils abroad to the danger at home. "Dear Birdsall," she wrote, "the 'flu' is still with us over here and, while no publicity is being given, I am inclined to believe that in some sections it is almost as bad as during the epidemic. I note the Dallas News indicates this morning that the country as a whole has sustained about 300,000 deaths by reason of the malady." Among them were their acquaintances, Charlie Giraud and Coke Burns.[57]

Despite the general malaise prompted by war and the very literal malaise of flu in the fall of 1918, Adele remained committed to finding a way to have the index for the *Southwestern Historical Quarterly* completed. "I am asked every now and then, when our Index will be completed, and must reply, 'I do not know,' for I have heard nothing about it since I met Mr. Winkler over a year ago at the meeting of the Texas Library Association in this city," she wrote to Ramsdell in mid-October. In response to her inquiry, Charles Ramsdell patiently reported that Ernest Winkler was simply too busy, and until he got some help, there seemed no chance that he could get the index ready for publication.[58] Adele was not in the mood for excuses. "I am sure Mr. Winkler is very busy, and it seems to me possible that he may be able to recommend someone who would be capable of completing the Index for a price," she replied. She reminded Ramsdell that the association had been promising an index to the *Quarterly* for two years. "The war conditions furnish a good reason for our failure, but, now that so many people are to be relieved from the government employ, there may be an opportunity to get on with this important work."[59] She continued in this vein a few days later when she wrote him again. "Without an Index," she argued, "the inestimable articles, the result of so much careful investigation and deep study, are, like unvalued jewels, scattered through hundreds of pages, and, while like this guarded and preserved, are unavailable to the new student." Innate kindness prevailed over impatience, and she closed on a conciliatory note: "I dislike to annoy you by my persistency on this subject; my habit of reading much by indexes of which I know the value must serve as an excuse."[60]

Adele's impatience, however, was not limited to the indexing project. Another perennial concern reasserted itself with word of the armistice on November 11: the matter of increasing membership and the number of subscribers. A year previously, she had recommended to Ramsdell that Gertrude Hobby of Ennis was willing to solicit subscribers for the *Quarterly*. "Can you tell me whether she accomplished anything; whether she finally undertook the task?" she inquired. "As the war seems to be really over, do you not think some steps could now be taken to increase our membership?" She urged Ramsdell to send her a list of present subscribers in Houston. She would see if Lewis R. Bryan might be willing to assist in getting new ones since he was now a vice president of the association.[61] The TSHA had comprised both amateur and academic historians from its inception, owing to George Garrison's realization that inclusiveness was the only likely path to success and his hope that other groups with a historical bent might eventually be guided to scholarly techniques of historical investigation and writing, thereby expanding the number of contributions to the *Quarterly*. The category of Fellows was created to incentivize and reward such activity. Eugene C. Barker, however, was less tolerant of amateurs. From the beginning of his tenure, he emphasized quality over quantity, and his adherence to this rule hampered Adele's recruiting efforts. To her, an interest in Texas history and a willingness to pay the annual membership dues and subscribe to the *Quarterly* were qualification enough. Limiting the membership to scholars narrowed the pool of recruits considerably.

The election of officers at the annual meeting in March 1919 reflected just how narrow the pool of active members had become: all of the current officers were reelected. The treasurer's report showed a deficit of some $350. There was nothing to do but reduce the size of the *Quarterly*, Barker told Adele. With a confidence born of limited experience in courting wealthy patrons, he wrote, "I am sure that there are wealthy men and women in the State who would be willing to endow the Association if the matter were properly presented to them." But, he admitted, his only wealthy acquaintance was Major Littlefield, and he did not want to ask him for more. At the same time he revealed his tendency toward academic snobbishness that left Adele handicapped when it came to recruitment. In response to an important lead she was tactfully cultivating, he wrote, "Who is Mrs. Erath, whose letter you sent me? She ought by all means to preserve the [memoirs] which her father dictated. It frequently happens that persons who have not had definite historical training lack appreciation of most important historical material. In some ways the original might be more valuable than the more finished literary copy that the daughter has rewritten."[62] Although that statement was true, finessing the originals when the daughter had been laboring over a manuscript was not so simple and required both patience and tact.

Adele was also hampered by her own prejudice for Texas history, which led her to focus her recruiting primarily on old Texas families while the *Southwestern Historical Quarterly*, under the influence of Herbert Bolton, borderlands historian and coeditor with Barker from 1912 to 1937, had long since expanded to include not just Texas but all the Spanish borderlands.[63] Ever since, Adele had felt that the journal was simply not Texan enough to attract her most desired prospects. "I sometimes hear people express regret that we do not publish more of Texas matter, as many here take little interest in Arizona, New Mexico, and California," she confided to Ramsdell. "But, I presume the majority of our subscribers may be from those states. Am I right?" She did not think her efforts to publicize the *Quarterly* in the daily newspapers were paying any real dividends, and that made her feel ineffectual and anxious. "Are we getting any new members?" she asked Ramsdell. "Is the old membership falling off? You are in a position to know."[64]

Ramsdell did take her concern seriously. Within a week he replied at length, but he offered no solutions. He was convinced that personal contact was the way to go about soliciting new members, but his experiment with student canvassers had been a failure and he had no time to make personal calls himself. A paid recruiter seemed the likeliest solution, but where was the money to come from? He threw the problem back to Adele.[65]

Charles Ramsdell, however, was not the only one with more than one thing on his plate. Adele still had a multitude of family matters that required constant attention. She had loaned money to a young couple, James and Mary Davis, to buy a home in Philadelphia. Now the wife was sick and James could barely manage to pay interest on the loan.[66] Adele's tenant on the farm in McLennan County was having trouble paying his rent. And poor Mary Looscan, Michael's niece, continued to struggle with declining health. Adele sent her a check from time to time to cover her needs. It was typical of her kindness, loyalty, and sense of responsibility.

"I received your kind letter with check which I thank you so much; was so kind of you to send so much," Mary wrote gratefully as the year drew to a close. She assured Adele that she was feeling better and getting stronger and walking better. She had not been able to do much work that year and had relied heavily on Adele's kindness and generosity both to herself and to Michael's sister, Winnie Looscan McAran, also more or less an invalid. "I feel when you send the money you are doing without things yourself. I know you done [sic] that for so many years," she told Adele, "you must not send it if you need it for yourself."[67]

Once Christmas was out of the way and family obligations at least temporarily met, Adele turned her attention again to Ramsdell's most recent letter. She called on the manager of the *Houston Post* and obtained a pledge of assistance—he agreed to publish anything that would be of assistance to the TSHA. Then, she volleyed the ball right back into Ramsdell's court. "Send him whatever you think suitable and he will publish it as an editorial at any time before the annual meeting, on that date, or afterward. So I leave this with you. It is an opportunity to make the public conversant with our objects and the work that is being done. We need more publicity than we are likely to obtain except through such means as this," she wrote.[68] As the date for the 1920 annual meeting drew closer, she wrote Ramsdell again, this time suggesting that if measures could be adopted authorizing the formation of branch societies in places with at least twelve members, she thought that might help build interest in the association; it was a model not unlike the one followed by the Daughters of the Republic of Texas three decades earlier.[69] She also wrote Kenneth Krahl, who worked in the legal department at Houston city hall, and persuaded him to get in touch with a number of the younger attorneys of the city with a view to having them join the Texas State Historical Association. He graciously agreed to help out in any way he could and sent solicitations to seventy of the younger lawyers in the city.[70]

At the same time, Adele had been corresponding with Dr. Alex Dienst in Temple, Texas. He was an enthusiastic student of Texas history and the deeply committed vice president of the TSHA. Her letter reminded him of his own shortcomings, and he assured her that he had just sent in his subscription for 1920. "I wish I could have a 'chat' with you concerning the welfare of the Association," he told her. An inveterate collector of Texana, Dienst had more on his mind than garnering new memberships. "I wanted to take up the possibilities and the feasibility of Texas having a grand store house of publicly displayed documents, portraits, relics, etc, etc, in its own building," he wrote. The Land Office Building, which had been proposed for that purpose previously, would be suitable only on a temporary basis, until something "worthy" was built. "Ever since I have seen the magnificent collections and proper housing in Forest Park, St. Louis, of the Missouri Historical Association, I have wanted a similar collection assembled of Texana," Dienst wrote. "I know it could be done," he insisted. "The Alamo exhibit is infinitesimally small compared to what Texas could do in six months if the matter was entered into with proper spirit—enthusiasm and faith—and have the backing of the Association. I do not want to get started on paper. It is too slow, but I could talk an hour on visions I have had of 'what might be' if such a project had the loyal support of the United Membership of our Association. Someday I hope to talk the matter over with you."[71]

Adele must have been frustrated by Dienst's words. The idea of a state museum had been a favorite of hers, too, but since taking on the presidency of the TSHA she had learned more than she ever wanted to know about the difference between the ideal and the possible. Dienst talked about the loyal support of the united membership of TSHA when she was wondering if there would be any membership at all. As dedicated as she was, she had always felt inadequate to deal effectively with the challenges the association faced. It would be a relief, she thought, to step down that year and give someone more qualified the leadership role. Her wish was not to be granted. When she expressed her thoughts to Barker, he replied, "We have never had a president who has felt the interest that you feel in the Association, and I am perfectly sincere in saying that I don't know where we should turn if you declined election."[72]

The TSHA met on March 2, 1920, with Adele presiding. Dienst read a paper titled "The Need of a Great Public Museum in Texas," and a committee was formed to pursue that objective. Word spread quickly. Before the week was out, Adele began receiving letters from collectors offering their treasures. Albert Schulze of Rosenberg wrote to inform her of his collection of more than nine thousand Indian relics from Texas alone. He had taken them to San Antonio to put them up for sale but would rather see them stay in the state. He invited her to come to San Antonio herself and take a look at them.[73]

In the midst of the excitement generated by talk of a museum, Adele's life was again interrupted by grief and loss. Her sister Jessie, lifelong confidant and the last of her immediate family, died in July, after a protracted illness officially described as pernicious anemia. Adele dutifully penned a memorial to her for the Daughters of the American Revolution: "She died at the home of her only child Joseph Milton Howe in the city of Houston. Her ancestors, the Briscoes and Harrises[,] were pioneers and builders of the Republic of Texas, and in the American Revolution. Historical records and family traditions disclose many acts of heroism on the part of the women as well as the men of these families."[74]

As she had done after each painful loss, Adele went back to work. Through the summer the museum committee, chaired by H. Y. Benedict, then dean of the College of Arts and Sciences at the University of Texas, brainstormed the problem of organizing a state museum and articulated a vision for the project. The purpose of the museum would be collecting, housing, arranging, and exhibiting material from the Texas region for diffusion and increase of knowledge. Incorporating Adele's long-standing concern, it was to house state archives as well as artifacts and books.[75]

Although the idea had many supporters in the TSHA, such an undertaking was fraught with obstacles. By November, Dr. Benedict had informed Adele that he was so overburdened by his university duties that he feared he would not be able to continue the work of getting the museum effort started. Adele hoped to induce him to continue as chair of the museum committee or suggest some suitable person to succeed him. In the meantime, she turned again to written appeals, writing to the managing editor of the *Dallas Morning News* to ask that he provide something for the public on the crowded conditions of the Texas State Library and the crying need for a new building. To Hally Bryan Perry, she confided, "I feel sure that the News will respond. We need a good publicity Secretary to put the subject forcibly before the public. It seems to me the Legislature will have to be appealed to first and failing in that, we'll get a memorial to Gov. Hogg."[76] A month later, she wrote Hally, "It is needless to tell anyone, who knows the difficulties attending the accomplishment of such public enterprises, that it will require perseverance, and no small amount of patience." Dr. Dienst seconded her assessment of the situation, noting, "Like you, I often think we as a Society are not active enough. But what can we do? Texas is not prosperous—We have no great champion or speaker for us in the House or Senate, and I am satisfied till someone [there] gets the vision we have of a great State Museum, there will be nothing doing."[77]

Adele had plenty doing, however. The historical association's financial situation had not improved measurably, and in the absence of significantly increased subscriptions the cost of publishing the *Quarterly* threatened the journal's very existence. In November 1920, Adele and the other members of the publication committee concluded that the cost of subscriptions would have to increase. The museum committee tried without great success to generate momentum behind the Texas museum movement. In 1921 Prof. James Pearce, who had taken Benedict's place as head of the museum committee, delivered a paper, "The Place and Function of Museums in the World of Learning," at the twenty-fifth annual meeting of the association in the hope of generating interest or at least keeping the idea of a museum at the forefront. Meanwhile, with no other candidates clamoring for the position of president, Adele once again agreed to stand for reelection. She reluctantly embarked on yet another year of the same challenges the association had faced in its quarter century of existence.[78]

It was a year of personal as well as institutional challenges. Before it was out, Adele's oldest friend, Carrie Ennis Lombardi, with whom she had worked so hard for a public library in Houston, had died in California. Adele eulogized her friend at a gathering of the Ladies' Reading Club of Houston, which the two of them had helped to organize sixty years before. "The great outstanding feature of her influence amoung [sic] us," she noted, "was her intense purpose and supreme appreciation of the work we had undertaken."[79]

With the closing of yet another chapter of her life, Adele turned her attention once more to the affairs of the TSHA. Although she had increased her own contribution to the endowment fund to one thousand dollars the previous year, large donations were scarce. She and Charles Ramsdell redoubled their efforts to build up a surplus fund by increasing membership in the association. Following up on her prior correspondence with Kenneth Krahl about contacting Houston attorneys, she sent a note to Clarence Wharton, a partner at the firm of Baker and Botts, whom she knew personally through church and business associations in Houston. Shortly before being elected for yet another term as president in 1922, Adele received a response from him indicating that he would enjoy participating in the organization of a Harris County historical society and would, when he had time, suggest it to fellow attorney Henry Borden.[80] Encouraged, she and other members of the executive committee, including Charles Ramsdell and Alex Dienst, eventually settled on a plan to encourage county historical societies to affiliate with the TSHA. They hoped that the organization of county societies would help to build membership, raise money, and "correct many errors current due to the manipulation of the facts of history by newspaper writers." Adele also noted to Ramsdell that the Panhandle-Plains Historical Society was making preparations to commemorate the 1874 Battle of Adobe

Walls.[81] She wrote to the society's president, Thomas F. Turner, mentioning the desire of the TSHA to have the cooperation of all county historical societies. He responded enthusiastically, assuring her that the Panhandle-Plains Historical Society would be very glad to cooperate with the TSHA in every way possible and would greatly appreciate the assistance the larger association would be able to give them.[82] In Belton, George Tyler, a Fellow and recently elected vice president of the TSHA, responded to her inquiry about the progress of his manuscript on the history of Bell County and expressed his pleasure to note everywhere in Texas a growing interest in both state and local history. He noted that the effort to celebrate the Texas centennial had already begun, and he believed it would arouse much enthusiasm all over the state. He, too, thought the association ought to adopt some plan of extension to all portions of the state and agreed to do what he could to help. Progress was discouragingly slow, however. "It is very difficult to go into a county and get other people to organize upon our mere request," he wrote Adele. "My idea has been simply to encourage every organization, city, county or regional, already in existence and every one that attempts to organize, with the view of bringing them into direct relation with our Association. Usually when an organization is established it is on the initiative of the people themselves and is therefore more likely to survive."[83]

People tended to be fickle, however, as the experience of the Texas Historical Society, founded at Galveston in 1871, had demonstrated. The need for promotion would be unrelenting, as unrelenting as the demands on Adele's time, which seemed not to change over the years. Her mail continued to bring a stream of requests for assistance. A Mrs. Mayfield of Houston wrote to complain that her grandfather's name had been omitted from the list of heroes at the San Jacinto Battlefield State Park. When she learned that Adele was president of the Texas State Historical Association, she wrote asking her to advise what steps were necessary to establish his claim.[84] Julia Beazley, a student of Frederick Eby at the University of Texas, wrote to Adele for personal recollections of the schools she had attended, which Beazley apparently wished to use in fulfilling advanced coursework requirements and which Eby also thought he might use in his book on the history of Texas education. Adele complied with the request as she had always done and received a more rewarding than usual reply. "When he [Eby] saw your letter he said, 'With Mrs. Looscan's help, the success of your attempt is assured.' I thought it was an exquisite compliment, an unconscious tribute to your position in the world of achievement that he could not have equaled by studied effort," Beazley wrote.[85]

Adele was not given to self-congratulation, but she was pleased, and the thought that at seventy-six she might still make a difference helped persuade her to continue as president for one more year. While the goals remained much the same—money, museum, membership—1924 brought its own distinctive challenges. Dr. Barker had taken on a new protégé, a young associate professor in the department of history at the University of Texas with some very ambitious ideas about fundraising. Thomas P. Martin, who had been involved with a fund drive for the Texas Memorial Stadium Association, urged a campaign modeled after that one to procure wealthy patrons willing to subscribe not less than $100 for the TSHA, rather than new members at $3 each. His goal was an ambitious $500,000. Since the stadium association was seeking a million dollars and might get it, he thought the greater interests of patriotism and the welfare of Texans justified the TSHA asking for half a million, and he believed they might also get it.[86] Adele, a veteran of more than one fundraising campaign, was skeptical. Her immediate response succinctly put the scheme in perspective. "Some of the methods of the Stadium people can be used in a drive for funds for the Texas State Historical Association," she wrote. "Careful planning and good campaigning certainly must be used. Expert guidance will be needed; time, money and workers will be needed. Can they be found?"[87] She then wrote Martin a much more detailed and more encouraging letter, spelling out what needed to be done and who would be needed to do it. She later cautioned that unless the other officers would unite with him in arousing some enthusiasm, she feared the scheme would fail. Nevertheless, she was resolved to support Martin's effort, so with characteristic efficiency she wrote, "Now, upon a careful inspection of the names comprising the Harris County members, I find at least half a dozen who have been dead several years. I presume you have a copy of this list furnished me by Dr. Ramsdell's clerk." She assured him of the cooperation of all of the TSHA officers in putting his plan for promoting the financial interests of the association into action. "Call upon me," she offered, "for information or any assistance within my power to render."[88]

Energized by Martin's enthusiasm, Adele peppered him with information. When he asked if she had seen the interview on the historical association, published in the *Austin Statesman* of November 9, in any other newspapers, she replied with a capsule analysis of the Texas press: "I am enclosing clippings from the two leading Houston papers to show you how differently they treat matter sent to them. The Galveston and Dallas News print everything sent to them just as it comes from the hands of the writer; so does the San Antonio Express. The [Houston] Post Dispatch is under a management which does not appreciate the patronage of our historical Association. I recommend that you get in touch with the Chronicle representative at Austin. I would like to see your interview," she told him. "Did you get replies to your letters from the respective Vice Presidents, as to the prospect for their attendance on the proposed meeting at Thanksgiving time? I observe that your correspondence is on old letterhead on which Dr. Dienst's name is the only correct one in the list of Vice Presidents, so, I am sending by same mail a few sheets of more recent date," she continued almost frenetically. Then, her tone sobered as she acknowledged his lingering worries over cooperation. "I regret that you are not getting encouragement equal to the importance of the movement you have in hand," she sympathized. "Unless the other officers will unite with you in arousing some enthusiasm before your proposed meeting, the little that I have to offer will prove insignificant, and contribute to failure. Drs. Barker and Ramsdell have witnessed and taken part in several failures of a financial character since I have been President," she warned. "I imagine their buoyancy cannot be revived, but I hoped that Judges [George] Tyler and [T. F.] Harwood might be enthused."[89]

Resolved to do everything she could to buoy Martin's flagging optimism and refine his technique, Adele wrote him a letter of encouragement every week, sometimes more than one. Upon hearing of his need for a paid secretary, she sent the professor her personal check for twenty-five dollars for that purpose and pledged a similar amount monthly until the end of March 1925, at which time she thought he ought to be able to estimate whether the expenditure was worth continuing. "I trust that you may not be discouraged by the indifference of the average Texan to the importance of the historical publications," she commiserated.[90]

When she thought Martin's ideas needed tempering, however, she was not shy about expressing her opinion or offering advice. When, in his draft prospectus, titled "Appeal for Subscription to the Patrons Endowment Fund," he proposed tying governing influence proportionately to endowment fund contributions, she quickly but tactfully responded, "I am inclined to think that the governing powers in the proportion of one vote for every hundred dollars paid in would be unwise. It might be interpreted as commercializing the primary objects of our Association. Let us consider this clause carefully before adopting it." She did approve his idea of including the list of Fellows and life members and a leaflet listing the tables of contents of the twenty-sixth and twenty-seventh volumes of the *Quarterly*, but when he proposed including the entirety of an article, "A Plea for County Historical Societies," in the prospectus, she questioned the necessity. "One reason is," she explained, "the people seem to be indifferent, and if they organize county or regional societies they formulate and adopt a Constitution of their own making." Making portions of the plea part of the leaflet might effect good results in stimulating interest, but to devote the whole thing to the plea seemed unwise. Not wishing to burden Barker and Ramsdell further with their fundraising experiment, Adele even offered to print the leaflet at her own expense. "When I hear from you in regard to number of copies desired," she wrote Martin, "I will present the matter to Mr. Cummings of the Southern Printing Company for his price."[91]

While Martin went back to the drawing board to revise his appeal to prospective patrons and consult with Eugene C. Barker about the appropriate quantity to print, Adele took the draft to attorney Clarence Wharton in hopes of getting his endorsement and permission to include his name as a member of the patron committee. "The lawyers are our best members, and with their support and influence, we may count upon success," she assured Martin. But Wharton's reaction was not all she had hoped for. He commended the prospectus as a worthy move in the right direction but expressed doubts that the historical association would get a substantial result from any circular sent by mail. With that, Adele decided, wisely, not to ask him to serve on the patron committee. "I felt that all on that Committee should believe it would accomplish the desired result," she explained to Martin. However, she acknowledged that there were some who would avoid the responsibility of serving on the committee but who might become patrons. "If you can succeed in awakening enthusiasm in a few leading men, enough to form a strong Committee, the acquisition of Patrons will be comparatively easy," she reassured him.[92]

As the year wound down, though, Adele sensed Martin's flagging confidence in the project and tried to bolster his spirits by providing perspective. "I have not lost interest in this worthy undertaking but realize that the end can be gained only by long continued efforts," she told him. "After the holiday season is over I will see what can be done here towards securing names of persons willing to serve on the

Committee of Patrons."[93] Unfortunately, Adele had business of her own to attend to. "Sundry domestic irregularities have prevented my giving the time it deserves to this matter," she explained apologetically. She had been appointed chair of the historical committee of the Texas Woman's Press Association, which was charged with getting the organization's archives up to date before the annual meeting.[94] In January, feeling a little guilty about having left Martin on his own for some weeks, she sent him a check for one hundred dollars to help in financing the patrons appeal and acknowledged receiving a copy of the appeal itself, which he had had mimeographed to save money. "I am writing very briefly, to show that I have not lost interest," she assured him, "for I have business on hand of some importance demanding attention." She was reading the Austin Papers, in both English and Spanish, and making slow progress, she confided to Martin. But, she emphasized, "[I] find the index accurate, so I select only what is of interest to me."[95]

In spite of her concerns over the TSHA and her busy schedule, Adele found time to enjoy her continued friendship with the De Zavala sisters. On a Friday afternoon in mid-February she settled into her most comfortable chair and read the cheerful letter from Mary De Zavala that had arrived with the day's mail. Mary complimented her on her "brilliant" article in the *Houston Chronicle* giving well-deserved credit to Ann Pamela Cunningham. Adina, it seemed, had bought an old stone house in San Antonio that she had fallen in love with and had moved most of her books and manuscripts over there, "but," wrote Mary, "she's been sick since the day after she bought it." The house was half a block back of the Menger Hotel and thus in a central location. It had six rooms and was all solid stone and in very good repair. "The abstract reads that it was donated to the Adaes Indians and no doubt the blood of martyrs was shed all around about and that was what made her like it, no doubt," Mary mused, knowing Adele would appreciate the humor.[96] If Adele was devoted to Texas history, Adina was obsessed with it.

The first two months of 1925 brought no significantly cheering news from the patrons committee, and Martin was clearly losing heart for the fund drive. When Alex Dienst, a vice president of the historical association, and Sam Asbury, a contributor to the *Quarterly* and vocal member, failed to respond to the appeal for patrons, Martin openly voiced his frustration. Adele did what she could to placate him. "These estimable members have been under the iron heel of 'fads' since their early boyhood," she explained. "These have given them too much pleasure to permit of their adopting any other. There is no hope of the 'fads' dying; they are valuable as promoters of long life for those who cherish them. One will work harder for a fad than for anything else, unless it may be an automobile." She wished she could be more encouraging. She knew her pep talks were sounding more feeble with every letter. "We are realizing that our scheme must work slowly," she offered, perhaps sensing how flimsy that sounded.[97]

Only a little more than a month later Martin's fundraising enthusiasm gave way to enthusiasm for a research fellowship in England. He resigned as chair of the patrons committee, pointing out that the raising of endowment funds was not properly the work of a university professor "but rather of the publicist and promoter," whether "in the guise of politician or president of an educational institution or statesman or simply as a public spirited citizen."[98]

With the departure of Martin, Adele finally did retire as president of the TSHA. After a decade, one in which she had been able to achieve few of her goals, she believed new leadership was needed, and her health was increasingly a hindrance. Still, she remained active in efforts to preserve and promote Texas history. She continued to serve on the executive council of TSHA. Her continued correspondence with Barker gave evidence of her undiminished enthusiasm for the pursuit of Texas history, as, for example, when she described her visit with the daughter of German pioneer leader John O. Meusebach during a four-week stay at Fredericksburg in the summer following her retirement as president of the association. "I met some interesting people and found some valuable manuscripts," she told Barker. "We, Mrs. Perry, Mrs. Hume, and I called on [her] at her house in Fredericksburg. She showed us some interesting documents related to her father's life."[99]

That year, 1925, she fulfilled her duties as chair of the historical committee of the Texas Woman's Press Association. She continued to contribute articles to the *Houston Chronicle* and other newspapers; to maintain a lively correspondence on matters of genealogy, history, and historic preservation; to tend personally to the management of family properties; and to support various family members with loans. She remained particularly interested and involved in the Texas Historical and Landmarks Association through her friendship with Adina De Zavala, whose effervescence never subsided. Texas in the mid-1920s was undergoing many changes, but Adina's energy, dedication, and enthusiasm did not change. As her sister Mary observed when first relating Adina's determination to have the stone house, "I can see no comfort or pleasure in the change but it must be I suppose as there is no other way out. I am quite convinced that Adina will keep on trying until it is either bought or she is incapacitated. It is marvelous how she can hold out! She was really very ill while I was gone and yet kept up her phoning, answering calls and efforts to organize permanent committees etc."[100] Mary could have just as easily been describing Adele. Perhaps that is what made the friendship between Adina and Adele so strong. Adina simply embraced and incorporated the changes the twentieth century brought and then eagerly shared her delight in them. On just such an occasion, in May 1926, Adina shared her newest discovery, the radio. "I am listening to Damrosch as I write," Adina confided.[101] "I have a little radio in my room—He is now giving 'The Beauty and the Beast.' I like the speeches and the classical music—but when the jazz comes on I turn it off. 'Half Hours with the U.S. Senators' I have heard once and enjoyed it—he was a Democrat. We are now listening to the chanting of the Italian pilgrims wending their way to a sanctuary on a high hill. You can read and write and yet have this classic music when it is on the air," she marveled.[102]

Adele had been amazed by the typewriter, which she had yet to employ regularly for personal correspondence, though she had engaged the services of a typist on occasion. She recalled with a trace of amused nostalgia Mary's fascination a decade earlier with that newfangled contraption, the automobile. "The only thing that I know of that I want really and truly is an automobile and only recently have I had this awful want," Mary had written. "I formerly thought a nice horse and carriage would be satisfying but the disease is certainly contagious, and I find I was not immune. My friends are just lovely to me but it is not like owning your own car and having it to take out others when one wants to. So when my ship arrives it is already bartered for a car."[103]

Adele may also have recalled with a twinge of irony her reaction to the suffragists back in 1915, the same year she became president of the TSHA. "Woman's suffrage, if it means the right and the privileges of woman to vote at any or all elections, as a male citizen is now entitled to, is all nonsense, and it never can and never will be," she had written back then. "This woman's suffrage is all right in theory," she'd continued. "If it could be put into practice, I am sure that the whiskey selling and all other evils that now exist would be suppressed; but alas! such a state of things can never exist, it has never existed from the days of Socrates, nor before, to the present time; no never will it exist, so long as man's nature is what it is."[104] But now it was 1930, and women had been voting for a decade.

There were changes at the Texas State Historical Association, too, in the five years that had passed since she had stepped down as president. Dr. Barker had stepped down, too, as chair of the University of Texas Department of History in 1927, and now focused all his attention on the association. Coral Horton Tullis was hired as corresponding secretary to relieve Dr. Ramsdell, at last, of some of the burden of his association duties, which he had to fulfill in addition to faculty responsibilities. Alex Dienst had succeeded T. F. Harwood as association president in 1929, with unfortunate results.[105]

In 1930 Adele turned eighty-two, and chronic pain in her hip made travel beyond Houston very difficult. In November she did manage to preside over the Pioneer Dinner, an event held at the annual meeting of the Texas Federation of Women's Clubs at Houston's Rice Hotel.[106] But by the following year she was largely homebound. What had not changed was her attention to her friends and her passionate interest in Texas. She might not get around as well as she once had, but there was nothing wrong with her writing hand. She continued to correspond, offering wisdom, comfort, and encouragement to friends and colleagues. "Beloved Friend," Adina De Zavala began in reply to one such letter in March 1931,

> This is the first day I have attempted to write. I am getting on wonderfully well, the doctor says—although I am still somewhat weak and "trembly." I am encouraged to believe that I shall soon be strong again.
>
> I have so much enjoyed your dear, sweet letters which Mary read to me and was much comforted by them.
>
> I enjoyed your last one enclosing the picture of the beautiful horse. I remember your last splendid buggy horse perfectly well.
>
> The Texas folk lore society will have its meeting here in April. I would like to be able to go to the meeting of the Texas State Historical Association but have no idea whether I shall be well enough. I attribute my recovery to the prayers of my dear friends.
>
> With my fondest love to you, little Annie [Hume], and all others of our mutual friends—and hoping to hear from you soon again. As ever, Adina.[107]

There is no evidence that Adele made any public appearances after 1930. She continued managing her business affairs and maintaining her correspondence. On the last day of March 1932, she met with her attorney, William H. Wilson, to make out her will. "Mrs. Looscan was a person of rather unusual intelligence, and a woman of very good and exact judgment in business matters," he later wrote of her.[108] Perhaps she was prescient as well, though for someone of her age making a will would not be considered unusual. In September of that same year, her bad hip finally gave out and she fell, breaking her femur right at the hip. Her faithful friends, Adina and Mary De Zavala, traveled to Houston to visit her and offer their comfort, perhaps fearing that it might be their last time to see her.[109] The fracture could not be healed, and Adele never recovered.[110] Her cousin, Annie Hume, assumed the responsibility for her day-to-day affairs and any necessary correspondence, with assistance from William Wilson, nephew Birdsall Briscoe, and great-nephew Knox Howe. The real properties and investments she owned in Harris, San Jacinto, and McLennan Counties had appreciated dramatically with the growth of the Houston area and wise management. Fortunately, therefore, finances posed no problem, even in the tough economic climate of the 1930s. At the time of her death, her assets were appraised at more than $191,000.[111]

In late 1935 Adele contracted pneumonia. She died on November 23, within a few months of her eighty-eighth birthday. She was buried in her family plot in Glenwood Cemetery, not far from her home.[112] Newspapers across Texas carried an obituary noting her many family and personal connections to famous people in early Texas history and her accomplishments as a historian and clubwoman.[113] The January 1936 issue of *Southwestern Historical Quarterly* carried the following notice on the last page:

> Mrs. Adele B. Looscan died at her home in Houston, Texas, on November 23, 1935. She was the daughter of Andrew Briscoe, a captain in the Battle of San Jacinto, and Mary Jane Harris, a pioneer resident of Harrisburg, Texas. She was President of the Texas State Historical Association from 1915 to 1925, and contributed liberally both labor and money to its maintenance. She was an able and singularly candid and detached student of Texas history. Many of her articles were published in the *Quarterly of the Texas State Historical Association*—the most notable being her "History of Harris County, 1822–1845." She contributed studies also to *A Comprehensive History of Texas* (edited by Dudley G. Wooten) and to local Houston papers. During the last six or eight years of her life, she was a helpless invalid.[114]

It was a graceless, not to mention inaccurate, understatement to sum up so vibrant a life. Adele Lubbock Briscoe Looscan was no swaggering adventurer, no romantic cowboy, no oil baron with a big cigar and a bigger car. She needed no manufactured identity or brand. A woman who moved at ease in the man's world of her day, she never sought to be a trailblazer, much less a feminist. Instead, she quietly did things that she thought needed to be done, and she ended up doing them better than most men could have, a fact acknowledged by the men, like George Garrison and Eugene Barker, who knew her best. If she had ever been asked about her identity, she might well have simply answered, "Texan."

Epilogue

Adele Lubbock Briscoe Looscan did not live to see many of the changes she had sought and for which she had worked so tirelessly come to fruition. The Texas Memorial Museum opened in January 1939. A printed index of the *Quarterly* did not appear until 1950. A state archives and library building, constructed with granite from the same quarry that supplied materials for the state capitol building, was dedicated on April 10, 1962. It boasted five main floors, with seven stack floors not open to the public. In 1980, the Educational Services Division of the TSHA, an outgrowth of the Junior Historians of Texas program, was established to encourage interest in Texas history among students in secondary schools. In 2012, with three thousand members, the association had assets totaling more than $4 million. Some challenges faced by modern Texas historians and the TSHA Adele Looscan would immediately recognize: the contentious relationship with the University of Texas (which in 2007 led to a split that lasted eight years), perennial apathy and indifference to the state's history by Texans in their pursuit of "business," and the continuous financial struggle to provide means to carry out the goals and ambitions of the association.

Although she devoted a large proportion of her energy and intellect to the Texas State Historical Association during the last decades of her life, Adele left an impressive legacy as a clubwoman, summed up in the Texas Federation of Women's Clubs "Who's Who" of 1923–24:

> Charter member of Texas State Historical Association; member of Daughters American Revolution, United Daughters of the Confederacy, Daughters of Republic of Texas, Ladies' Reading Club, Texas Woman's Press Association; first President Houston City Federation of Women's Clubs, Vice-President of T.F.W.C. in its first year. She organized the Ladies' Reading Club in 1885 and was instrumental in founding other literary clubs some years before the organization of the Texas Federation. Mrs. Looscan's contributions to Texas history have appeared in many papers and in the *Southwestern Historical Quarterly*, which is issued by the State Historical Association, of which she is President. It was largely through her efforts as a member of the Daughters of the Republic of Texas that some of the historic Spanish Missions at San Antonio were preserved and restored. Her influence in all educational work, especially the encouragement of public education and of the preservation of historic land-marks, relics and documents, has been invaluable. The keen analytical mind, the fire of patriotism, with which Mrs. Looscan is endowed, makes one feel that if suffrage had come to woman a quarter of a century earlier, here might have found a leader and statesman.[1]

A history of the City Federation of Women's Clubs of Houston in 1961 remembered, "Mrs. M. Looscan was the first president of C.F.W.C. and served one year. She served as first vice-president to TFWC and was called 'The Mother of Women's Clubs' in Texas."[2]

Adele Looscan's career as a clubwoman grew out of her earliest experiences with her mother and the Texas Veterans Association in working to preserve the San Jacinto battleground and memorialize the participants of the battle. She identified herself as "Texan" throughout her life. That was her identity. Her devotion to preserving and promoting the history of Texas had a lasting impact on the perception and perpetuation of Texans' historical consciousness long after her name faded from memory. Her background as a granddaughter of Texas pioneer John Richardson Harris, as a daughter of Andrew Briscoe, veteran of the Battle of San Jacinto and signer of the Texas Declaration of Independence, and as one who looked to Francis R. Lubbock as a father figure shaped her destiny. She did not know her father or grandfather. She knew them only through the memories handed down by her mother and grandmother. Those memories had to be heroic. In a time when female identities were closely associated with the men in their lives, men were often portrayed as heroes, even if they did not always live up to that image. "Memory," some memory theorists have argued, "is the source of our special access to our own identities," and "personal identity must involve spatiotemporal continuity." Of course, like an ancient vase found in pieces and then restored by museum technicians, that continuity is not identical to the original but a link between its past and future.[3] Adele Looscan was thus, literally and figuratively, a daughter of the Republic of Texas, providing a link to Texas's storied past and nourishing the memory of it for future Texans.

Like most of her peers, Adele Briscoe Looscan was a romantic; perhaps she could never have been anything else. She was affected by most of the same cultural forces as her predecessors and contemporaries: by the Texas story of heroism and individualism, by the southern milieu into which she was born and lived, by the emergence of women from private lives into public activism, by the experience of maintaining social standing through education and club affiliation. She wrote the same kinds of articles that her contemporaries did: primarily about Texas pioneers, especially her own family members, but also about the history of broader subjects such as the Spanish missions and the Texas flags. In that she wrote about people who had played a role in the battles of the Texas Revolution or in the government of the Republic of Texas, she seemed to subscribe to the lingering nineteenth-century idea of the "Great Man." Her work in many cases is still the most thorough and in some cases the only published biographical account of these individuals. Her article "Pioneer Harrises of Harris County" remains one of the most detailed descriptions of Harris County environs during the era of the Republic of Texas.[4]

She differed from other female writers focusing on Texas history, notably Anna J. Pennybacker, who were storytellers. She wrote primarily to preserve original sources and the lives and deeds of individuals. Sinclair Moreland, Texas state archivist during the first years of Adele's presidency of the TSHA, described the mementos and pictures of family homes clustered about the home in Houston she had shared with her mother, Mary Jane Briscoe, that told the "tale of pioneer life running through many generations." She pursued with sincere dedication the causes most meaningful to her: education, libraries, writing, and history. Even in her club activities she remained focused on history. The history was more important to her than any organization. She associated herself with organizations that allowed her to pursue and promote this interest, and if an organization competed with it, she would choose her devotion to history over her devotion to the organization. Moreland, in his biographical sketch of her for *Texas Women's Hall of Fame*, noted that though she maintained her membership and held offices in other organizations, her best efforts were dedicated to the history of Texas.[5] This devotion was, in essence, Eugene C. Barker's reason for appointing and keeping her as president of the TSHA. She was actively involved in promoting the organization, not just a token woman on the executive council. She actively contributed to the *Southwestern Historical Quarterly* while other clubwomen in the association served as board members and officers but rarely, if ever, contributed to the journal. Several of her articles were published as monographs. These included *The Beginnings of Houston* (1910), an extract from her larger work, "Harris County 1822–1845," including bibliographical references; *Harris County, 1822–1845* (1915); *Micajah Autry: A Soldier of the Alamo* (1915); and *The Journal of Lewis Birdsall Harris, 1836–1845* (1922), all published by the Texas State Historical Association; *The Battle of Sabine Pass*, published by the *Texas Magazine* Company in Dallas in 1897; *Heroes of Texas: Micajah Autry, a Soldier of the Alamo*, reprinted from the *Quarterly* by the Union National Bank in Houston; *A brief sketch of the life and characteristics of Mrs. Mary Jane Briscoe : showing the estimation in which she was held by her friends and the public generally*, printed in Houston by A. C. Gray in 1904 and reprinted in 1930; and several other self-published works, chiefly *A correct statement of the intention and purpose of the state in buying the Alamo Mission property at San Antonio*, which she and her sister, Jessie Wade Briscoe Howe, produced in 1913.

She differed from her peers in the women's club movement in that she did not participate in order to empower herself. While she shared their social mores and observed them, in a practical, day-to-day sense, she simply did whatever she needed to do without much deference because of her sex. Unlike even Bride Neill Taylor, who rose to speak "with a timidity characteristic of the era" at the first organizational meeting of the TSHA, Adele was not timid or uncomfortable in the company of men.[6] She respected their knowledge and expertise that exceeded hers in scholarship, business, or politics, and she respected their claim to those areas, but she never considered herself less than an intellectual and social equal.

Although her health declined with old age, she continued managing her business affairs and maintaining her correspondence until she could no longer do so and her cousin and longtime companion, Annie Hume, had to do it for her. She died of pneumonia in November 1935, but like the true historian she was, she saved her research, her drafts, and her correspondence, and they remain her legacy along with the organizations she helped to found: the Houston Public Library, Ladies' Reading Club of Houston, Texas Woman's Press Association, Texas Federation of Women's Clubs,

Texas State Historical Association, and Daughters of the Republic of Texas.

"Family portraits look down upon the old mahogany furniture," wrote Sinclair Moreland of the Briscoe home, "and closets and chests hold in their keeping letters and documents which could many a tale unfold of personages who played an important part in the history of Texas."[7] They also tell a tale of Adele Briscoe Looscan, first woman president of Texas State Historical Association, a true daughter of the Republic of Texas.

Notes

Introduction

1. "Mrs. Looscan Made President," *San Antonio Express*, Mar. 3, 1915, http://texashistory.unt.edu/ark:/67531/metapth432275/, University of North Texas Libraries, Portal to Texas History, crediting Abilene Library Consortium, Abilene, TX.
2. Looscan to Barker, Mar. 5, 1915, Eugene Campbell Barker Papers, Dolph Briscoe Center for American History, University of Texas at Austin (hereinafter cited as Barker Papers, CAH).
3. Barker to Looscan, Mar. 6, 1915, Barker Papers, CAH.
4. Barbara Welter, "The Cult of True Womanhood: 1820–1860," *American Quarterly* 18 (Summer 1966): 151–74.
5. Ibid., 152.
6. Margaret A. Nash, *Women's Education in the United States, 1780–1840* (New York: Palgrave Macmillan, 2005), 10.
7. Elizabeth Fox-Genovese, "Texas Women and the Writing of Women's History," *Women and Texas History: Selected Essays*, ed. Fane Downs and Nancy Baker Jones (Austin: Texas State Historical Association, 1993), 4 (first quote), 13 (second quote), 5 (third quote), 8–9 (fourth quote).
8. Mary P. Ryan, *Women in Public: Between Banners and Ballots, 1825–1880* (Baltimore: Johns Hopkins University Press, 1990), quoted in Nash, *Women's Education*, 9.
9. Nash, *Women's Education*, 9.
10. Karen J. Blair, *The Clubwoman as Feminist: True Womanhood Redefined, 1868–1914* (New York: Holmes & Meier Publishers, 1980), 1–2.
11. "Daughters of the Republic of Texas," *Galveston Daily News*, Nov. 7, 1891, http://texashistory.unt.edu/ark:/6753/metaphth468350/m1/5/zoom/?q=Daughters, University of North Texas Libraries, Portal to Texas History, crediting Abilene Library Consortium, Abilene, TX (first quote); "The Public School Flag Raising, Interesting Exercises of Texas Independence Day," *Brenham Daily Banner*, Mar. 3, 1900, http://texashistory.unt.edu/ark:/67531/metapth484724/ University of North Texas Libraries, Portal to Texas History, crediting Abilene Library Consortium, Abilene, TX (second quote).
12. Audrey Crawford, "A Women's History Tour of Early Houston," Summer Seminar for Public School History Teachers, University of Houston, June 10, 2002, http://path.coe.uh.edu/seminar2002/week1/tour.html.
13. Blair, *Clubwoman as Feminist*, 1–2; Adele L. Briscoe, Senior's Address, manuscript, July 1864, Box 120, Adele Briscoe Looscan Papers, San Jacinto Museum

of History, La Porte, TX (hereinafter cited as Adele Briscoe Looscan Papers, SJMH).

14. Barbara Welter, *Dimity Convictions: The American Woman in the Nineteenth Century* (Athens: Ohio University Press, 1976), 4; Adrienne Caughfield, *True Women and Westward Expansion* (College Station: Texas A&M University Press, 2005), viii.
15. Julie Des Jardins, *Women and the Historical Enterprise in America: Gender, Race, and the Politics of Memory, 1880–1945* (Chapel Hill: University of North Carolina Press, 2003), 3–4.
16. Nash, *Women's Education*, 4.
17. Blair, *Clubwoman as Feminist*, 9.
18. Welter, *Dimity Convictions*, 4.
19. Nash, *Women's Education*, 10, 39.
20. Megan Seaholm, "Earnest Women: The White Woman's Club Movement in Progressive Era Texas, 1880–1920" (PhD diss., Rice University, 1988), 204.
21. Crawford, "Women's History Tour of Early Houston"; Adele B. Looscan, "Miss Mary B. Brown's Young Ladies' School," manuscript, n.d., Box 119, Adele Briscoe Looscan Papers, MC046, SJMH.
22. Frederick Eby, *The Development of Education in Texas* (New York: Macmillan, 1925), 112.
23. Ibid., 150.
24. Blair, *Clubwoman as Feminist*, 7, 12–13.
25. Anne Firor Scott, *Natural Allies: Women's Associations in American History* (Urbana: University of Illinois Press, 1993), 77.
26. Blair, *Clubwoman as Feminist*, 5.
27. "Literary Association," *Houston Telegraph*, July 6, 1871, edition 1, http://texashistory.unt.edu/ark:/67531/metapth234975/, University of North Texas Libraries, Portal to Texas History, crediting Dolph Briscoe Center for American History, University of Texas at Austin.
28. Seaholm, "Earnest Women," 10–11.
29. Carl N. Degler, *At Odds: Women and the Family in America from the Revolution to the Present* (New York: Oxford University Press, 1980), 16.
30. Blair, *Clubwoman as Feminist*, 100.
31. Stella L. Christian, ed., *The History of the Texas Federation of Women's Clubs* (Houston: Texas Federation of Women's Clubs, 1919), 352.
32. Quoted in Barbara J. Howe, "Women in Preservation: The Legacy of Ann Pamela Cunningham," *Public Historian* 12 (Winter 1990): 32.
33. Annette K. Baxter, preface to *The Clubwoman as Feminist: True Womanhood Redefined, 1868–1914*, by Karen J. Blair (New York: Holmes & Meier Publishers, 1980), xi–xii.
34. Frank W. Jennings and Rosemary Williams, "Adina De Zavala: Alamo Crusader," *Texas Highways Magazine*, Mar. 1995, 14–21,

http://www.tamu.edu/faculty/ccbn/dewitt/adp/history/bios/zavala/zavala.html

35. Seaholm, *Earnest Women*, 11.
36. Des Jardins, *Women and the Historical Enterprise*, 1.
37. Blair, *Clubwoman as Feminist*, 101.
38. Richard R. Flores, "Private Visions, Public Culture: The Making of the Alamo," *Cultural Anthropology* 10, no. 1 (Feb. 1995): 104.

Chapter One: Antecedents

1. Adele B. Looscan, "Mrs. Mary Jane Briscoe," *Quarterly of the Texas State Historical Association* 7 (July 1903): 67.
2. Jane Ingersoll to Mary Jane Harris, June 8, 1835, Mary Jane (Harris) Briscoe Papers, MC056, San Jacinto Museum of History, La Porte, TX (hereinafter cited as Mary Jane Briscoe Papers, SJMH). Egbert Benson Birdsall (b. Oct. 10, 1797, Dutchess, NY, d. Mar. 4, 1845, Saint Augustine, FL), was buried in Glendale Cemetery, Harrisburg, Texas.
3. Looscan, "Mrs. Mary Jane Briscoe," 67; Lewis Birdsall Harris, "Journal of Lewis Birdsall Harris, 1836–1845," *Southwestern Historical Quarterly* 25, no. 3 (Jan. 1922): 188; John W. Clark Jr., review of *A History of Quintana: A Nineteenth-Century Coastal Port in Brazoria County, Texas*, by Martha Doty Freeman with co-principal investigators Elton R. Prewitt and Ross C. Fields (Austin: Prewitt and Associates, 1998), *Southwestern Historical Quarterly* 103 (Oct. 1999): 265–67.
4. Marie Beth Jones, "Quintana, TX," *Handbook of Texas Online*, accessed Oct. 16, 2011, http://www.tshaonline.org/handbook/online/articles/hnq03, published by the Texas State Historical Association (hereinafter, TSHA).
5. Looscan. "Mrs. Mary Jane Briscoe," 67–68.
6. J. C. Clopper's description of Jane Long quoted in Ann Fears Crawford, *Women in Texas: Their Lives, Their Experiences, Their Accomplishments* (Burnet, TX: Eakin Press, 1982), 6.
7. Looscan, "Mrs. Mary Jane Briscoe," 68.
8. Ibid., 66; "Mary Jane Harris Briscoe," HistoricTexas.net, accessed Dec. 28, 2011, http://www.historictexas.net/bios/2b/briscoe-mary-jane-harris.html.
9. Lewis Birdsall Harris, "Journal," *Southwestern Historical Quarterly* 25 (July 1921): 140.
10. "Mary Jane Harris Briscoe," HistoricTexas.net; L. B. Harris, "Journal," 185–86.
11. L. B. Harris, "Journal," 187n. After John R. Harris's death, his heirs filed suit against the estate's administrator, as well as [William] Harris and [Robert] Wilson, begging the court to set aside all former proceedings on account of fraud. Postponements from time to time kept the case pending for years, until finally in 1838 it was settled by compromise. This litigation, more than anything else, prevented the location of the new seat of government at Harrisburg

at the time when this honor was bestowed upon Houston. Its situation at the head of navigation on Buffalo Bayou made it by far the better site at a period when water transportation had little competition.

12. Andrew Forest Muir, "The Municipality of Harrisburg," *Southwestern Historical Quarterly* 56, no. 1 (July 1952): 38.
13. Ibid., 38–39; Feris A. Bass Jr. and B. R. Brunson, eds., *Fragile Empires: The Texas Correspondence of Samuel Swartwout and James Morgan, 1836–1856* (Austin: Shoal Creek Publishers, 1978), xxi.
14. Henry Teal had come to Texas before 1826 with his father, Edward Teal. He made a name for himself during the siege of Bexar and afterward, when he and Henry Wax Karnes were sent to Matamoros to negotiate with Gen. José de Urrea for the return of prisoners under the treaties of Velasco. The exact nature of Teal's business with Briscoe, Allen, and Raguet is unknown but was presumably related to Raguet's mercantile business. Henry Raguet had come to Nacogdoches in March 1833 from Ohio, where he had been unsuccessful in business. Briscoe, in seeking to establish a mercantile enterprise in Texas, had done business with Raguet, among others. Robert Bruce Blake, "Henry Teal," *Handbook of Texas Online*, accessed Nov. 20, 2011 http://www.tshaonline.org/handbook/online/articles/fte02, published by the TSHA; Robert Bruce Blake, "Henry Raguet," *Handbook of Texas Online*, accessed Nov. 9, 2011, http://www.tshaonline.org/handbook/online/articles/fra12, published by the TSHA.
15. José María Carbajal (or Carvajal) was also a friend of Stephen F. Austin and official surveyor for Martín de León, an early empresario who laid out the town of Victoria. Ernest C. Shearer, "The Carvajal Disturbances," *Southwestern Historical Quarterly* 55, no. 2 (1951): 201–30.
16. Andrew Briscoe to A. C. and J. K. Allen, Jan. 24, 1834, Andrew Briscoe Papers, MC055, San Jacinto Museum of History, La Porte, TX (hereinafter cited as Andrew Briscoe Papers, SJMH).
17. Andrew Briscoe to J. K. Allen, Apr. 14, 1835, Andrew Briscoe Papers, SJMH.
18. Margaret Swett Henson, "Anahuac Disturbances," *Handbook of Texas Online*, accessed Oct. 23, 2011, http://www.tshaonline.org/handbook/online/articles/jca01, published by the TSHA.
19. Lewis W. Newton, "Briscoe, Andrew," *Handbook of Texas Online*, accessed Oct. 23, 2011, http://www.tshaonline.org/handbook/online/articles/fbr58, published by the TSHA.
20. Andrew Briscoe to J. K. Allen, Apr. 14, 1835, Andrew Briscoe Papers, SJMH.
21. Andrew Briscoe to DeWitt Clinton Harris, Nov. 26, 1836, quoted in Muir, "Municipality of Harrisburg," 48; Sallie Latimer Harris, "Harris Family, Harrisburg, Pennsylvania, and Harris County, Texas," manuscript, Sept. 2,

1915, 2R34, Harris Family Papers, Dolph Briscoe Center for American History, University of Texas at Austin; William Fairfax Gray, *From Virginia to Texas, 1835: Diary of Col. Wm. F. Gray* (1909; reprint, Houston: Fletcher Young Publishing, 1965), 120; Lewis W. Newton, "Briscoe, Andrew," *Handbook of Texas Online*, accessed Nov. 8, 2011, http://www.tshaonline.org/handbook/online/articles/fbr58, published by the TSHA.

22. Mary Jane Briscoe, Journal, Dec. 31, 1885, Mary Jane Briscoe Papers, SJMH.
23. Muir, "Municipality of Harrisburg," 50.
24. Marguerite Johnston, *Houston: The Unknown City, 1836–1946* (College Station: Texas A&M University Press, 1991), 16.
25. Ibid., 16–17.
26. Ibid., 17.
27. Ibid.
28. Ibid.
29. L. B. Harris, "Journal," 188.
30. Quoted in Francis Richard Lubbock, *Six Decades in Texas: Or, Memoirs of Francis Richard Lubbock, Governor of Texas in Wartime, 1861–1863; A Personal Experience in Business, War, and Politics*, ed. C. W. Raines (Austin: Ben C. Jones & Co., 1900), 48.
31. Andrew Forest Muir, "Railroad Enterprise in Texas, 1836–1841," *Southwestern Historical Quarterly* 47, no. 4 (Apr. 1944): 345.
32. Ibid., 346.
33. Ibid., 356–57.
34. Mary Jane Briscoe to Andrew Briscoe, Dec. 10, 1840, Andrew Briscoe Papers, SJMH.
35. Lubbock, *Six Decades in Texas*, 125.
36. Ibid., 102–6.
37. Quoted in Harriet Smither, ed., "The Diary of Adolphus Sterne: XIV," *Southwestern Historical Quarterly* 33 (Jan. 1930), 231, digital images, http://texashistory.unt.edu/ark:/67531/metapth101090, University of North Texas Libraries, Portal to Texas History, http://texashistory.unt.edu, crediting Texas State Historical Association, Denton, TX.
38. Gifford White, ed., *The 1840 Census of the Republic of Texas* (Austin: Pemberton Press, 1966), 62; Muir, "Railroad Enterprise in Texas," 359; Parmenas Briscoe, "The First Texas Railroad," *Southwestern Historical Quarterly* 7 (Apr. 1904): 281 (quote).
39. Muir, "Railroad Enterprise in Texas," 366–69; P. Briscoe, "First Texas Railroad," 282.
40. Mary Jane Briscoe to James M. Briscoe, Oct. 17, 1849, Mary Jane Briscoe Papers, SJMH; Anna J. Hardwicke Pennybacker, *A New History of Texas for Schools*, rev. ed. (Austin: Mrs. Percy V. Pennybacker, 1898), 256–57; Lubbock,

Six Decades in Texas, 125; Sinclair Moreland, "Adele Lubbock Briscoe Looscan," *The Texas Women's Hall of Fame* (Austin: Biographical Press, 1917), 194; Lewis W. Newton, "Briscoe, Andrew," *Handbook of Texas Online*, accessed May 13, 2011, http://www.tshaonline.org/handbook/online/articles/fbr58, published by the TSHA.

41. Johnston, Houston, 51; Lubbock, *Six Decades in Texas*, 122, 123–24 (quotes).
42. A. Briscoe to James M. Briscoe, Feb. 5, 1849, Andrew Briscoe Papers, SJMH.
43. A. Briscoe to Parmenas Briscoe, July 9, 1849, Andrew Briscoe Papers, SJMH.
44. Parmenas Briscoe to Andrew Briscoe, Feb. 11, 1849, Andrew Briscoe Papers, SJMH.
45. A. Briscoe to Parmenas Briscoe, Apr. 2, 1849; A. Briscoe to Parmenas Briscoe, July 9, 1849; Parmenas Briscoe to Andrew Briscoe, Aug. 26, 1849, all in Andrew Briscoe Papers, SJMH.
46. Sources vary slightly as to the exact date of Andrew Briscoe's death. Mary Jane Briscoe gives the date of death as October 2, 1849, in "Biography of Andrew Briscoe," n.d., Box 132, Mary Jane Briscoe Papers, SJMH. Adele B. Looscan describes his death as occurring October 4, 1849. Looscan, "Mrs. Mary Jane Briscoe," 69.

Chapter Two: Early Days in Texas

1. Mary Jane Briscoe to James M. Briscoe, Oct. 17, 1849; James M. Briscoe to Mary Jane Briscoe, Nov. 7, 1849, both in Box 132, Mary Jane (Harris) Briscoe Papers, MC056, San Jacinto Museum of History, La Porte, TX (hereinafter cited as Mary Jane Briscoe Papers, SJMH); Adele B. Looscan, "Mrs. Mary Jane Briscoe," *Quarterly of the Texas State Historical Association* 7 (July 1903): 69.
2. Hadley and Terry were T. J. B. Hadley and his nephew by marriage, David Smith Terry. Terry lost the election for district attorney of Galveston in 1847, and in 1849 he joined the gold rush to California. Kenneth W. Hobbs, "Terry, David Smith," *Handbook of Texas Online*, accessed Nov. 26, 2011, http://www.tshaonline.org/handbook/online/articles/fte29, published by the Texas State Historical Association (hereinafter, TSHA).
3. A. Briscoe to James M. Briscoe, Feb. 5, 1849, Box 93, Andrew Briscoe Papers, MC055, San Jacinto Museum of History, La Porte, TX (hereinafter cited as Andrew Briscoe Papers, SJMH).
4. James M. Briscoe to Mary Jane Briscoe, Nov. 7, 1849, Mary Jane Briscoe Papers, SJMH.
5. Ibid.
6. Ibid.
7. James M. Briscoe to Mary Jane Briscoe, Nov. 8, 1849, Mary Jane Briscoe Papers, SJMH.

8. James M. Briscoe to Mary Jane Briscoe, Jan. 4, 1850, Mary Jane Briscoe Papers, SJMH.
9. Ibid.
10. Parmenas Briscoe to Andrew Briscoe, Aug. 26, 1849, Andrew Briscoe Papers, SJMH.
11. Mary Jane Briscoe to James M. Briscoe, undated, but sometime after Parmenas Briscoe's death in summer 1851, Mary Jane Briscoe Papers, SJMH.
12. Frederick Eby, *The Development of Education in Texas* (New York: Macmillan, 1925), 142.
13. See Andrea L. Turpin, "Ideological Origins of Women's College: Religion, Class, and Curriculum in the Educational Visions of Catharine Beecher and Mary Lyon," *History of Education Quarterly* 50 (May 2010): 133, doi:10.1111/j.1748-5959.2010.00257.x.
14. Adele Briscoe Looscan, "My First Recollections of Christmas," manuscript, n.d., Box 119, Adele Briscoe Looscan Papers, MC041, San Jacinto Museum of History, La Porte, TX (hereinafter cited as Adele Briscoe Looscan Papers, SJMH); Dan Ferguson, "St. Paul's College," *Handbook of Texas Online*, accessed June 2, 2011, https://tshaonline.org/handbook/online/articles/kbs49, published by the TSHA; Adele Briscoe Looscan, "Mrs. Mary Jane Briscoe," *Southwestern Historical Quarterly* 7 (July 1903): 69.
15. Ellen Garwood, "Early Texas Inns: A Study in Social Relationships," *Southwestern Historical Quarterly* 60 (Oct. 1952): 239.
16. Francis Richard Lubbock, *Six Decades in Texas: Or, Memoirs of Francis Richard Lubbock, Governor of Texas in Wartime, 1861–1863; A Personal Experience in Business, War, and Politics*, ed. C. W. Raines (Austin: Ben C. Jones & Co., 1900), 239.
17. "Camp Verde," *Handbook of Texas Online*, accessed Mar. 25, 2015, http://www.tshaonline.org/handbook/online/articles/qbc29, published by the TSHA.
18. All four children would remain lifelong friends. Ella Hutchins Steuart in 1885 became the first woman to compile and edit a book specifically about Texas, *Gems from a Texas Quarry; Or Literary Offerings by and Selections from Leading Writers and Prominent Characters of Texas, Being a Texas Contribution to the World's Industrial Exposition at New Orleans, 1884–85*, and she became, like Adele, a member of the Texas Woman's Press Association. Sylvia Grider and Lou Rodenberger, "Women and Literature," *Handbook of Texas Online*, accessed Mar. 25, 2015, http://www.tshaonline.org/handbook/online/articles/kzwcu, published by the TSHA.
19. Lubbock, *Six Decades in Texas*, 239; Adele Looscan to Judge C. W. Raines, Jan. 29, 1899, quoted in Lubbock, *Six Decades in Texas*, 241–42.
20. See Eby, *Development of Education in Texas*, 112, 116, 125.

21. Ibid., 115.
22. The first railroad in Texas was the Buffalo Bayou, Brazos, and Colorado. A charter was applied for and obtained under that name by an act of the third legislature, Feb. 11, 1850. The company was organized June 1, 1850. The incorporators were Sidney Sherman, Hugh McLeod, John G. Todd, John Angier, Jonathan F. Barrett, E. A. Allen, Wm. M. Rice, W. A. Van Alstyne, James H. Stevens, B. A. Shepherd, and W. J. Hutchins. In the early spring of 1851 John A. Williams of Boston, Massachusetts, as locating engineer, began surveying the west bank of Buffalo Bayou near Harrisburg. Late in 1852, the first locomotive and iron were received, and track laying commenced; by the first of August, 1853, twenty miles had been completed. Parmenas Briscoe, "The First Texas Railroad," *Quarterly of the Texas State Historical Association* 7 (Apr. 1904): 283.
23. Adele B. Looscan, Notes, n.d., Box 1, Adele Looscan Papers, MSS37, Houston Metropolitan Research Center, Houston, TX (hereinafter cited as Adele Looscan Papers, HMRC).
24. Adele B. Looscan, "Schools at Harrisburg and Houston," manuscript, n.d., Box 120, Adele Briscoe Looscan Papers, SJMH.
25. Looscan, "Mrs. Mary Jane Briscoe"; Adele Briscoe Looscan, "Schools at Harrisburg and Houston."
26. Adele B. Looscan, "Professor Reuter's School," manuscript, n.d., Box 119, Adele Briscoe Looscan Papers, SJMH.
27. Eby, *Development of Education in Texas*, 118.
28. Adele B. Looscan, "Miss Mary B. Brown's Young Ladies' School," manuscript, n.d., Box 119, Adele Briscoe Looscan Papers, SJMH.
29. Ibid.
30. Ibid.
31. Ibid.
32. Christie Ann Farnam, *The Education of the Southern Belle: Higher Education and Student Socialization in the Antebellum South* (New York: New York University Press, 2004), 18, 136.
33. Eighth Census of the United States, 1860; Precinct 5, Harris, TX; roll M653_1296, p. 351, image 146; Family History library film 805296, provided by Ancestry.com.
34. "Andrew Birdsall Briscoe," Online Archives of Terry's Texas Rangers, accessed Nov. 27, 2011, http://www.terrystexasrangers.org/biographical_notes/b/briscoe_ab.htm; Sarah Canby Jackson, Biographical Note, Parmenas Briscoe Papers, MC058, San Jacinto Museum of History, La Porte, TX (hereinafter cited as Parmenas Briscoe Papers, SJMH).
35. Thomas Carothers to Mary Jane Briscoe, Mar. 27, 1861, Mary Jane Briscoe Papers, SJMH. The governor of Texas in 1861 was Edward Clark.
36. Mary Jane Briscoe, correspondence with William R. DeVoe, Jan. 5, 1864,

through May 27, 1864, Mary Jane Briscoe Papers, SJMH.

37. Lubbock, *Six Decades in Texas*, 328.
38. Ibid., 328, 345, 347, 377, 386, 463; F. R. Lubbock to Mary Jane Briscoe, Mar. 11, 1863, Mary Jane Briscoe Papers, SJMH.
39. Adele L. Briscoe, Senior's Address, manuscript, July 1864, Box 120, Adele Briscoe Looscan Papers, SJMH.
40. Adele L. Briscoe, Valedictory of Adele L. Briscoe, Miss Brown's Young Ladies' School, manuscript, July 1866, Box 120, Adele Briscoe Looscan Papers, SJMH.
41. Andrew Forest Muir, "Harris, Lewis Birdsall," *Handbook of Texas Online*, accessed Nov. 28, 2011, http://www.tshaonline.org/handbook/online/articles/fha87, published by the TSHA; Ninth Census of the United States, 1870; Sacramento Ward 4, Sacramento, CA; roll M593_77; p. 306A; image 610; Family History Library Film 545576, provided by Ancestry.com.
42. Mary Jane Briscoe to Parmenas Briscoe, Aug. 1870, Box 70, Parmenas Briscoe Papers, SJMH.
43. Brownson Malsch, "Indianola, TX," *Handbook of Texas Online*, accessed Nov. 28, 2011, http://www.tshaonline.org/handbook/online/articles/hvi11, published by the TSHA.
44. Geoff Winningham, *Traveling the Shore of the Spanish Sea: The Gulf Coast of Texas and Mexico* (College Station: Texas A&M University Press, 2010), 94.
45. Jessie Wade Briscoe to Adele Briscoe, Feb. 13, 20, 1870, Adele Briscoe Looscan Papers, SJMH.
46. Mary Jane Briscoe, Journal, May 28, 1870, Mary Jane Briscoe Papers, SJMH.
47. Milton Grosvenor Howe (1839–1902) studied civil engineering at Dartmouth College before becoming employed in railway construction. Howe worked in Illinois until the outbreak of the Civil War, after which he joined the Confederate Army as a captain in the First Battalion of Engineers. After the war, Howe became chief engineer and superintendent for the Texas Central Railroad. John H. Lienhard, "No. 2033: Milton Grosvenor Howe," *Engines of Our Ingenuity*, Houston Public Media, 2005.
48. Jessie Wade Briscoe to Adele Briscoe, June 21, 1870, July 24, 31, 1870, Adele Briscoe Looscan Papers, SJMH.
49. Muir, "Harris, Lewis Birdsall," *Handbook of Texas Online*; Mary Jane Briscoe to Parmenas Briscoe, Aug. 1870, Parmenas Briscoe Papers, SJMH.
50. Adele Briscoe to Jessie Wade Briscoe, Oct. 12, 1870, Jessie Wade Briscoe Howe Papers, MC057, San Jacinto Museum of History, La Porte, TX.
51. Adele L. Briscoe to Mark Kelly, May 1, 1871, Adele Briscoe Looscan Papers, SJMH.
52. Adele L. Briscoe to Mark Kelly, June 1871, Adele Briscoe Looscan Papers, SJMH.
53. "Literary Association," *Houston Telegraph*, July 6, 1871,

http://texashistory.unt.edu/ark:/67531/metapth234975/, University of North Texas Libraries, Portal to Texas History, http://texashistory.unt.edu, crediting Dolph Briscoe Center for American History, Austin, TX.

54. "Michael Looscan," *The National Cyclopaedia of American Biography* (New York: James T. White & Co., 1900), 8:486.
55. Michael Looscan to Mrs. Briscoe, July 4, 1870, Adele Looscan Papers, HMRC. According to correspondence between Major Looscan and Mary Jane Briscoe, the Texas Historical Society was organized in Galveston. According to the *Houston Evening Telegraph*, June 16, 1870, the Texas Historical Society was organized at Houston on May 23, 1870, with Col. J. C. McCoy of Dallas as one of the vice presidents. *Evening Telegraph*, June 16, 1870, edition 1, http://texas-history.unt.edu/ark:/67531/metapth232586, University of North Texas Libraries, Portal to Texas History, http://texashistory.unt.edu, crediting Dolph Briscoe Center for American History, Austin, TX.
56. Marilyn M. Sibley, "Houston Ship Channel," *Handbook of Texas Online*, accessed Dec. 2, 2011, http://www.tshaonline.org/handbook/online/articles/rhh11, published by the TSHA.
57. Frank W. Johnson, *A History of Texas and the Texans*, ed. Eugene C. Barker and Ernst W. Winkler (Chicago and New York: American Historical Society, 1916), 2:731.
58. Leonly B. Harrison to Mary Jane Briscoe, Jan. 21, 1855, Mary Jane Briscoe Papers, SJMH. Leonly Stewart Briscoe Harrison was married to Andrew's brother, William, who died in 1853. She then married David Harrison, whose late wife, Mary Ann, was Andrew's sister. Mary Ann also died in 1853.
59. Adele Briscoe to Mary Jane Briscoe, Oct. 10, 1876, Mary Jane Briscoe Papers, SJMH.
60. Jessie Wade Briscoe to Adele Lubbock Briscoe, June 21, 1870, Box 107, Adele Briscoe Looscan Papers, SJMH; Tenth Census of the United States, 1880; Houston, Harris, TX; enumeration district 75, roll 1309; p. 105B; Family History Film 1255309, provided by Ancestry.com; "Michael Looscan," *National Cyclopaedia of American Biography*, 8:486.

Chapter Three: Woman of the Club

1. William L. Foley, Statements of Account, 1881, Adele Briscoe Looscan Papers, San Jacinto Museum of History, La Porte, TX (hereinafter cited as Adele Briscoe Looscan Papers, SJMH).
2. J. David Hacker estimates mean age at marriage for white women to have been between twenty-one and twenty-three for the period from 1850 to 1890. Hacker, "Rethinking the Early Decline of Marital Fertility in the United States," *Demography* 40, no. 4 (Nov. 2003): 605–20, accessed Feb. 12, 2012, at

www2.binghamton.edu/.../Hacker-RethinkingUSFertilityDecline.pdf.

3. Jessie Wade Briscoe to Adele Briscoe, Feb. 21, 1870, Adele Briscoe Looscan Papers, SJMH.
4. Adele Briscoe to Mark Kelly, May 1, 1871, Adele Briscoe Looscan Papers, SJMH.
5. Mary Jane Briscoe, Journal, Sept. 13, 1885, Mary Jane (Harris) Briscoe Papers, MC056, San Jacinto Museum of History, La Porte, TX (hereinafter cited as Mary Jane Briscoe Papers, SJMH).
6. Barbara Welter, *Dimity Convictions: The American Woman in the Nineteenth Century* (Athens: Ohio University Press, 1976), 4; "Education of Women," *Peterson's Magazine* 11 (1842): 75 (quote). See Joan Marie Johnson, *Southern Ladies, New Women: Race, Region, and Clubwomen in South Carolina, 1890–1930* (Gainesville: University Press of Florida, 2004), for a discussion of typical southern clubwomen and what distinguished them from their northern counterparts, and also Elizabeth Hayes Turner, *Women, Culture, and Community: Religion and Reform in Galveston, 1880–1920* (New York: Oxford University Press, 1997), for an analysis of the rise of the women's club movement in Galveston.
7. Folder 46, 1866–92, Box 2, Looscan Papers, Heritage Society of Harris County, Houston, TX.
8. Marguerite Johnston, *Houston: The Unknown City, 1836–1946* (College Station: Texas A&M University Press, 1991), 91–92, 113.
9. Ibid., 92–95. The Houston Light Guard was organized by Confederate veterans in the fall of 1872. It was the first uniformed militia company in post-Reconstruction Houston and is one of the oldest national guard companies in the state. It won its first prize for drill competition at the Austin Capital Fair in 1875, and by 1885 "the company enjoyed renown like that of a sports team." Bruce A. Olson, "Houston Light Guards," *Handbook of Texas Online*, accessed July 22, 2015, http://www.tshaonline.org/handbook/online/articles/qjh02, published by the Texas State Historical Association (hereinafter, TSHA).
10. Johnston, *Houston*, 57; Anne Firor Scott, *The Southern Lady: From Pedestal to Politics, 1830–1930*, expanded ed. (Charlottesville: University Press of Virginia Press, 1995), 135.
11. Jan DeVault, comp., *The Ladies and the Battlefield: A Partial Chronology of the Efforts of the San Jacinto Chapter, Daughters of the Republic of Texas, to Save and Preserve the San Jacinto Battlefield, 1891 to 1999* ([Houston]: San Jacinto Chapter, Daughters of the Republic of Texas, 1999), introduction; Galveston Veterans Association to Mrs. M. J. Briscoe, Mar. 3, 1884, Mary Jane Briscoe Papers, SJMH.
12. Nancy M. Theriot, *Mothers and Daughters in Nineteenth-Century America: The Biosocial Construction of Femininity* (Lexington: University Press of Kentucky, 1996), 78–79; Judith N. McArthur, *Creating the New Woman: The Rise of Southern Women's Progressive Culture in Texas, 1893–1918* (Urbana: University

of Illinois Press, 2003), 1, 3.

13. Audrey Crawford, "A Women's History Tour of Early Houston," Summer Seminar for Public School History Teachers, University of Houston, June 10, 2002, http://path.coe.uh.edu/seminar2002/week1/tour.html; Johnston, *Houston*, 91, 95; Johnson, *Southern Ladies, New Women*, 1; Turner, *Women, Culture, and Community*, 152.
14. Scott, *Southern Lady*, 153. The Ladies Literary Club of Spartanburg, South Carolina, had been formed in 1884 for a similar purpose. *Annual Report of the Ladies' Reading Club of Houston*, 1885–86, Box 119, Adele Briscoe Looscan Papers, SJMH; "The Ladies' Reading Club," *Houston Chronicle*, May 19, 1997.
15. Adele Briscoe Looscan, quoted in "The Ladies' Reading Club," *Houston Chronicle*, May 19, 1997; Welter, *Dimity Convictions*, 76 (quoted phrases). According to Welter, somehow through this mixture of challenge and acceptance, of change and continuity, the "True Woman" evolved into the "New Woman"—a transformation as startling in its own way as the abolition of slavery or the coming of the machine age (41).
16. Adele B. Looscan, "Address of the President," presented to the Ladies' Reading Club of Houston, Apr. 2, 1886, Box 117, Adele Briscoe Looscan Papers, SJMH.
17. Mary Jane Briscoe, Journal, May 2, 1885, Mary Jane Briscoe Papers, SJMH.
18. Quote from "Address of Mrs. M. Looscan to the Ladies Reading Club on its 10th Anniversary, April 1895," Box 120, Adele Briscoe Looscan Papers, SJMH; "The Ladies Reading Club," *Houston Chronicle*, May 19, 1997; "Club Women Sponsor Library 29 Years Ago; Federation Is Formed," *Houston Post-Dispatch*, Mar. 25, 1928, clipping from Scrapbook #3647, Houston Club Women, Box 115, Adele Briscoe Looscan Papers, SJMH.
19. Mrs. J. C. Croly (Jennie June), *The History of the Woman's Club Movement in America* (New York: Henry G. Allen & Co., 1898), 1096; "Club Women Sponsor Library 29 Years Ago; Federation Is Formed," *Houston Post-Dispatch*, Mar. 25, 1928; quotes from Adele Looscan to Hally Bryan, Jan. 30, 1900, Hally Ballinger Bryan Perry Papers, Dolph Briscoe Center for American History, University of Texas at Austin.
20. Johnson, *Southern Ladies, New Women*, 139.
21. "Club Women Sponsor Library 29 Years Ago; Federation Is Formed," *Houston Post-Dispatch* Mar. 25, 1928.
22. Johnson, *Southern Ladies, New Women*, 130. Johnson observes the same phenomenon in white clubwomen in South Carolina, who moved naturally from self-education to social reform, most often justifying their new role as one that amounted to being municipal housekeepers. See also Adrienne Caughfield, *True Women and Westward Expansion* (College Station: Texas A&M University Press, 2005), 7, 14, 59–62.
23. "Club Women Sponsor Library 29 Years Ago; Federation Is Formed," *Houston*

Post-Dispatch, Mar. 25, 1928.

24. "Mrs. Adele L. Briscoe Looscan, Widow of Major Michael Looscan," undated manuscript, Folder 9, Adele Looscan Papers, MSS37, Houston Metropolitan Research Center, Houston, TX (hereinafter cited as Adele Looscan Papers, HMRC); Sinclair Moreland, "Adele Lubbock Briscoe Looscan," *The Texas Women's Hall of Fame* (Austin: Biographical Press, 1917), 195.
25. See Turner, *Women, Culture, and Community*, 166.
26. Betty Trapp Chapman, *Houston Women: Invisible Threads in the Tapestry* (Virginia Beach, VA: Donning Company, 2000), 118–19. See also Mary Jane Briscoe, Journal, Jan. 5, 1885, Mary Jane Briscoe Papers, SJMH.
27. Articles by "Texan" in the *Ladies' Messenger* include: "The First Anniversary Ball of the Battle of San Jacinto," Apr. 1887; "Reminiscences of Mrs. Briscoe's Early Life in Houston," May 1887; "Decoration Day," June 1887; "Home Patronage," July 1887; "The Impolicy of Educating Texas Youth Abroad," Aug. 1887; "Industries for Women," Sept. 1887; "Some of the Properties of Coal," read before the Ladies' Reading Club of Houston Oct. 22, 1887, published Nov. 1887; "Mrs. Long at Bolivar Point Sixty Six Years Ago," Dec. 1887; "A Sketch of the Early Settlement of Harris County," Jan. 1888; "Early History of Harris County," Apr. 1888; "The Runaway Scrape of 1836," Apr. 1888; "Advice to a Young Housekeeper," Apr. 1888; "Letter from Bandera, Texas," July 1888; "Report of the Directors of the Woman's Exchange Sewing Class—October 4th," Oct. 1888; "Trip Up the Medina River, August 1888," Oct. 1888. Other works include: Mrs. M. Looscan, "The Battle of Sabine Pass, September 8, 1863," *Texas Magazine*, Nov. 1897; and Mrs. M. Looscan, "The Capture of the *Morning Light*, U.S. Warship, and Schooner *Velocity*," *Houston Post*, May 23, 1895, incorporated into Gov. O. M. Roberts, *Confederate Military History* (Atlanta, GA: Confederate Publishing, 1899), 98.
28. Stacy A. Cordery, "Pennybacker, Anna J. Hardwicke," *Handbook of Texas Online*, accessed Mar. 26, 2015, http://www.tshaonline.org/handbook/online/articles/fpe30, published by the TSHA.
29. Anna J. Pennybacker to Mrs. Looscan, Jan. 1 1893, Adele Briscoe Looscan Papers, SJMH; Adele B. Looscan to Mrs. P. Pennybacker, May 14, 1894, Mar. 19, 1895, both in 2M17, General Correspondence, Mrs. Percy V. Pennybacker Papers, Dolph Briscoe Center for American History, University of Texas at Austin.
30. William G. Scarff to Adele Looscan, Jan. 1894, Feb. 2, 14, 1894, Adele Briscoe Looscan Papers, SJMH; Dudley G. Wooten, *A Comprehensive History of Texas, 1685–1897*, vol. 2 (Dallas: William G. Scarff, 1898), chaps. 12, 16, and 17.
31. Sara Hartman to Adele Looscan, Aug. 20, 1894; and Dora Fowler Arthur to Adele Looscan, Mar. 28, 1893, both in Adele Briscoe Looscan Papers, SJMH.

32. Dora Fowler Arthur to Adele Looscan, May 19, 1897, Folder 7, Box 97, Adele Briscoe Looscan Papers, SJMH.
33. I. D. Affleck to Adele Looscan, May 25, 1905, June 10, 1905, Oct. 11, 1905 (quote), Folder 2, Box 97, Adele Briscoe Looscan Papers, SJMH.
34. F. R. Lubbock to Mary Jane Briscoe, May 4, 1900; Adele Looscan to Mary Jane Briscoe, May 21, 1900; and Adele Looscan to Mary Jane Briscoe, Apr. 23, 1900, respectively, all in Mary Jane Briscoe Papers, SJMH.
35. Adina De Zavala to Mary Saunders, May 24, 1902 (quotes), Folder 9, Box 123, Adele Briscoe Looscan Papers, SJMH. The title "Texas Kalevala," references a nineteenth-century work of epic poetry from Finnish and Karelian oral folklore and mythology. Originally published in 1835 and again in 1849, it is regarded as the national epic of Finland. Interestingly enough, in June 1969, the Texas Senate passed Concurrent Resolution No. 8 naming "The Legend of Old Stone Ranch," by John Worth Cloud, the official "Texas Kalevala." See "Texas Kalevala," Netstate.com, accessed Mar. 29, 2012, http://www.netstate.com/states//symb/poems/tx_legend_of_old_stone_ranch.htm.
36. Adele Looscan to Mary Jane Briscoe, June 25, 1900, Mary Jane Briscoe Papers, SJMH.
37. Ibid. "Mollie" was Mollie Evelyn Moore Davis (1844–1909), poet and editor.
38. Adele Looscan, "Historic Shrines," paper read before Alexander Love Chapter of the DAR, Houston, Feb. 1923, Box 119, Adele Briscoe Looscan Papers, SJMH.
39. Adele B. Looscan, "Mrs. Mary Jane Briscoe," *Quarterly of the Texas State Historical Association* 7 (July 1903): 71.
40. Margaret L. Watson, "Tribute to Miss Adelia Dunovant," *Proceedings of the Thirty-First Annual Convention (1926–1927) of the Texas Division United Daughters of the Confederacy* (Wichita Falls: Texas Div UDC, 1927), 77, accessed Sept. 8, 2012, http://www.lksfriday.com/UDC/UDC-030.htm.
41. Adina De Zavala to Adele Looscan, Nov. 27, 1907, Folder 5, Box 99, Adele Briscoe Looscan Papers, SJMH.
42. Turner, *Women, Culture, and Community*, 167; Kelly McMichael, *Sacred Memories: The Civil War Monument Movement in Texas* (Denton: Texas State Historical Association, 2009), 8.
43. Andrea Kökény, "The Construction of Anglo-American Identity in the Republic of Texas, as Reflected in the *Telegraph* and *Texas Register*," *Journal of the Southwest* 46, no. 2 (Summer 2004): 298, accessed June 27, 2010, http://www.jstor.org/stable/40170291; Mrs. M. Looscan, "President's Address," *Annual Reports of the Ladies' Reading Club of Houston, Texas* (Houston: Gray's Printing Office, 1890), 13–14, Box 117, Adele Briscoe Looscan Papers, SJMH; Adelia A. Dunovant, "Study of History," Proceedings of the Fourth Annual Convention, United Daughters of the Confederacy, Texas Division, 1900, 1–5, Box 118, Adele Briscoe Looscan Papers, SJMH. For comments on the differ-

ences among southern clubwomen, see Francesca Morgan, *Women and Patriotism in Jim Crow America* (Chapel Hill: University of North Carolina Press, 2005), 30–31. See also Karen L. Cox, Dixie's *Daughters: The United Daughters of the Confederacy and the Preservation of Confederate Culture* (Gainesville: University Press of Florida, 2003), 65.

44. Adina De Zavala to Adele Looscan, June 3, 1902, Folder 2, Box 99, Adele Briscoe Looscan Papers, SJMH.
45. McMichael, *Sacred Memories*, 15. Also see Gregg Cantrell, "The Bones of Stephen F. Austin: History and Memory in Progressive-Era Texas," *Lone Star Pasts: Memory and History in Texas*, ed. Gregg Cantrell and Elizabeth Turner (College Station: Texas A&M University Press, 2007), 42.
46. The *Silver Cross* was the weekly organ of the International Order of the King's Daughters and Sons, an interdenominational Christian service organization founded on January 13, 1886, in the New York City home of Margaret Bottome, a Methodist minister's wife.
47. Adele B. Looscan, "The Daughters of the Republic of Texas," *Silver Cross*, Texas Number, 11, no. 42 (Aug. 13, 1898): 9–10.

Chapter Four: Daughter of the Republic

1. Elizabeth Hayes Turner, "Ballinger, Betty Eve," *Handbook of Texas Online*, accessed Aug. 29, 2011, https://tshaonline.org/handbook/online/articles/fba51, published by the Texas State Historical Association (hereinafter, TSHA); Nancy Baker Jones, "Perry, Hally Ballinger Bryan," *Handbook of Texas Online*, accessed Aug. 29, 2011, https://tshaonline.org/handbook/online/articles/fpe41, published by the TSHA. A longer chapter on Betty Ballinger and women's clubs, including the DRT, can be found in Elizabeth Hayes Turner, *Women, Culture, and Community: Religion and Reform in Galveston, 1880–1920* (New York: Oxford University Press, 1997), 158, 169–74.
2. Betty Ballinger quoted in Turner, "Ballinger, Betty Eve," accessed November 7, 2010.
3. First quote, Anna Ehinger to Adele B. Looscan, Dec. 1, 1892, Box 99, Adele Briscoe Looscan Papers, San Jacinto Museum of History, La Porte, TX (hereinafter cited as Adele Briscoe Looscan Papers, SJMH); second quote, Nettie Houston Bringhurst to Adele B. Looscan, Nov. 28, 1891; and third quote, Nettie Houston Bringhurst to Adele Looscan, Jan. 23, 1893, both in Box 97, Adele Briscoe Looscan Papers, SJMH.
4. Marie Bennett Urwitz to Mrs. Looscan, Mar. 13, 1893, Box 103, Adele Briscoe Looscan Papers, SJMH.
5. L. Robert Ables, "Zavala, Adina Emilia De," *Handbook of Texas Online*, accessed Mar. 26, 2015, http://www.tshaonline.org/handbook/online/articles/fzafg, published by the TSHA.

6. Adina De Zavala to Adele B. Looscan, Feb. 6, 1893, Box 99, Adele Briscoe Looscan Papers, SJMH.
7. Mrs. J. R. Fenn, "Chapter Report," in *Proceedings of the Second Annual Meeting of the Daughters of the Republic of Texas, held at Houston, Texas, April 20 and 21, 1893*, 5, in Jan DeVault, comp., *The Ladies and the Battlefield: A Partial Chronology of the Efforts of the San Jacinto Chapter, Daughters of the Republic of Texas to Save and Preserve the San Jacinto Battlefield—1891 to 1899* ([Houston]: San Jacinto Chapter: Daughters of the Republic of Texas, 1999), n.p.
8. Mary Saunders to Adele Looscan, Nov. 24, 1894, Box 102, Adele Briscoe Looscan Papers, SJMH; Andrew Forest Muir, "San Jacinto Battleground State Historical Park," *Handbook of Texas Online*, accessed Aug. 29, 2011, https://tshaonline.org/handbook/online/articles/gks04, published by the TSHA.
9. L. W. Yarrington to Mrs. Looscan, May 29, 1895, Box 103, Adele Briscoe Looscan Papers, SJMH.
10. H. A. McArdle to Adele Looscan, Apr. 4, 1895, Box 101, Adele Briscoe Looscan Papers, SJMH.
11. Claudia Hazlewood, "McArdle, Henry Arthur [Harry]," *Handbook of Texas Online*, accessed Mar. 26, 2015, http://www.tshaonline.org/handbook/online/articles/fmc03, published by the TSHA.
12. "Fisher, Rebecca Gilleland," *Handbook of Texas Online*, accessed Mar. 26, 2015, http://www.tshaonline.org/handbook/online/articles/ffi22, published by the TSHA.
13. Rebecca J. Fisher to Mrs. Looscan, Jan. 27, 1897, Box 100, Adele Briscoe Looscan Papers, SJMH.
14. Dora Fowler Arthur to Mrs. M. Looscan, Oct. 27, 1896, Box 97, Adele Briscoe Looscan Papers, SJMH.
15. "*Texas Magazine*, Austin," *Handbook of Texas Online*, accessed Mar. 27, 2015, http://www.tshaonline.org/handbook/online/articles/edt06, published by the TSHA.
16. Dora F. Arthur to Mrs. M. Looscan, Oct. 27, 1896, Box 97, Adele Briscoe Looscan Papers, SJMH.
17. Dora Fowler Arthur to Mrs. M. Looscan, Jan. 27, 1897, Box 97, Adele Briscoe Looscan Papers, SJMH.
18. Dora Fowler Arthur to Adele Looscan, Feb. 13, 20, Box 97, Adele Briscoe Looscan Papers, SJMH.
19. Dora Fowler Arthur to Mrs. Looscan, Mar. 9, 1897, Box 97, Adele Briscoe Looscan Papers, SJMH.
20. William G. Scarff to Adele B. Looscan, correspondence, Jan. 5, 1894–Mar. 14, 1896, Box 102, Adele Briscoe Looscan Papers, SJMH.

21. Mrs. A. V. Winkler to George P. Garrison, Feb. 24, 1897, General Correspondence, 1897–1926, Texas State Historical Association Records, Dolph Briscoe Center for American History, University of Texas at Austin (hereinafter cited as TSHA Records, CAH).
22. Dudley G. Wooten to George P. Garrison, Feb. 16, 1897, TSHA Records, CAH.
23. Anne A. Brindley, "Galveston Historical Foundation," *Handbook of Texas Online*, accessed Apr. 14, 2012, http://www.tshaonline.org/handbook/online/articles/vrg01, published by the TSHA.
24. Marie Bennett Urwitz et al., to Mrs. M. Looscan, Apr. 1, 1897, Box 103; and Jessie Wade Briscoe Howe to Adele Looscan, Apr. 5, 1897, Box 107, both in Adele Briscoe Looscan Papers, SJMH.
25. Mary Saunders to Adele Looscan, Apr. 14, 1897, Box 102, Adele Briscoe Looscan Papers, SJMH.
26. James S. Hogg to Mrs. Michael Looscan, Apr. 23, 1897, Box 101, Adele Looscan Papers, SJMH.
27. Marie Bennett Urwitz to Mrs. Looscan, Apr. 14, 1897, Box 103, Adele Briscoe Looscan Papers, SJMH.
28. Susan Prendergast Schoelwer, "San Antonio de Valero Mission," *Handbook of Texas Online*, accessed Feb. 3, 2013, http://www.tshaonline.org/handbook/online/articles/uqs08, published by the TSHA.
29. L. Robert Ables, "The Second Battle for the Alamo," *Southwestern Historical Quarterly* 70 (Jan. 1967): 376.
30. Mrs. Willard E. Simpson Jr., "Fiesta San Antonio," *Handbook of Texas Online*, accessed Mar. 26, 2015, http://www.tshaonline.org/handbook/online/articles/lkf02, published by the TSHA.
31. Adina De Zavala to Adele Looscan, May 2, 1897, Box 97, Adele Briscoe Looscan Papers, SJMH.
32. Belle Blandini to Adele Looscan, Apr. 16, 1897, Box 97, Adele Briscoe Looscan Papers, SJMH.
33. Dora Fowler Arthur to Adele Looscan, June 2, 1897, Box 99, Adele Briscoe Looscan Papers, SJMH.
34. Jessie Briscoe Howe to Dell, July 30, 1897, Adele Briscoe Looscan Papers, SJMH.
35. Ibid.
36. Norma Bonner to Adele Looscan, Aug. 14, 1897, Adele Briscoe Looscan Papers, SJMH.
37. Norma Bonner to Adele Looscan, Sept. 4, 1897, Adele Briscoe Looscan Papers, SJMH.
38. George P. Garrison to Mrs. Adele Looscan, Oct. 13, 1897, Adele Briscoe Looscan

Papers, SJMH.

39. George P. Garrison to Adele B. Looscan, Dec. 21, 1897, Box 100, Adele Briscoe Looscan Papers, SJMH; Mary Jane Briscoe, Journal, Feb. 2, 1890, Box 135, Mary Jane (Harris) Briscoe Papers, MC056, San Jacinto Museum of History, La Porte, TX.
40. Mary Saunders to Adele Looscan, Nov. 24, 1897, Box 102, Adele Briscoe Looscan Papers, SJMH.
41. Ibid.
42. Mary Saunders to Adele Looscan, Jan. 3, 1898, Box 102, Adele Briscoe Looscan Papers, SJMH.
43. Winnefred Looscan McAran to Adele Looscan, Feb. 21, 1898, Box 107, Adele Briscoe Looscan Papers, SJMH.

Chapter Five: Disillusionment and Change

1. Adele Looscan, "Daughters of the Republic of Texas," *Silver Cross* 11 (Aug. 13, 1898): 9–10.
2. Adina De Zavala to Adele Looscan, May 30, 1902, June 3, 1902, Adele Briscoe Looscan Papers, San Jacinto Museum of History, La Porte, TX (hereinafter cited as Adele Briscoe Looscan Papers, SJMH).
3. Adina De Zavala to Adele Looscan, Dec. 17, 1896. Adele Briscoe Looscan Papers, SJMH.
4. L. Robert Ables, "The Second Battle for the Alamo," *Southwestern Historical Quarterly* 70 (Jan. 1967): 378.
5. Ibid., 380–81.
6. Adina De Zavala to Adele Looscan, Mar. 31, 1903, Box 99, Adele Briscoe Looscan Papers, SJMH.
7. Adina De Zavala to Adele Looscan, Oct. 29, 1903, Box 99, Adele Briscoe Looscan Papers, SJMH.
8. Adina De Zavala to Adele Looscan, Jan. 24, 1904, Box 99, Adele Briscoe Looscan Papers, SJMH.
9. Adina De Zavala to Adele B. Looscan, Feb. 10, 1904, Box 99, Adele Briscoe Looscan Papers, SJMH. George Brackenridge was one of San Antonio's most powerful businessmen. He had a demonstrated interest in philanthropy, and his sister, Mary Eleanor Brackenridge, was a member of the DRT.
10. Adina De Zavala to Adele B. Looscan, Feb. 10, 1904, Box 99, Adele Briscoe Looscan Papers, SJMH.
11. Richard R. Flores, "Private Visions, Public Culture: The Making of the Alamo," *Cultural Anthropology* 10, no. 1 (Feb. 1995): 103–7.
12. Ibid., 103.
13. Adina De Zavala, *Anniversary of the Victory of San Jacinto* (1904), pamphlet, Folder 55, Box 5, Adina Emilia De Zavala Collection, Dolph Briscoe Center for

American History, University of Texas at Austin (hereinafter cited as Adina De Zavala Collection, CAH).

14. Adina De Zavala, "Texas History—Written and Unwritten," *Texas Talks* 1 (June 1904): 5.
15. Adele B. Looscan, "The Work of the Daughters of the Republic of Texas in Behalf of the Alamo," *Quarterly of the Texas State Historical Association* 8 (July 1904): 79–80.
16. *Fort Worth Record*, Jan. 22, 1905.
17. *San Antonio Express*, Jan. 29, 1905.
18. Adina De Zavala to Adele B. Looscan, Feb. 1, 1905, Adele Briscoe Looscan Papers, SJMH.
19. Adina De Zavala to Adele B. Looscan, Feb. 25, 1905, Adele Briscoe Looscan Papers, SJMH.
20. Adina De Zavala to Adele B. Looscan, Mar. 11, 1905, Adele Briscoe Looscan Papers, SJMH.
21. Ables, "Second Battle for the Alamo," 384–85.
22. George P. Garrison to Mrs. Adele Looscan, Apr. 27, 1905, Adele Briscoe Looscan Papers, SJMH.
23. I. D. Affleck to Mrs. A. Looscan, May 25, 1905, June 10, 1905, Adele Briscoe Looscan Papers, SJMH.
24. Ables, "Second Battle for the Alamo," 386.
25. *San Antonio Express*, Oct. 10, 1905.
26. "Plaintiff's Petition," *Daughters of the Republic of Texas v. Adina De Zavala*, Docket No. 18471, Thirty-Seventh District Court of Texas, Bexar County, Texas, quoted in Ables, "Second Battle for the Alamo," 387.
27. Ables, "Second Battle for the Alamo," 388.
28. Mary De Zavala to Mrs. Looscan, Oct. 18, 1905, Adele Briscoe Looscan Papers, SJMH.
29. Adina De Zavala to Mrs. Looscan, Oct. 23, 1905, Adele Briscoe Looscan Papers, SJMH.
30. Adina De Zavala to Mrs. Looscan, Nov. 10, 1905, Adele Briscoe Looscan Papers, SJMH.
31. Quoted in Ables, "Second Battle for the Alamo," 388.
32. Adina De Zavala to Mrs. Looscan, Nov. 10, 1905, Adele Briscoe Looscan Papers, SJMH.
33. Julia Ideson to Mrs. Looscan, Nov. 20, 1905, Adele Briscoe Looscan Papers, SJMH.
34. Cornelia Branch Stone to Mrs. Adele Looscan, Dec. 19, 1905, Adele Briscoe Looscan Papers, SJMH. It is interesting to note that Cornelia Stone seemed to identify with Adele Looscan through Michael Looscan, a Civil War veteran, in view of her devotion to the United Daughters of the Confederacy, of which she served as president (1907–9).

35. Adele B. Looscan to Charles Merritt Barnes, Feb. 6, 1906, Adele Briscoe Looscan Papers, SJMH.
36. Gwynn Briscoe to Cousin Dell, Mar. 6, 1906, Adele Briscoe Looscan Papers, SJMH.
37. Nettie Houston Bringhurst to Adele Looscan, Mar. 18, 1906, Adele Briscoe Looscan Papers, SJMH.
38. Ables, "Second Battle for the Alamo," 388–89.
39. Ibid.
40. Ibid., 391.
41. Ibid., 392.
42. Adina De Zavala to Mrs. Looscan, Apr. 27, 1906, Adele Briscoe Looscan Papers, SJMH. J. W. Campbell, a Fort Worth businessman who was on the first board of directors of the Nueces Valley, Rio Grande, and Mexico Railway Company, was their legal adviser and a business acquaintance of Adele Looscan.
43. Adina De Zavala to Mrs. Looscan, May 3, 1906, Adele Briscoe Looscan Papers, SJMH.
44. Adele B. Looscan to J. W. Campbell, May 13, 1906, Adele Briscoe Looscan Papers, SJMH.
45. Ables, "Second Battle for the Alamo," 392–94; *Notes and Corrections of the Report of the Fifteenth Annual Meeting of the Daughters of the Republic of Texas* (San Antonio: Alamo Printing, 1906), 17–18.
46. Katie Daffan to Mrs. A. B. Looscan, June 10, 1906, Adele Briscoe Looscan Papers, SJMH.
47. Ables, "Second Battle for the Alamo," 395–96.
48. Adina De Zavala to Mrs. Looscan, Aug. 3, 1906, Adele Briscoe Looscan Papers, SJMH.
49. Ibid.
50. Nettie Houston Bringhurst to Adele Looscan, Aug. 6, 1906, Adele Briscoe Looscan Papers, SJMH.
51. Adina De Zavala to Mrs. Looscan, Aug. 3, 1906, Adele Briscoe Looscan Papers, SJMH.
52. Adele B. Looscan, "Sketch of the Life of Oliver Jones, and of His Wife, Rebecca Jones," *Quarterly of the Texas State Historical Association* 10 (Oct. 1906): 172–80.
53. Kate Briscoe Shaifer Sholars [to Adele Looscan], Sept. 23, 30, 1906, Adele Briscoe Looscan Papers, SJMH.
54. Adina De Zavala to Mrs. Looscan, Sept. 10, 1906, Adele Briscoe Looscan Papers, SJMH.
55. Andrew Birdsall Briscoe to Delly, Nov. 25, 1906, Adele Briscoe Looscan Papers, SJMH.
56. Adina De Zavala [to Adele Looscan], Oct. 12, 1906, Adele Briscoe Looscan Papers, SJMH.

57. Adele Looscan to Adina De Zavala, Oct. 27, 1906, Adele Briscoe Looscan Papers, SJMH.
58. Adina De Zavala to Mrs. Looscan, Nov. 12, 1906, Adele Briscoe Looscan Papers, SJMH; photo caption, *San Antonio Express*, Nov. 11, 1906, p. 10.
59. Adina De Zavala to Mrs. Looscan, Nov. 12, 1906, Adele Briscoe Looscan Papers, SJMH.
60. Nellie Steadman Cox to Adele Looscan, Dec. 26, 1906, Adele Briscoe Looscan Papers, SJMH. The Brownsville Affair occurred in August 1906, when a unit of black troops from the Twenty-Fifth Infantry (known as the Buffalo Soldiers) was falsely accused of killing a white bartender. Pres. Theodore Roosevelt then summarily ordered the dishonorable discharge of 167 of the unit's soldiers.
61. Nellie Steadman Cox to Adele Looscan, Dec. 26, 1906, Adele Briscoe Looscan Papers, SJMH.
62. Andrew Birdsall Harris to Sister Delly, Jan. 26, 1907, Adele Briscoe Looscan Papers, SJMH.
63. Katie Daffan to Mrs. Looscan, Feb. 26, 1907, Adele Briscoe Looscan Papers, SJMH.
64. Adina De Zavala to Mrs. Looscan, Jan. 9, 1907, Adele Briscoe Looscan Papers, SJMH.
65. Adina De Zavala to Mrs. Looscan, Jan. 10, 1907, Adele Briscoe Looscan Papers, SJMH.
66. Adina De Zavala to Mrs. Looscan, Jan. 14, 1907, Adele Briscoe Looscan Papers, SJMH.
67. Adele Looscan to Jessie [Wade Howe], Mar. 7, 1907, Adele Briscoe Looscan Papers, SJMH.
68. Quoted in *San Antonio Express*, Apr. 16, 1907.
69. Adina De Zavala to Mrs. Looscan, Apr. 11, 1907, Adele Briscoe Looscan Papers, SJMH.
70. *Houston Post*, Apr. 20, 1907.
71. *Austin Statesman*, Apr. 20, 1907.
72. *Houston Post*, Apr. 20, 1907.
73. *Austin Statesman*, Apr. 20, 1907.
74. Ables, "Second Battle for the Alamo," 400–401; Stone quoted in *DRT Report*, 1907, in ibid., 401.
75. L. de L. Tuttle to Mrs. Looscan, July 1, 1907, Adele Briscoe Looscan Papers, SJMH.
76. See Ables, "Second Battle for the Alamo," 402.
77. Celicia D. Redding to Mrs. Looscan, July 10, 1907, Adele Briscoe Looscan Papers, SJMH.
78. Adele B. Looscan to Mrs. Bringhurst, July 19, 1907, Adele Briscoe Looscan Papers, SJMH.

79. Ibid.
80. Adele B. Looscan to Mrs. Huber, July 27, 1907, Adele Briscoe Looscan Papers, SJMH.
81. Ibid.
82. Adele B. Looscan, "Elizabeth Bullock Huling: A Texas Pioneer," *Quarterly of the Texas State Historical Association* 11 (July 1907): 66–69.
83. Mary Looscan to Adele B. Looscan, Aug. 27, 1907, Adele Briscoe Looscan Papers, SJMH. Adele Looscan was the executrix of Michael Looscan's estate.
84. Mary Looscan to Adele B. Looscan, Aug. 27, 1907, Adele Briscoe Looscan Papers, SJMH.
85. Adele B. Looscan to Mrs. Foster, Sept. 5, 1907, Adele Briscoe Looscan Papers, SJMH.
86. Adele B. Looscan to Adina De Zavala, Dec. 31, 1907, Adina De Zavala Collection, CAH.
87. Mary De Zavala to Adele B. Looscan, Jan. 24, 1908, Adele Briscoe Looscan Papers, SJMH.
88. Betty Ballinger to Adele Looscan, Jan. 28, 1908, Adele Briscoe Looscan Papers, SJMH.
89. Ibid.
90. Ibid.
91. Mary Looscan to Adele Looscan, Feb. 8, 1908, Adele Briscoe Looscan Papers, SJMH.
92. Adina De Zavala to Adele Looscan, Feb. 10, 1908, Adele Looscan Papers, MSS37, Houston Metropolitan Research Center, Houston, TX (hereinafter cited as Adele Looscan Papers, HMRC).
93. Executive Committee of the DRT statement quoted in Ables, "Second Battle for the Alamo," 404.
94. *San Antonio Light*, Feb. 11, 1908, quoted in Ables, "Second Battle for the Alamo," 404.
95. Adele B. Looscan to Mrs. Huber, July 22, 1908, Adele Briscoe Looscan Papers, SJMH.
96. Betty Ballinger to Adele Looscan, Mar. 5, 1909, Adele Looscan Papers, HMRC.
97. Andrew Birdsall Briscoe to Adele Looscan, May 2, 1909, Adele Briscoe Looscan Papers, SJMH.
98. George P. Garrison to Adele B. Looscan, July 19, 1909, Adele Briscoe Looscan Papers, SJMH.
99. Adele B. Looscan to O. B. Colquitt, July 3, 1911, Adele Briscoe Looscan Papers, SJMH.
100. Ables, "Second Battle for the Alamo," 412.
101. Mrs. L. de L. Tuttle to Mrs. Looscan, July 21, 1913, Adele Briscoe Looscan Papers, SJMH.

Chapter Six: Madame President

1. George P. Garrison to Adele Looscan, Nov. 28, 1898, Box 100, Adele Briscoe Looscan Papers, San Jacinto Museum of History, La Porte, TX (hereinafter cited as Adele Briscoe Looscan Papers, SJMH).
2. Adele Looscan to George P. Garrison, Dec. 6, 1898, General Correspondence, 1897–1926, Texas State Historical Association Records, Dolph Briscoe Center for American History, University of Texas at Austin (hereinafter cited as TSHA Records, CAH).
3. See Adele Looscan to Lester Bugbee, Sept. 9, 1899, TSHA Records, CAH.
4. Adele B. Looscan, "The Old Mexican Fort at Velasco," *Quarterly of the Texas State Historical Association* 1 (Apr. 1898): 282–84; Looscan, "The Old Fort at Anahuac," *Quarterly of the Texas State Historical Association* 2 (July 1898): 21–28; Looscan, "The Old Fort on the San Saba River as Seen by Dr. Ferdinand Roemer in 1847," *Quarterly of the Texas State Historical Association* 5 (Oct. 1901): 134–41; Debbie Mauldin Cottrell, "Casis, Lilia Mary," *Handbook of Texas Online*, accessed Mar. 25, 2015, http://www.tshaonline.org/handbook/online/articles/fcace, published by the Texas State Historical Association (hereinafter, TSHA).
5. Herbert H. Lang, "Harris, Dilue Rose," *Handbook of Texas Online*, accessed Mar. 26, 2015, http://www.tshaonline.org/handbook/online/articles/fha89, published by the TSHA; Texas Historical Marker—Stafford's Point, accessed Mar. 27, 2015, http://www.9key.com/markers/marker_detail.asp?atlas_number=5157009068.
6. Adele B. Looscan, "The Work of the Daughters of the Republic of Texas on Behalf of the Alamo," *Quarterly of the Texas State Historical Association* 8 (July 1904): 79–82.
7. George P. Garrison to Adele B. Looscan, June 12, 1902, Box 100, Adele Briscoe Looscan Papers, SJMH.
8. John A. Lomax to Adele Looscan, Apr. 11, 1911, Adele Looscan Papers, MSS37, Houston Metropolitan Research Center, Houston, TX (hereinafter cited as Adele Looscan Papers, HMRC).
9. Richard B. McCaslin, *At the Heart of Texas: 100 Years of the Texas State Historical Association, 1897–1997* (Austin: Texas State Historical Association, 2007), 64-65.
10. Kelley M. King, *Call Her a Citizen: Progressive-Era Activist and Educator Anna Pennybacker* (College Station: Texas A&M University Press, 2010), 41.
11. Mrs. M. Looscan, "President's Address," *Annual Reports of the Ladies' Reading Club of Houston, Texas* (Houston: Gray's Printing Office, 1890), 13–14, in Adele Briscoe Looscan Papers, SJMH.
12. King, *Call Her a Citizen*, 50.

13. Adele B. Looscan to Mrs. Pennybacker, Aug. 5, 1903, Adele Briscoe Looscan Papers, SJMH.
14. King, *Call Her a Citizen*, 58.
15. McCaslin, *At the Heart of Texas*, 65.
16. Adele B. Looscan to Eugene C. Barker, June 26, 1914, Eugene Campbell Barker Papers, Dolph Briscoe Center for American History, University of Texas at Austin (hereinafter cited as Barker Papers, CAH).
17. Adele B. Looscan to Eugene C. Barker, Aug. 22, 1914, Barker Papers, CAH.
18. Ibid.
19. Ibid.
20. Eugene C. Barker to Adele B. Looscan, Mar. 6, 1915, Adele Looscan Papers, HMRC.
21. Adele B. Looscan to Eugene C. Barker, Mar. 5, 1915, Barker Papers, CAH.
22. Adele B. Looscan to Eugene C. Barker, Nov. 17, 1915, Barker Papers, CAH.
23. Elizabeth Brooks, *Prominent Women of Texas* (Akron, OH: Werner Company, 1906), 179; "Nellie Branch: The Brainiest Girl in Texas," typescript, n.d., Mss. 32, Series 6, Biographical Files, Texas Federation of Women's Clubs, Woman's Collection, Texas Woman's University, Denton, TX.
24. Eugene C. Barker to Adele Looscan, Apr. 16, 1915, Adele Looscan Papers, HMRC.
25. Claudia N. Norvell to Adele Looscan, May 3, 1915, Adele Looscan Papers, HMRC.
26. Adele B. Looscan to Eugene C. Barker, June 11, 1915, Sept. 23, 1916, Barker Papers, CAH.
27. Ben Campbell to Adele Looscan, May 23, 1915, Adele Looscan Papers, HMRC.
28. Quote from file copy of letter from Adele B. Looscan to friends in the UDC, Dec. 6, 1915, Adele Looscan Papers, HMRC; McCaslin, *At the Heart of Texas*, 55–58, 60.
29. Ben Campbell to Adele Looscan, Jan. 14, 1916, Adele Looscan Papers, HMRC.
30. Adele B. Looscan to Charles W. Ramsdell, Mar. 6, 13, 1916, TSHA Records, CAH.
31. Adele B. Looscan to Charles W. Ramsdell, July 19, 1916, TSHA Records, CAH.
32. Adele B. Looscan to Charles W. Ramsdell, Feb. 11, 1917, TSHA Records, CAH.
33. Louis J. Hennessey to Adele B. Looscan, Feb. 5, 1917, Adele Looscan Papers, HMRC.
34. Adele B. Looscan to Charles W. Ramsdell, Feb. 11, 1917, TSHA Records, CAH.
35. Adele B. Looscan to Doctor Barker, Jan. 13, 1917, Barker Papers, CAH.
36. Ibid.
37. McCaslin, *At the Heart of Texas*, 68–69; Lewis L. Gould, "The University Becomes Politicized: The War with Jim Ferguson, 1915–1918," *Southwestern Historical Quarterly* 86 (Oct. 1982): 255–58 (Bailey quote).
38. Gould, "University Becomes Politicized," 260–68.

39. Adele B. Looscan to Charles W. Ramsdell, Mar. 27, 1917, TSHA Records, CAH.
40. Adele B. Looscan to Charles W. Ramsdell, May 24, 1917, TSHA Records, CAH.
41. Adele B. Looscan to Charles W. Ramsdell, May 27, 1917, TSHA Records, CAH.
42. Charles W. Ramsdell to Adele B. Looscan, July 14, 1917, TSHA Records, CAH. Ramsdell is undoubtedly referring to Gov. Jim Ferguson's ongoing battle with the University of Texas in the summer of 1917. At the July meeting in Galveston, the board of regents fired six faculty members whom Ferguson disliked, including John Lomax. Unrelated to Ferguson, the regents fired another faculty member, Lindley M. Keasbey, for his activism in an antiwar organization. See Gould, "University Becomes Politicized," 272–73.
43. Adele B. Looscan to Charles W. Ramsdell, Nov. 14, 1917, TSHA Records, CAH.
44. Charles W. Ramsdell to Adele B. Looscan, Nov. 17, 1917, TSHA Records, CAH.
45. David B. Gracy, *The State Library and Archives of Texas: A History, 1835–1962* (Austin: University of Texas Press, 2010), 11.
46. Harriet Smither and Dorman H. Winfrey, "Texas State Library," *Handbook of Texas Online*, accessed Mar. 26, 2015, http://www.tshaonline.org/handbook/online/articles/lct02), published by the TSHA; Gracy, *State Library and Archives of Texas*, 22, 41 (Winkler quote).
47. Governor Ferguson had been impeached and convicted in September 1917.
48. First quote, Adele B. Looscan to Charles W. Ramsdell, Feb. 7, 1918; subsequent quotes, Charles W. Ramsdell to Adele B. Looscan, Feb. 9, 1918, both in TSHA Records, CAH.
49. Adele B. Looscan to Charles W. Ramsdell, Feb. 27, 1918, TSHA Records, CAH (both quotations).
50. Adele B. Looscan to Charles W. Ramsdell, Feb. 27, 1918, TSHA Records, CAH (first quote); Charles W. Ramsdell to A. B. Looscan, Mar. 6, 1918, TSHA Records, CAH (second quote).
51. Charles W. Ramsdell to A. B. Looscan, Mar. 6, 1918, TSHA Records, CAH.
52. Adele B. Looscan to Texas State Landmark Association [sic], Apr. 13, 1918, Adele Looscan Papers, HMRC.
53. Charles W. Ramsdell to Adele B. Looscan, Apr. 16, 1918, TSHA Records, CAH.
54. Adele B. Looscan to Charles W. Ramsdell, Aug. 6, 1918, TSHA Records, CAH.
55. Pat M. Neff to Adele B. Looscan, Aug. 18, 1918, Adele Looscan Papers, HMRC.
56. US Department of Health and Human Services, "The Great Pandemic: The United States in 1918–1919," accessed Oct. 24, 2013, http://www.flu.gov/pandemic/history/1918/your_state/southwest/texas/.
57. Adele B. Looscan to Maj. Birdsall P. Briscoe, Oct. 2, 1918, Dec. 5, 1918, both in Looscan Papers, Harris County Heritage Society, Houston, TX.
58. Adele B. Looscan to Charles W. Ramsdell, Oct. 12, 1918, TSHA Records, CAH; Charles W. Ramsdell to Adele B. Looscan, Oct. 30, 1918, Adele Looscan Papers, HMRC.
59. Adele B. Looscan to Charles W. Ramsdell, Nov. 20, 1918, TSHA Records, CAH.

60. A. B. Looscan to Charles W. Ramsdell, Nov. 23, 1918, TSHA Records, CAH.
61. Ibid.
62. E. C. Barker to Adele B. Looscan, Mar. 8, 1919, Adele Looscan Papers, HMRC. "Mrs." Erath was Lucy Erath, daughter of George B. Erath. The memoirs were eventually published in the *Southwestern Historical Quarterly* in 1923.
63. McCaslin, *At the Heart of Texas*, 56.
64. Adele B. Looscan to Charles W. Ramsdell, Nov. 13, 1919, TSHA Records, CAH.
65. Charles W. Ramsdell to Adele B. Looscan, Nov. 20, 1919, TSHA Records, CAH.
66. James T. Davis to Adele Looscan, Feb. 22, 1919, Adele Briscoe Looscan Papers, SJMH.
67. Mary Looscan to Adele B. Looscan, Dec. 16, 1919, Adele Briscoe Looscan Papers, SJMH.
68. Adele B. Looscan to Charles W. Ramsdell, Feb. 3, 1920. TSHA Records, CAH.
69. Adele B. Looscan to Charles W. Ramsdell, Feb. 26, 1920, TSHA Records, CAH.
70. Kenneth Krahl to Adele B. Looscan, Feb. 18, 1920, TSHA Records, CAH.
71. Alex Dienst to Adele B. Looscan, Jan. 16, 1920, TSHA Records, CAH.
72. Eugene C. Barker to Adele B. Looscan, Feb. 25, 1920, Adele Briscoe Looscan Papers, SJMH.
73. "Affairs of the Association," *Southwestern Historical Quarterly* 23 (Apr. 1920): 313; Albert W. Schulze to Mrs. A. B. Looscan, Mar. 7, 1920, TSHA Records, CAH.
74. Adele Looscan, Jessie Briscoe Howe memorial to the DAR, July 9, 1920, Adele Briscoe Looscan Papers, SJMH.
75. H. Y. Benedict to Adele B. Looscan, Aug. 10, 1920, Adele Briscoe Looscan Papers, SJMH.
76. Adele Looscan to Hally Bryan Perry, Nov. 15, 1920, Hally Ballinger Bryan Perry Papers, Dolph Briscoe Center for American History, University of Texas at Austin (hereinafter cited as Hally Bryan Perry Papers, CAH).
77. Adele Looscan to Hally Bryan Perry, Dec. 13, 1920, Hally Bryan Perry Papers, CAH; Alex Dienst to Adele Looscan, Dec. 6, 1921, Adele Briscoe Looscan Papers, SJMH.
78. "Affairs of the Association," *Southwestern Historical Quarterly* 25 (July 1921): 78.
79. [Adele B. Looscan], Carrie G. Ennis Lombardi eulogy delivered before the Ladies' Reading Club, Nov. 29, 1921, Adele Briscoe Looscan Papers, SJMH.
80. C. R. Wharton to Adele B. Looscan, Mar. 20, 1922, Adele Looscan Papers, HMRC.
81. Adele B. Looscan to Charles Ramsdell, June 27, 1923, TSHA Records, CAH.
82. Thomas Turner to Adele Looscan, June 16, 1923, Adele Looscan Papers, HMRC.
83. George W. Tyler to Adele Looscan, Jan. 20 (quotes), 26, 1924, Adele Looscan Papers, HMRC.

84. Mrs. J. W. Mayfield to Mrs. A. B. Looscan, June 14, 1924, Adele Looscan Papers, HMRC.
85. Julia Beazley to Adele Looscan, June 19, 27 (quote), 1924, Adele Looscan Papers, HMRC.
86. Thomas P. Martin to Adele B. Looscan, October 7, 1924, TSHA Records, CAH.
87. Adele B. Looscan to Thomas P. Martin, n.d., TSHA Records, CAH.
88. Adele B. Looscan to Thomas P. Martin, Oct. 8, 1924 (first quote); Adele B. Looscan to Thomas P. Martin, Nov. 13, 1924; Adele B. Looscan to Thomas P. Martin, Oct.13, 1924 (second quote), all in TSHA Records, CAH.
89. Adele B. Looscan to Thomas P. Martin, Nov. 13, 1924, TSHA Records, CAH.
90. Adele Looscan to Thomas P. Martin, Nov. 19, 1924, TSHA Records, CAH.
91. A. B. Looscan to Thomas P. Martin, Nov. 25, 1924, TSHA Records, CAH. See also "A Plea for County Historical Societies," *Southwestern Historical Quarterly* 27 (July 1923): 74–76.
92. A. B. Looscan to Thomas P. Martin, Dec. 8 (first quote), 9 (second and third quotes), 1924, TSHA Records, CAH.
93. A. B. Looscan to Thomas P. Martin, Dec. 17, 1924, TSHA Records, CAH.
94. A. B. Looscan to Thomas P. Martin, Dec. 9, 1924 (quote), TSHA Records, CAH; A. B. Looscan to Thomas P. Martin, Jan. 14, 1925, Adele Briscoe Looscan Papers, SJMH.
95. A. B. Looscan to Thomas P. Martin, Jan. 19, 1925, TSHA Records, CAH.
96. Mary De Zavala to Adele Looscan, Feb. 17, 1925, Adele Briscoe Looscan Papers, SJMH.
97. A. B. Looscan to Thomas P. Martin, Feb. 6, 1925, TSHA Records, CAH.
98. Thomas P. Martin to Adele B. Looscan, Mar. 23, 1925, TSHA Records, CAH.
99. A. B. Looscan to E. C. Barker, Nov. 10, 1925, Barker Papers, CAH.
100. Mary De Zavala to Adele Looscan, Jan. 18, 1925, Adele Briscoe Looscan Papers, SJMH.
101. Walter Johannes Damrosch was a German-born American conductor and composer best remembered as a longtime director of the New York Symphony Orchestra and for conducting the world premiere performances of George Gershwin's Piano Concerto in F (1925) and *An American in Paris* (1928).
102. Adina De Zavala to Adele Looscan, Mar. 30, 1926, Adele Briscoe Looscan Papers, SJMH.
103. Mary De Zavala to Adele Looscan, n.d. [Dec. 1914], Adele Briscoe Looscan Papers, SJMH.
104. Adele B. Looscan, "Woman's Suffrage," undated manuscript, Box 122, Adele Briscoe Looscan Papers, SJMH.
105. McCaslin, *At the Heart of Texas*, 79. Alex Dienst had become increasingly deaf and difficult to deal with, and Barker did not want to deal with him. J. Evetts Haley led a successful movement to remove Dienst as president of TSHA, to the outrage of Dienst's supporters, and the resulting conflict continued for some

time afterward.

106. *San Antonio Express*, Nov. 16, 1930.
107. Adina De Zavala to Adele B. Looscan, Mar. 28, 1931, Adele Briscoe Looscan Papers, SJMH.
108. Harris County, Texas, Probate Records, Case no. 23,005, 125: 664, William H. Wilson, affidavit, Dec. 17, 1935, County Clerk's Office, Houston, TX.
109. *San Antonio Light*, Sept. 22, 1932.
110. Harris County, Texas, Probate Records, Case no. 23,005, 125: 664.
111. Harris County, Texas, Probate Records, Case no. 23,005, 128: 21–22, Apr. 6, 1936, County Clerk's Office, Houston, TX.
112. Texas, Death Certificates, 1903–82, provided by Ancestry.com.
113. For example, "Texas Historian Dies in Houston," *San Antonio Express*, Nov. 24, 1935.
114. "Mrs. Adele B. Looscan," *Southwestern Historical Quarterly* 39 (Jan. 1936): 253. The announcement erred in stating that she had been a helpless invalid for the last six or eight years of her life, as she clearly remained active through 1930 and was not incapacitated until about three years before her death.

Epilogue

1. "Looscan, Adele Briscoe (Mrs. Michael)," Mss. 32, Series 6, Biographical Files, Texas Federation of Women's Clubs, Woman's Collection, Texas Woman's University, Denton, TX (hereinafter cited as Texas Federation of Women's Clubs, TWU).
2. "City Federation of Women's Clubs," typescript, n.d., Mss. 32, Series 6 (Alphabetical by City), Texas Federation of Women's Clubs, TWU.
3. Theodore Scaltsas, "Identity, Origin, and Spatiotemporal Continuity," *Philosophy* 56 (July 1981): 395.
4. Adele B. Looscan, "The Pioneer Harrises of Harris County," *Southwestern Historical Quarterly* 31, no. 4 (April 1928): 365–73.
5. Sinclair Moreland, *The Texas Women's Hall of Fame* (Austin: Biographical Press, 1917), 197.
6. Bride Neill Taylor, "The Beginnings of the State Historical Association," *Southwestern Historical Quarterly* 33, no. 1 (July 1929): 4.
7. Moreland, *Texas Women's Hall of Fame*, 197.

Bibliography

Primary Sources

Unpublished

Barker, Eugene Campbell. Papers. Dolph Briscoe Center for American History, University of Texas at Austin.

Birdsall, John. Papers. Manuscript Collection MC067. San Jacinto Museum of History, Houston (La Porte), TX.

Birdsall, Lewis. Family Papers. Manuscript Collection MC069. San Jacinto Museum of History, Houston (La Porte), TX.

Briscoe, Andrew. Papers. Manuscript Collection MC055. San Jacinto Museum of History, Houston (La Porte), TX.

Briscoe, Andrew Birdsall. Family Papers. Manuscript Collection MC093. San Jacinto Museum of History, Houston (La Porte), TX.

Briscoe, Mary Jane Harris. Papers. Dolph Briscoe Center for American History, University of Texas at Austin.

Briscoe, Mary Jane Harris. Papers. Manuscript Collection MC056. San Jacinto Museum of History, Houston (La Porte), TX.

Briscoe, Parmenas [B.]. Papers. Manuscript Collection MC058. San Jacinto Museum of History, Houston (La Porte), TX.

Briscoe Family. Papers. Manuscript Collection MC074. San Jacinto Museum of History, Houston (La Porte), TX.

De Zavala, Adina. Collection, 1828–1955. Dolph Briscoe Center for American History, University of Texas at Austin.

Garrison, George P. Papers, 1836–1925. Dolph Briscoe Center for American History, University of Texas at Austin.

Harris, DeWitt Clinton. Papers. Manuscript Collection MC064. San Jacinto Museum of History, Houston (La Porte), TX.

Harris, John R., and Jane. Papers. Manuscript Collection MC063. San Jacinto Museum of History, Houston (La Porte), TX.

Harris, Lewis Birdsall. Papers. Manuscript Collection MC066. San Jacinto Museum of History, Houston (La Porte), TX.

Harris, William Plunkett. Papers. Manuscript Collection MC065. San Jacinto Museum of History, Houston (La Porte), TX.

Harris County, Texas, Probate Records. Case no. 23,005, 1935–1936. County Clerk's Office, Houston, TX.

Harris Family. Papers, 2R34. Dolph Briscoe Center for American History, University of Texas at Austin.

Harris Family. Papers. Manuscript Collection MC062. San Jacinto Museum of History, Houston (La Porte), TX.

Hogg, James Stephen. Papers, 1836–1969. Dolph Briscoe Center for American History, University of Texas at Austin.

Howe, Jessie Wade Briscoe. Papers. Manuscript Collection MC057. San Jacinto Museum of History, Houston (La Porte), TX.

Ladies' Reading Club. Records. RG E.0026. Houston Metropolitan Research Center, Houston Public Library, Houston, TX.

Looscan, Adele. Texana Collection. Manuscript Collection MC059. San Jacinto Museum of History, Houston (La Porte), TX.

Looscan, Adele Briscoe. Papers. Manuscript Collection MC041. San Jacinto Museum of History, Houston (La Porte), TX.

Looscan, Adele Briscoe. Papers. Manuscript Collection MSS37. Houston Metropolitan Research Center, Houston Public Library, Houston, TX.

Looscan, Adele Lubbock Briscoe. Papers. Dolph Briscoe Center for American History, University of Texas at Austin.

Looscan, Michael. Papers. Manuscript Collection MC054. San Jacinto Museum of History, Houston (La Porte), TX.

Looscan Papers. Harris County Heritage Society, Houston, TX.

Pennybacker, Mrs. Percy V. Papers. Dolph Briscoe Center for American History, University of Texas at Austin.

Perry, Hally Ballinger Bryan. Papers. Dolph Briscoe Center for American History, University of Texas at Austin.

Texas Federation of Women's Clubs. Records. The Woman's Collection. Texas Woman's University, Denton, TX.

Texas State Historical Association. Records, 1897–2004. General Correspondence, 1897–1926. Dolph Briscoe Center for American History, University of Texas at Austin.

Winegarten, Ruthe. Papers. Dolph Briscoe Center for American History. University of Texas at Austin.

Winkler, Ernest William. Collection, 1846–1972. Dolph Briscoe Center for American History, University of Texas at Austin.

Published

"Affairs of the Association." *Southwestern Historical Quarterly* 23 (April 1920): 313.

"Affairs of the Association." *Southwestern Historical Quarterly* 25, no. 1 (July 1921): 78–80.

Asbury, Samuel E. "The Amateur Historian." *Southwestern Historical Quarterly* 28 (October 1924): 89–97.

Briscoe, Parmenas. "The First Texas Railroad." *Quarterly of the Texas State Historical*

Association 7 (April 1904): 279–86.
De Zavala, Adina. "Texas History—Written and Unwritten." Texas Talks 1 (June 1904): 5.
Dickinson, Ellen E. "New York Exchange for Women's Work." Art Amateur 1 (July 1879): 35. http://www.jstor.org/stable/25626812.
"Education of Women." Peterson's Magazine 11 (1842): 75.
Gray, William Fairfax. From Virginia to Texas, 1835: Diary of Col. Wm. F. Gray. Houston: Fletcher Young Publishing, 1965.
Johnson, Frank W. A History of Texas and the Texans. Volume 2. Edited by Eugene C. Barker and Ernst W. Winkler. Chicago and New York: American Historical Society, 1916.
Looscan, Adele B. "The Daughters of the Republic of Texas." *Silver Cross* Texas 11 (August 13, 1898): 9–10.
———. "Elizabeth Bullock Huling, a Texas Pioneer." *Quarterly of the Texas State Historical Association* 11, no. 1 (July 1907): 66–69.
———. "Journal of Lewis Birdsall Harris, 1836–1845." *Southwestern Historical Quarterly* 25 (Jan. 1921; Oct. 1921; Jan. 1922): 63–71; 131–46; 185–97.
———. "Miles Squier Bennet." *Quarterly of the Texas State Historical Association* 7 (October 1903): 166–68.
———. "Mrs. Mary Jane Briscoe." *Quarterly of the Texas State Historical Association* 7 (July 1903): 65–71.
———. "The Old Fort at Anahuac." *Quarterly of the Texas State Historical Association* 2 (July 1898): 21–28.
———. "The Old Fort on the San Saba River as Seen by Dr. Ferdinand Roemer in 1847." *Quarterly of the Texas State Historical Association* 5 (October 1901): 134–41.
———."The Old Mexican Fort at Velasco." *Quarterly of the Texas State Historical Association* 1 (April 1898): 282–84.
———. "Sketch of the Life of Oliver Jones, and of His Wife, Rebecca Jones." *Quarterly of the Texas State Historical Association* 10, no. 2 (October 1906): 172–80.
———. "The Work of the Daughters of the Republic of Texas in Behalf of the Alamo." *Quarterly of the Texas State Historical Association* 8 (July 1904): 79–82.
Lubbock, Francis R. *Six Decades in Texas: Or, Memoirs of Francis Richard Lubbock, Governor of Texas in Wartime, 1861–1863; A Personal Experience in Business, War, and Politics.* Edited by C. W. Raines. Austin: Ben C. Jones & Co., 1900.
Notes and Corrections of the Report of the Fifteenth Annual Meeting of the Daughters of the Republic of Texas. San Antonio: Alamo Printing, 1906.
Pennybacker, Anna J. Hardwicke. *A New History of Texas for Schools.* Rev. ed. Austin: Mrs. Percy V. Pennybacker, 1898.
"A Plea for County Historical Societies." *Southwestern Historical Quarterly* 27 (July

1923): 74–76.

Smither, Harriet, ed. "The Diary of Adolphus Sterne XIV." *Southwestern Historical Quarterly* 33 (January 1930): 231–42.

Thomas, Joseph, and Thomas Baldwin. *A Complete Pronouncing Gazetteer, or Geographical Dictionary of the World.* Philadelphia: Lippincott & Co., 1856.

United States of America. Bureau of the Census. *Seventh Census of the United States, 1850.* Washington, DC: National Archives and Records Administration, 1850. M432, 1,009 rolls.

United States of America. Bureau of the Census. *Eighth Census of the United States, 1860.* Washington, DC: National Archives and Records Administration, 1860. M653, 1,438 rolls.

United States of America. Bureau of the Census. *Tenth Census of the United States, 1880.* NARA microfilm publication T9, 1,454 rolls. Records of the Bureau of the Census, Record Group 29. Washington, DC: National Archives and Records Administration, 1880.

Watson, Margaret L. "Tribute to Miss Adelia Dunovant." *Proceedings of the Thirty-First Annual Convention (1926–1927) of the Texas Division United Daughters of the Confederacy*, 77. Wichita Falls: Texas Div. UDC, 1927. http://www.lksfriday.com/UDC/UDC-030.htm.

White, Gifford, ed. *The 1840 Census of the Republic of Texas.* Austin: Pemberton Press, 1966.

Winters, James Washington. "An Account of the Battle of San Jacinto." *Quarterly of the Texas State Historical Association* 6 (October 1902): 139–44.

Newspapers

Austin [American] Statesman
Austin Weekly Democratic Statesman
Bartlett Tribune
Bastrop Advertiser
Brenham Daily Banner
Brenham Enquirer
Brownsville Daily Herald
Brownwood Daily Bulletin
Denison Daily News
Dublin Progress
El Paso Daily Times
El Paso Morning Times
Fort Worth Gazette
Fort Worth Record
Galveston Daily News
Houston Chronicle
Houston Daily Mercury
Houston Daily Post
Houston Evening Telegraph
Houston Post
Houston Post-Dispatch
Houston Telegraph
Houston Tri-Weekly Telegraph
Meridian Tribune
Orange Leader, Citizen-Record Consolidated
San Antonio Express
San Antonio Light
Schulenburg Sticker
Velasco Times

Secondary Sources

Articles

Adams, Nicholas. "Lucy Maynard Salmon: A Lost Parent for Architectural History." *Journal of the Society of Architectural Historians* 55 (March 1996): 4–5, 108. http://www.jstor.org/stable/991052.

Ables, L. Robert. "The Second Battle for the Alamo." *Southwestern Historical Quarterly* 70 (January 1967): 372–413.

Baker, Paula. "The Domestication of Politics: Women and American Political Society, 1780–1920." *American Historical Review* 89 (June 1984): 620–47.

Boylan, Anne M. "Women and Politics in the Era before Seneca Falls." *Journal of the Early Republic* 10 (Autumn 1990): 363–82. http://www.jstor.org/stable/3123393.

Burkhart, J. A. "Texas, Texans, and Texanism." *Antioch Review* 9 (Autumn 1949): 316–31. http://www/jstor.org/stable/4609358.

Clark, John W. Review of *A History of Quintana: A Nineteenth-Century Coastal Port in Brazoria County, Texas,* by Martha Doty Freeman, with co-principal investigators Elton R. Prewitt and Ross C. Fields. *Southwestern Historical Quarterly* 103 (October 1999): 265–67.

Coughlin, Mimi. "Women and History: Outside the Academy." *History Teacher* 40 (August 2007): 471–79. http://www.jstor.org/stable/30037044.

Crane, Susan A. "Writing the Individual Back into Collective Memory." *American Historical Review* 102 (December 1997): 1872–35. http://www.jstor.org/stable/2171068.

Crawford, Audrey. "Women's History Tour of Houston." Summer Seminar for Public School History Teachers at the University of Houston, June 10, 2002. http://path.coe.uh.edu/seminar2002/week1/tour.html.

Flores, Richard. R. "Memory-Place, Meaning, and the Alamo." *American Literary History* 10 (Autumn 1998): 428–45. http://www.jstor.org/stable/490104.

———. "Private Visions, Public Culture: The Making of the Alamo." *Cultural Anthropology* 10 (February 1995): 99–115. http://www.jstor.org/stable/656233.

Furer, Howard B. "The American City: A Catalyst for the Women's Rights Movement." *Wisconsin Magazine of History* 42 (Summer 1969): 285–305. http://www.jstor.org/stable/4634459.

Gamm, Gerald, and Robert D. Putnam. "The Growth of Voluntary Association in America, 1840–1940." *Journal of Interdisciplinary History* 29 (Spring 1999): 511–57. http://www.jstor.org/stable/206973.

Garwood, Ellen. "Early Texas Inns: A Study in Social Relationships." *Southwestern Historical Quarterly* 60 (October 1952): 219–44.

Goggin, Jacquelin. "Challenging Sexual Discrimination in the Historical Profession:

Women Historians and the *American Historical Association*, 1890–1940." American Historical Review 97 (June 1992): 769–802. http://www.jstor.org/stable/2164780.

Gould, Lewis L. "The University Becomes Politicized: The War with Jim Ferguson, 1915–1918." *Southwestern Historical Quarterly* 86 (October 1982): 255–76.

Hacker, J. David. "Rethinking the Early Decline of Marital Fertility in the United States." *Demography* 40, no. 4 (November 2003): 605–20.

Howe, Barbara J. "Women in Preservation: The Legacy of Ann Pamela Cunningham." *Public Historian* 12 (Winter 1990): 31–61. http://www.jstor.org/stable/3378321?seq=1#page_scan_tab_contents.

Isenberg, Nancy. "The Personal Is Political: Gender, Feminism, and the Politics of Discourse Theory." *American Quarterly* 44 (September 1992): 449–58.

Jennings, Frank W., and Rosemary Williams. "Adina De Zavala: Alamo Crusader." *Texas Highways Magazine*, March 1995, 14–21.

Kerber, Linda K. "Separate Spheres, Female Worlds, Woman's Place: The Rhetoric of Women's History." *Journal of American History* 75 (June 1988): 9–39.

Kökény, Andrea. "The Construction of Anglo-American Identity in the Republic of Texas, as Reflected in the 'Telegraph and Texas Register.'" *Journal of the Southwest* 46 (Summer 2004): 283–308. http://www.jstor.org/stable/40170291.

Library of Congress. "Walter Damrosch, 1862–1950." *Encyclopedia of Performing Arts*. Accessed March 26, 2015. http://lcweb2.loc.gov/diglib/ihas/loc.natlib.ihas.200035728/default.html.

Lowenthal, David. "History and Memory." *Public Historian* 19 (Spring 1997): 30–39. http://www.jstor.org/stable/3379138.

Marks, Paula. "Davy Crockett, Texas, and Shared Identities." *Western Historical Quarterly* 33 (Winter 2002): 478–84. http://www.jstor.org/stable/4144769.

Miri, Mrinal. "Memory and Personal Identity." *Mind* 82 (January 1973): 1–21. http://www.jstor.org/stable/2252498.

Muir, Andrew Forest. "The Municipality of Harrisburg." *Southwestern Historical Quarterly* 56 (July 1952): 36–50.

———. "Railroad Enterprise in Texas, 1836–1841." *Southwestern Historical Quarterly* 47 (April 1944): 339–70.

Salvucci, Linda K. "'Everybody's Alamo': Revolution in the Revolution, Texas Style." *Reviews in American History* 30 (June 2002): 236–44. http://www.jstor.org/stable/30031272.

Scaltsas, Theodore. "Identity, Origin, and Spatiotemporal Continuity." *Philosophy* 56 (July 1981): 395–402. http://www.jstor.org/stable/3750280.

Schwartz, Barry. "The Social Context of Commemoration: A Study in Collective Memory." *Social Forces* 61 (December 1982): 374–402. http://www.jstor.org/stable/2578232.

Shearer, Ernest C. "The Carvajal Disturbances." *Southwestern Historical Quarterly* 55

(1951): 201–30.

Sklar, Kathryn Kish. "American Female Historians in Context, 1779–1930." *Feminist Studies* 3 (Autumn 1975): 171–84.

Smith, Bonnie G. "The Contribution of Women to Modern Historiography in Great Britain, France, and the United States, 1750–1940." *American Historical Review* 89 (June 1984): 709–32. http://www.jstor.org/stable/1856122.

Stagner, Stephen. "Epics, Science, and the Lost Frontier: Texas Historical Writing, 1836–1936." *Western Historical Quarterly* 12 (April 1981): 165–81.

Tolley, Kim. "Science for Ladies, Classics for Gentlemen: A Comparative Analysis of Scientific Subject in the Curricula of Boys' and Girls' Secondary Schools in the United States, 1794–1850." *History of Education Quarterly* 36 (Summer 1966): 129–53. http://www.jstor.org/stable/369502.

Turpin, Andrea L. "Ideological Origins of Women's College: Religion, Class, and Curriculum in the Educational Visions of Catharine Beecher and Mary Lyon." *History of Education Quarterly* 50 (May 2010): 133. doi:10.1111/j.1748-5959.2010.00257.x.

Welter, Barbara. "The Cult of True Womanhood: 1820–1860." *American Quarterly* 18 (Summer 1966): 151–74.

White, Geoffrey M. "Emotional Remembering: The Pragmatics of National Memory." *Ethos* 27 (December 1999): 505–29. http://www.jstor.org/stable/640711.

———. "Histories and Subjectivities." *Ethos* 28 (December 2000): 493–510. http://www.jstor.org/stable/640613.

Books

Appleton, Thomas H., and Angela Boswell. *Searching for Their Places: Women in the South across Four Centuries.* Columbia: University of Missouri Press, 2003.

Bass, Feris A., Jr. and B. R. Brunson, eds. *Fragile Empires: The Texas Correspondence of Samuel Swartwout and James Morgan, 1836–1856.* Austin: Shoal Creek Publishers, 1978.

Blair, Karen J. *The Clubwoman as Feminist: True Womanhood Redefined,* 1868–1914. New York: Holmes & Meier Publishers, 1980.

Brooks, Elizabeth. *Prominent Women of Texas.* Akron, OH: Werner Company, 1906.

Cantrell, Gregg, and Elizabeth Turner, eds. *Lone Star Pasts: Memory and History in Texas.* College Station: Texas A&M University Press, 2007.

Carrington, Evelyn M., ed. *Women in Early Texas.* Austin: Pemberton Press, 1975.

Caughfield, Adrienne. *True Women and Westward Expansion.* College Station: Texas A&M University Press, 2005.

Chapman, Betty Trapp. *Houston Women: Invisible Threads in the Tapestry.* Virginia Beach, VA: Donning Company, 2000.

Christian, Stella L., ed. *The History of the Texas Federation of Women's Clubs.* Houston: Texas Federation of Women's Clubs, 1919.

Crawford, Ann Fears. *Women in Texas: Their Lives, Their Experiences, Their Accomplishments.* Burnet, TX: Eakin Press, 1982.

Croly, Mrs. J. C. (Jennie June). *The History of the Woman's Club Movement in America.* New York: Henry G. Allen & Co., 1898.

Degler, Carl. *At Odds: Women and the Family in America from the Revolution to the Present.* New York Oxford: Oxford University Press, 1980.

Des Jardins, Julie. *Women and the Historical Enterprise in America: Gender, Race, and the Politics of Memory, 1880–1945.* Chapel Hill: University of North Carolina Press, 2003.

DeVault, Jan, comp. *The Ladies and the Battlefield.* Houston: San Jacinto Chapter, Daughters of the Republic of Texas, 1999.

Downs, Fane, and Nancy Baker Jones, eds. *Women and Texas History: Selected Essays.* Austin: Texas State Historical Association, 1993.

Eby, Frederick. *The Development of Education in Texas.* New York: Macmillan, 1925.

Farnam, Christie Ann. *The Education of the Southern Belle: Higher Education and Student Socialization in the Antebellum South.* New York: New York University Press, 1994.

Gracy, David B. *The State Library and Archives of Texas: A History, 1835–1962.* Austin: University of Texas Press, 2010.

Houghton, Dorothy Knox Howe, Barrie M. Scardino, Sadie Gwin Blackburn, and Katherine S. Howe. *Houston's Forgotten Heritage: Landscape, Houses, Interiors, 1824–1914.* Houston: Rice University Press, 1991.

Hughes, Fannie Mae Barbee. *History of the Texas Woman's Press Association.* Huntsville: Texas Woman's Press Association. 1935. Available at East Texas Research Center, Ralph W. Steen Library, Stephen F. Austin University, Nacogdoches, TX.

Johnson, Joan Marie. *Southern Ladies, New Women: Race, Region, and Clubwomen in South Carolina, 1890–1930.* Gainesville: University Press of Florida, 2004.

Johnston, Marguerite. *Houston: The Unknown City, 1836–1946.* College Station: Texas A&M University Press, 1991.

King, Kelley M. *Call Her a Citizen: Progressive-Era Activist and Educator Anna Pennybacker.* College Station: Texas A&M University Press, 2010.

McArthur, Judith N. *Creating the New Woman: The Rise of Southern Women's Progressive Culture in Texas, 1893–1918.* Urbana: University of Illinois Press, 2003.

McCaslin, Richard B. *At the Heart of Texas: 100 Years of the Texas State Historical Association, 1897–1997.* Austin: Texas State Historical Association, 2007.

McElhaney, Jacquelyn Masur. *Pauline Periwinkle and Progressive Reform in Dallas.* College Station: Texas A&M University Press, 1998.

McMichael, Kelly. *Sacred Memories: The Civil War Monument Movement in Texas.* Denton: Texas State Historical Association, 2009.

Moreland, Sinclair. *The Texas Women's Hall of Fame.* Austin: Biographical Press, 1917.

Morgan, Francesca. *Women and Patriotism in Jim Crow America.* Chapel Hill: University of North Carolina Press, 2005.

Nash, Margaret A. *Women's Education in the United States, 1780–1840.* New York: Palgrave Macmillan, 2005.

The National Cyclopaedia of American Biography. Volume 8. New York: James T. White & Co., 1900.

Pickrell, Annie Doom. *Pioneer Women in Texas. 1929.* Reprint, Austin: State House Press, 1991.

Ryan, Mary P. *Women in Public: Between Banners and Ballots, 1825–1880.* Baltimore: Johns Hopkins University Press, 1990.

Sander, Kathleen Waters. *The Business of Charity: The Woman's Exchange Movement, 1832–1900.* Urbana: University of Illinois Press, 1998.

Scott, Anne Firor. *Natural Allies: Women's Associations in American History.* Urbana: University of Illinois Press, 1993.

———. *The Southern Lady: From Pedestal to Politics, 1830–1930.* Expanded ed. Charlottesville: University Press of Virginia Press, 1995.

Theriot, Nancy M. *Mothers and Daughters in Nineteenth-Century America: The Biosocial Construction of Femininity.* Lexington: University Press of Kentucky, 1996.

Turner, Elizabeth Hayes. *Women, Culture, and Community: Religion and Reform in Galveston, 1880–1920.* New York: Oxford University Press, 1997.

Welter, Barbara. *Dimity Convictions: The American Woman in the Nineteenth Century.* Athens: Ohio University Press, 1976.

Winningham, Geoff, *Traveling the Shore of the Spanish Sea: The Gulf Coast of Texas and Mexico.* College Station: Texas A&M University Press, 2010.

Wooten, Dudley G. *A Comprehensive History of Texas, 1685–1897.* 2 vols. Dallas: William G. Scarff, 1898.

Dissertations

Seaholm, Megan. “Earnest Women: The White Woman's Club Movement in Progressive Era Texas, 1880–1920.” PhD diss., Rice University, 1988.

Radio Programs

Lienhard, John H. "No. 2033: Milton Grosvenor Howe." *Engines of Our Ingenuity.* Houston Public Media (KUHF), 2005.

Websites

Ancestry.com. www.ancestry.com.
Encyclopædia Britannica Online. http://www.britannica.com.
Handbook of Texas Online. https://tshaonline.org/handbook.
International Order of the King's Daughters and Sons. http://www.iokds.org/index.php/homepage/a-brief-history.
"Texas Biographies." www.historictexas.net/bios/.
"Texas Kalevala." http://www.netstate.com/states//symb/poems/tx_legend_of_old_stone_ranch.htm.
Oran M. Roberts Chapter, United Daughters of the Confederacy. http://www.lksfriday.com/UDC/UDC-030.htm.
Portal to Texas History. www.texashistory.unt.edu.
Texas Historical Marker—Stafford's Point. http://www.9key.com/markers/marker_detail.asp?atlas_number=5157009068.

Index

ABL – Adele Briscoe Looscan
DAR – Daughters of the American Revolution
DRT –Daughters of the Republic of Texas
TSHA – Texas State Historical Association
UDC – United Daughters of the Confederacy